THE LIFE AND TIMES OF THOMAS SPENCE

by

P. M. ASHRAF

Published by Frank Graham,
6 Queen's Terrace, Newcastle upon Tyne NE2 2PL

First Published in 1983
I.S.B.N. 0 85983 172 8

Dedicated
to
Ruth and Edmund Frow

Printed by Howe Brothers (Gateshead) Limited, Swan Street, Gateshead

Contents

Introduction
Professor Mary Kemp-Ashraf made a significant contribution to Marxist scholarship in the field of working-class literature and poetry in relation to the history of the time.

Born in England in the industrial North West, studied comparative linguistics at London University and, with a command of many languages, travelled to Austria and Yugoslavia during the twenties gathering material for a thesis on Albanian place names.

Her experiences during the economic crises of the thirties when she was unable to obtain academic work led her to join the Communist Party in 1934 and she undertook work in the National Unemployed Workers' Movement, the Anti-Fascist Movement and held leading positions in various local Party organisations. During the war she worked in industry and continued her political activity in the factory. When the war ended, Mary Kemp returned to Yugoslavia. She met and married K. M. Ashraf, a founder member of the Indian Communist Party and a well known authority on Indian History. Together they went to India where he participated as a prominent political leader as well as being Head of the Department of History in Delhi University. Mary Kemp-Ashraf became Head of the European Languages Department in the same University. In addition, she undertook ethnological field work into the vast jungle of Indian languages.

When the Ashraf's left India, they spent a year in Moscow where Mary worked at the Institute for Marxism-Leninism and where her work on the participation of black radicals in British history was published.

K. M. Ashraf was then offered the Chair of Indian History at the Department of Indology at Humboldt University and they moved to Berlin. There, Mary Ashraf became Senior Lecturer and subsequently Professor in the English/American Department. Teaching English Literature and Essay writing from 1962-1967, she founded the research group on English working-class literature which, in 1966 published **Essays In Honour of William Gallacher.** The life-long interest which Mary Ashraf devoted to Thomas Spence whom she considered to be one of the most important contributors to radical thought was first made public in that volume. She wrote a short introduction to a selection of extracts from his most important work and that has been reprinted in this volume. In that assessment of his work she shows that Spence's ideas were well in advance of his time. The concept of the General Strike, for example, was outlined in his **Jubilee** many years before Benbow announced his scheme for a National Holiday. His advocacy of a fusion of political and social-economic aims was nearly half a century in advance of the Chartists.

In 1966, Mary Ashraf characterised Spence as "evidence that a consciously working-class point of view was taking shape and becoming articulate. Its actual demands naturally rejected the liberalism of the new democratic ideology of capitalism. But the conflict was often expressed as a condemnation of the old order which still prevailed, or in passionate denunciations that made no distinction between one method of accumulation and another". The present volume is the development of her research into that conclusion and her evidence in support of it.

Possibly Mary Ashraf's most important contribution to working-class history, apart from Spence, was **The History Of English Working-Class Literature.** This was the fruit of years spent searching for and reading poetry and prose often published in small prints locally and rarely finding a place in the Libraries. She rescued much of it from obscurity and in the two published volumes, one on Prose and the other on Poetry, she laid the basis for further research into this important aspect of labour history.

Mary Ashraf died in Berlin in March, 1983. Her last moments were given to completing this work on Spence, but correction and preparation of the manuscript have had to be left to her friends. This has been done with as little alteration as possible to indicate Professor Ashraf's contribution to the re-assessment of the development of radical ideas and their influence on the formation of working-class consciousness.

Published Work

Black Radicals In Great Britain In The 18th Century Moscow 1962.

Essays In Honour of William Gallacher (edited by Professor Ashraf and including an essay on Thomas Spence and a selection of his works) Berlin 1966

A Young Revolutionary In 19th Century England: selected writings of Georg Weerth (article on Georg Weerth in Bradford) Berlin. 1971

1872-1972 Bradford Trades Council 100 Years. Bradford. 1972.

Political Verse and Song From Britain and Ireland. (Edited) Berlin 1975

Introduction To Working-class Literature In Great Britain. Berlin. Vol. 1 and 2 1978/1979

Englische Arbeiterliteratur vom Ende des 18. Jh. bis zum ersten Weltkreig Berlin-Weimar. 1980 (revised and enlarged German edition of Introduction)

Illustrations

Thanks for permission to reproduce these illustrations
Mr. Frank Graham (1)
Newcastle Public Library (2)
The British Museum (3,4,5,6,7,8,9,10,11,16,17,19)
Goldsmith's Library (12,14,15,18)
Institute of Marxism-Leninism, Moscow (20)

BIOGRAPHICAL NOTES

The main sources for Spence's biography are the materials collected by Francis Place and his own recollections; a memoir by John Mitchell in the *Newcastle Magazine* (1821); Thomas Evan's *Life of Mr. Thomas Spence;* the account published by Eneas Mackenzie in his *History of Newcastle* and as a separate brochure, and Allen Davenport's *Life, Writings and Principles of Thomas Spence,* which reproduces most of Evans's tract almost word for word but is interesting for associating Spence's teachings with workingclass demands in the eighteen-thirties. There are references to Spence in official records, Parliamentary reports, newspapers, contemporary memoirs etc., and in books on Newcastle, such as Thomas Bewick's *Memoir.*[1]

Later accounts were based on the earlier memoirs. A dozen or more can be found, including quite a long entry in the *Dictionary of National Biography,* but these add little or nothing to first sources. Most of the known facts and anecdotes were put together with a description of Spence's Plan in an article in the *Newcastle Weekly Chronicle,* 26 January, 1884, reprinted on the occasion of Henry George's visit to Newcastle, 4 November, 1888. It is just possible that this article was written by Julian Harney. It quotes direct from Spence's works and from Davenport's *Life.* It also gives a handbill issued by the Society of Spencean Philanthropists soon after Spence's death. A similar article by Morrison Davidson appeared in *The Star* also in 1888. The same material with additional comments was used later for his book on land reformers.[2] Reliable summaries of the lives of Spence and James Murray were compiled by Welford in 1895.[3]

The only comprehensive modern study is Olive Rudkin's *Thomas Spence and his Connections.*[4] It has stood the test of time as regards the general outline of Spence's life and the accuracy of its bibliographical data. It also covered the additional information given in A. Water's edition of some of Spence's works.[5] On the other hand, the author relied mainly and uncritically on Place's statements and even on his opinions and did not consult either Newcastle or central Government records. The present author also has not exhausted all the possible sources of further information.

Far from leaving a bad reputation in Newcastle, Spence had had the support and friendship of the most accomplished Newcastle scholar, James Murray, and of the benevolent and respected Thomas Saint. Among his own generation he won the lasting affection of the great woodcut artist, Thomas Bewick. In later years Bewick recalled that boyhood friendship and particularly happy days together on a visit to Spence at Haydon Bridge. Bewick left near a dozen Spence items among his books including London publications which must have been sent to him from there.[6] It seems probable that they kept contact for some years after Spence had left Newcastle — Bewick had never agreed with Spence's utopian and revolutionary ideas, but as sincere radical democrat he shared some of his opinions on other matters and wrote of him as follows:—

> "He was one of the warmest philanthropists in the world. The happiness of mankind seemed with him to absorb every other consideration.

He was of a cheerful disposition, warm in his attachment to his friends, and in his patriotism to his country; but he was violent against people whom he considered of an opposite character. With such he kept no bounds".[7]

The best local historians did not deal unsympathetically with Spence's memory. Mackenzie's account is conscientious. Oliver quoted from his works, in particular the remark in *The Restorer of Society* that the Plan would be the Millenium for the religious, the Age of Reason for the philosopher and the Golden Age for the poets.[8] With time his name was honoured by his fellow-townsmen. Paraphrasing the funeral oration the *Newcastle Weekly Chronicle* wrote:

"He was poor and despised but not despicable; for he was sincere, stoical, persevering, single-minded and self-approved. He set forth a distinct and intelligible system; he knew what he aimed at, and honestly declared it, in defiance of persecution and odium. He showed himself all along more anxious for the extension of what he considered useful truths, than for the establishment of his own influence as the head of a party. He had an open and expressive countenance, great liveliness of temper, a fund of mild humour, and manners peculiarly affable and pleasing".[9]

It is seen from Place's various notes that his feelings about Spence were mixed. He wrote that Spence was "one of those class of extraordinary men from whom the greatest changes in society have proceeded. Had he lived in times propitious to his views it is probable he would have been of considerable consequence".

But he regretted that Spence could not be persuaded to seek better company than his ignorant followers.

"He was unknown to such philosophical men as would have formed a true estimate of his worth, made allowance for his infirmities, rendered him the assistence he ought to have received, and led him to a better knowledge of the world, ameliorated his manners, soothed his care, made him as comfortable as he really deserved to be made. Ordinary men could not be the friends of one whom they could not appreciate and he on his part despised such men, he thought their vulgar notions were of by far too servile a cast, he looked upon them as despicable willing slaves, who deserved no better treatment than they met with and he frequently told them so".

If this was the advice Place offered to him it was not surprising that he found "Spence was irritable, he was uncourteous and he used harsh words". He added: "He was therefore vulgar and ought to be condemned". But he crossed out this last sentence and went on to say that for all his defects Spence was far better than those who abused him.

Twenty-five years after Spence's death, Place wrote in a letter: "It is my hope and belief that the time will come when men will be sufficiently wise to agree that all the land shall belong to the people, and that upon the plan or some such plan, as Mr. Spence has promulgated, by which the people shall be the sole landlord and receive all the rent".[10]

Spence did not record what he thought about Place.

THE LIFE AND WORKS OF THOMAS SPENCE

NEWCASTLE PERIOD

1

Thomas Spence was born at Newcastle-on-Tyne, 21 June 1750. His father Jeremiah Spence, a netmaker, came from Aberdeen about 1739. He had nineteen children, and his second wife, Margaret Flet of Orkney, was the mother of Thomas. Later Jeremiah sold hardware in a booth on Sandhill and Margaret kept a stocking stall. They were among those poor Scots immigrants who largely populated Sandgate, the Quayside and adjoining chares, the overcrowded home of waterside workers, keelmen and labourers.[11] Spence's recollections of these surroundings in one of his rare personal references, recalled the grim struggle to exist by honest labour, the endless toil and austere lives of his parents and others like him.

Spence (in his *Defence,* 1801) described how Jeremiah made his sons read and questioned them on what they had read at the end of every chapter. A habit of reasoning about all happenings and of reflecting on what he read was formed early, and Spence continued this dispassionate search for truth. This exercise of free opinion among serious-minded Scots like Jeremiah Spence was at that time no doubt stimulated by the popular struggles to preserve the rights of congregations to choose their own ministers, and current doctrinal controversies that had begun a series of secessions from the Church of Scotland. Spence's father and his family followed James Murray when some of the Scottish Presbyterians broke away from the Silver Street Meeting House to form an independent congregation of their own.

Later Thomas's brother Jeremiah and some others of the family went a step further in independency and joined the Glassite community, whose Meeting House in Forster Street had been founded about 1766/7. He became a leading Glassite elder, "a man of most distinguished worth",[12] and closely associated with William Leighton, a surgeon, who was later a trustee of their meeting house. Jeremiah was a slop seller (dealer in seamen's clothing.) at Sandhill Corner.[13] His verses *On Reading the History of Crusonia* and tokens which he had struck for Thomas before the latter left his home town for good, show that he accepted Spence's Plan as compatible with Glassite precepts, with the primitive-christian communism and absolute equality of the sect.[14]

A Jeremiah Spence was buried in 1791 in the Ballast Hills Cemetery, the resting place of paupers, workers and many dissenting ministers, where James Murray's widow, Sarah, was later interred. This could have been Thomas Spence's father.[15]

Spence began his working life at his father's trade of netmaking at the age of ten after some schooling. For a poor father of nineteen children in those days this was evidence of Jeremiah's care for their education. Spence is said to have followed various occupations at Newcastle. The only precise statement of his first biographers is that he was at some time clerk to a respectable smith, Mr. Hedley, on North Shore. There are Common Council entries for 1777 and 1784 showing that a Thomas Spence and a Jeremiah Spence were called by a master mariner and a sailmaker respectively and duly admitted to Freemanship by servitude.[16] It is not impossible that Spence served an apprenticeship of some kind and worked as a journeyman. The Mariners' Company covered more than navigation and the callings of the two Jeremiah's were trades connected with ships and seafaring. But even if there had been no regular apprenticeship, since the wealthy Aldermen made new freemen to suit their own convenience regardless of rules and qualifications, lesser masters may well have done as much with appropriate greater caution. Spence's many references to ships and seamen show familiarity with the sea and sympathy for seamen generally. Freemanship was a valuable privilege and would have been an asset when he applied for a post under the Corporation, as well as giving a Parliamentary and a Court of Guild vote.

The first evidence of Spence as a schoolmaster is the information on the title page of his *The Grand Repository of the English Language* (1775) that he taught his new system of reading "in his school in the Keyside" (Peacock's Entry). Thomas Saint printed the book, and from Thomas Bewick's account it may be conjectured that Spence had known Saint for some time.

In the same year, on 8th of November, he delivered his famous lecture to the recently formed Philosophical Society, in which he first formulated his proposals to abolish private property and to establish equal common rights to the land.

The birthday of the Plan was afterwards recorded on the title pages of various editions of the Lecture, and on a political token die.

The Philosophical Society was a frail blossom in the early spring of Newcastle radicalism. They supported American independence in line with the Newcastle Constitutional Club; by a majority of two, declared that a republic was superior to limited monarchy; and queried Church establishment. The Rev. James Murray and Spence were members.[17]

Encouraged by Murray and other friends, according to Evans and later writers, Spence published his lecture in a pamphlet. The next meeting of the Society passed a resolution expelling him, on the grounds that publication without the Society's approval and passing off as an original contribution to their proceedings a paper that had already been read elsewhere, were a breach of rules. It was also implied that the Society had been brought into disrepute. The reason for the strict application of rules is left in no doubt; the resolution expresses the strongest disapproval of Spence's pernicious doctrines.[18]

Every debate closed with a vote recorded in reports of the meetings usually published in the newspaper. There was no report of the meeting on 8 November but the resolution duly appeared as part of the proceedings of the next meeting. In spite of the formalities having been observed, some people must have felt that Spence had been shabbily treated and had he not been a poor man he certainly would have had a case to sue for a published libel.

Murray, the most formidable of polemicists, addressed twenty-two written questions to the Society challenging the expulsion and the sophistry of Spence's critics. These queries, forming a sort of catechism of Natural Right, were later published in *Pigs' Meat* and on other occasions. A handwritten copy survived in Place's papers. The unsigned endorsement reads as follows:—

> "Received this from Mr. M——y Dec. 23rd 1775. To the Philosophical Society in Newcastle Dec. 26th 1775. You will much oblige justice by returning *pertinent* answers to the above directed for him to the care of Mr. Thomas Bewick Engraver with Mr. Beilby, Newcastle".[19]

It is not clear who is meant by "for him" or why an answer to Murray should be sent via Bewick. Evidently Murray gave a copy of his *Queries* either to Spence or Bewick to be sent to the Society, perhaps to stop the spread of scandal due to the newspaper report. It shows that Bewick stood by Spence when he was under attack although he had laughed at his friend's theories to his face until Spence lost his temper, challenged him to settle the argument with cudgels, and lost.

Murray continued to attend the Society's meetings but the level of debate declined into harmless generalities like "What is virtue?". The Society's rules, published about fifteen months later (February 1777), showed that Spence's lecture had been a warning not to venture too far in discussing the nature of liberty. These rules allowed "freedom of debate that is consistent with a decent attention to those established opinions on the keeping of which the welfare of society in a great measure depends", but banned matters "too freely and incautiously calling in question the fundamental principles of Religion and Good Government".[20]

Later Mitchell and others explained that the Society had resented the insult to their dignity when the Lecture was hawked in the streets like a halfpenny ballad and read in taverns.[21] To which Place, painfully literal, objected that this was unlikely because it could not have been printed at that price! But this detail, no doubt authentic, is evidence that Spence really intended his Lecture for that audience and that he had started as an active agitator among the poorer classes when he began his career as a political author.

The publicity given to Spence's expulsion from the Philosophical Society in the press could only have been prejudicial and it may be true that it resulted in the loss of some of his pupils. However, Evan's story, repeated by Davenport and by some modern writers, that he encountered downright hostility on a scale that drove him out of Newcastle, was an exaggeration.[22] The days of martyrdom were not yet. In the seventies "levelling" doctrines were so far removed from reality that however wild and undesirable, they could pass as personal eccentricity. In the acute crisis of the nineties such talk could have dangerous consequences. Evans himself had suffered perhaps worse treatment than Spence, and when he wrote he may simply have taken it for granted that Spence would have been persecuted in Newcastle. The story belonged to the image of the persecuted pioneer, but can be traced to slanders circulated by the new Philosophical and Literary Society of Newcastle (founded in 1793). In reply to statements in the press and in Parliament in 1797 and again in 1817 they disclaimed any connection with Spence, saying that he had been driven out of Newcastle long before their Society had come into existence.[23]

The fact is that less than six months after his Lecture Spence was appointed as schoolmaster to the new Free Grammar School built at Haydon Bridge by the subscriptions of "all the most considerable inhabitants" to provide education for their own children. The governors must have been satisfied that Spence was able to produce "a sufficient character (i.e. testimonial) of his abilities and also of his sobriety and good morals". They promised "every possible encouragement to a deserving Master; no other need to apply whose continuance in that station must entirely depend on his own future good behaviour".

In the little world of eighteenth century Newcastle even this humble post was news. Spence's appointment at £15 for the first year "exclusive of quarterages and a schoolhouse fitted up", was given a paragraph in the local newspaper.[24] But no upholder of private property denounced him.

In April 1779 — the year in which he published his next political tract — he was appointed by the Newcastle Corporation as under-master to St. Ann's Chapel School, known as Sandgate Chapel School.

The school was built by the Corporation in 1682. It catered for the keelmen and was partly maintained by the Corporation and partly by pupils fees. The governor was the Mayor and the assistant governor was the Governor of the powerful Hoastmen's Company, with sixteen other trustees and visitors from among the Newcastle oligarchy, the hard core of all reaction and their hangers-on.[25] It can hardly be imagined that they would have tolerated anyone of whose political character there was the least doubt, especially as the vacancy was due to the misbehaviour of the last occupant. Spence and scandals in the Philosophical Society would have been far beneath their notice. By a decision of 12 April 1779, Spence became the regular under-master, under William Curry, the writing and arithmetic master, at the usual salary of £16. 16s. per annum, and shortly after (20 September) was made collector of the pew rents of St. Ann's Chapel, with the additional salary of £10 out of the rents. He held both these posts for eight years, until December 1787.[26]

Meanwhile he published two political works — *The Poor Man's Advocate* (1779) and *A Supplement to the History of Robinson Crusoe* (1782), and advertised an evening school of his own, in Head of the Side, where he taught reading by his own system of phonetic spelling.[27]

The title page of the *Supplement* mentions a storm at sea which set 'Captain Wishit' (Spence) off course in May 1781. This crisis whatever it was does not seem to connect with any public event or anything that is known about Spence's circumstances. As a precise date is given it might record the birth of his son, which would fit the statement that he was twelve years old when he was arrested for selling ballads in the street in 1793 or '94.

The Common Council minute shows that Spence left St. Ann's School on 17 December, 1787.[28] The word 'discharged' is used, but this was merely the proper form for such an entry. No one ever discharged himself from the service of that august body. In the case of dismissal due to misdemeanour the reasons were always recorded in detail, as in the case of Spence's predecessor. The matter of the pew rents was not overlooked. Spence rendered a satisfactory account.

Introduction to Politics

Biography should help to give concreteness to the way in which overall changes work and what is carried over from past conflicts. Spence was in his fortieth year at the beginning of the French Revolution. His life spanned a period of decisive economic and political change fecund in revolutionary speculation. To appreciate his response to all this and thus to place his own contribution, the environment in which he came to political consciousness is significant.

The new opposition forming among politicians had begun to arouse wider echoes. By coincidence Spence's Lecture appeared almost simultaneously with two memorable tracts by John Cartwright which, with other well-known documents of advanced democratic thought in the second half of the seventies, formed a great part of the permanent ideological equipment of the Parliamentary Reform movements. When a distinct workingclass political movement emerged it inherited on the one hand the democratic struggle with its legacy of constitutional theory, and on the other, tendencies to more fundamental social criticism with the seeds of utopian socialism represented in the first place by Spence.

Typical of the first decades of the agrarian and industrial revolution were natural right egalitarian tendencies spreading among the lower classes — small producers, artisans, pre-proletariat and petty bourgeois intellectuals. The stress was on the guide of reason, on civic rights, individualist independence and 'mediocrity' — the ideal of sufficiency without extremes of wealth and poverty — hence opposition to enclosures, large farms, monopolies. Connected with these ideas were traces of submerged notions of property levelling and land redistribution. Spence's early contact with this line of eighteenth century thinking was provided, for example, by Gilbert Gray.

Gilbert Gray (1709—1794) liked to help young people to develop. A group of lads used to meet in his bookbinding workshop to read the books sent for binding and listen to his teachings. That was where Spence and Bewick first met.

Formerly a shopman of Alan Ramsay and a man of superior education and ability, Gray chose to remain a humble journeyman. "Be neither slave nor tyrant" he taught his young friends.[29] A skilled workman or independent artisan could enjoy modest independence without directly exploiting others. Gray gave away much of his income to pay the debts of imprisoned journeymen and lived very simply, only eating whatever came to hand when he felt hungry, but was able to place his sons in Newcastle Grammar School.[30] One of them became a successful fruit painter and his son-in-law, also a bookbinder, was at one time a partner of Bewick.

Gray's *History of England* for the young went through at least three editions in the seventies.[31] It was unusual in that it combined narrative with political instruction. The Introduction outlined the Constitution and showed how the legal and political system was weighted against the poor. It draws attention to the growth of the Crown's influence and the standing army, and in a final review of recent developments, George III and his ministers are accused of introducing a new system "as unfavourable as it was contrary to the spirit of our constitution", "the first dangerous attack on the liberty of the subject" being the use of the General Warrant to suppress Wilkes. From which it is clear that Gray was a supporter of the extreme anti-Court opposition and of traditional Whig constitutionalism, while arranging his personal life in conformity with ideals of reason enlightenment, social obligation and the dignity of labour.

There was nothing strikingly original in these ideas, but one wonders how many such enlighteners there were among the lower ranks who taught libertarian politics and encouraged independent thinking, who brought into the beginnings of the Reform movement egalitarian attitudes which were not shared by the first leaders.

THE BIRTH OF THE PLAN

2

James Murray

The Rev. James Murray (1732—1782), the only distinguished scholar in eighteenth-century Newcastle, was the most important friend of Spence's youth. He was a leader, perhaps the foremost leader, in the first political struggles in which Spence could have participated; and who but Murray could have introduced him in the first place to so much old and new political literature?[32]

Murray published no systematic treatise. He has been completely overlooked by historians. Most of his ideas were derivative but they appeared in an unusual combination and with unusual vigour. Hone was probably right that no sooner was this formidable champion of liberty dead, than those who had feared him in life hastened to obliterate his memory. Even his son made no effort to preserve it.[33]

Born at Fans, Roxburghshire, in a clerical family with a Covenanter history, Murray himself belonged to the Presbyterian Church of Scotland. The violence of religious persecution in Scotland may account for his passionate denunciation of all war and particularly of war and intolerance in the name of religion, together with every form of "political church" and of clergy in state functions, whether as Bishops in the House of Lords or as Magistrates with authority to punish in this world and the next. He was licensed as a Minister of the Church of Scotland (1760) but never recognized the authority of any Presbytery. In his first clerical post, as assistant to the Minister of Bondgate Meeting House, Alnwick, his new ideas displeased the Minister and Elders, but a large part of the congregation thought he was ill-used, separated and chose him for their Minister. When some of these admirers moved to Newcastle, he was invited to Silver Street Meeting House as a lecturer (occasional preacher). Before long a break-away congregation again formed, including the Spence family, and "called" Murray. In 1764/5 they built High Bridge Meeting House, where Murray officiated until his death sixteen years later.[34]

His success was spectacular. Sermons and weekday lectures announced and reported in the newspapers, drew packed audiences. There were requests for repeat performances of favourite items. Murray demonstrated the equality of all men in his friendly and candid dealings with them, and was liked for his good humour, wit and generosity. High Bridge achieved a reputation for advanced opinion. Descendents of High Bridge families were prominent among radicals of later days and the name of their main society in the second decade of the nineteenth century, The Political Protestants, suggests memories of Murray's militant protestantism. James Morrison, the syndicalist leader, editor of *The Pioneer,* and his parents had belonged to that congregation when he broke into radical polemics at the early age of fifteen.[35]

In England, Presbyterians shared the disabilities of dissenters and were in practice Congregationalist. Murray preached and practised the fullest congregational independency, condemned both Episcopacy and Presbytery, covenants, articles of faith and hierarchy as all equally unscriptural, and looked back to the Apostolic Church. This was possible because there was no Presbytery in Newcastle.[36] Here in the time of secessions and popular struggle against patronage in Scotland, he could avoid courts and synods by living outside their jurisdiction. He attacked ecclesiastical tyranny in Scotland, particularly the scandal of inducting patron-sponsored ministers under military protection, as fiercely as the Erastianism and luxury of English bishops, and was one of the first to advocate united action by all dissenters to petition for the removal of disabilities.

What High Bridge paid their minister cannot have been much. It was supplemented by week-day ticket lectures and authorship. Some of Murray's works were issued in sixpenny, threepenny and even penny parts. When subscriptions did not come in punctually, he was in difficulties to find the money to print the next instalment. He published about three dozen items but none can have been very profitable. When his health was already failing he advertised an Academy for pupils of both sexes. Illness delayed the opening and he died suddenly the following year — when it appeared that he had lived up to his precepts and stored up remarkably little corruptible treasure. His total estate, including personal effects, was valued at less than £5. [37]

People who knew him, including Thomas Bewick,[38] described Murray as "playful" or "facetious" in company, but deadly earnest in defence of principle. The two moods mixed in his sermons — clowning, even references to ladies' legs, at one minute, and grim admonition at the next. The Bible story in his hands was history not mystery and mostly about sinful people. Murray made them living types, added entertaining detail, justified ridicule and laughter in the service of truth. Simple language and matter-of-factness corresponded to his crusade against hypocritical piety and "enthusiasm" (which he associated above all with Methodism and the sycophantic Toryism of Wesley — that "low and puny tadpole in divinity") and against those whom he regarded as conceited ignoramuses, like Bishop Warburton. Like Milton he used homely English where the Hebrew required it. In his sermon on the text "And the dirt came out" he built up comic suspense to the grand climax when the King of Moab shit himself on his golden throne, terrified by the rebellion which his tyranny had provoked. "I should beg the reader's pardon... but as it is the excrement of kings and great men, I hope I shall be excused".[40] He goes on with a mock philosophical discussion of the infinite divisibility of dirt, i.e. the ramifications of bribery and patronage. But his audience liked primitive jokes, recognized Lord North and other great men in the characters and got the message that corruption polluted thrones. As one authority has it, in the 18th century "political and social association was enlivened by the political sermon".[41]

Murray's portraits show a long, boney, serious face with a large nose. His voice was said to be harsh, his gestures wide and clumsy, he continually took snuff which fell in showers on his gown and his audience. Sneezing — laughter — for it is not to be supposed that suppressed sniggers would have been the right response. People were reminded that their everday frailities were not transformed by meeting-house decorum. After the purgation of laughter the admonition may have worked the stronger.

Ridiculing the great and insisting that every man's reason and conscience was as good as another's helped to free common people from servile awe, which held back not only the labouring poor but the lesser freeholders and burgesses. But since passivity was active sin, Murray likewise ridiculed and reproached the patient ass. The Church, said he, was only the clergy and the State only the richest men in it. The people burdened with taxes and tithes pay for their two-fold establishment. On the title-page engraving to his *Sermons to Asses,* the Ass has sunk down between two heavy panniers labelled "Religion" and "Politics". A copy of the Sermons lies open between his hooves but he gazes vacantly into space placidly chewing a whisp of hay. Spence adopted the ass symbol, adding double panniers to hold rents and profits, familiar to token collectors.

Murray encouraged Bible reading by making it a book of entertaining stories. No doubt his interpretations influenced Jeremiah Spence's method when he taught his sons to reason about the Bible chapter by chapter.[43] Murray said that whoever could help the poor to enjoy the Scriptures would be a great benefactor; Spence set out to simplify reading and to publish a phonetic Bible.

Murray called himself "a Hanoverian", supported the Settlement of 1707 and what were called "Revolution principles". But he was well to the left of Whig tradition, an advanced democrat, very near the mixture of constitutionalism and natural right doctrine later typical of the Society for Constitutional Information and the London Corresponding Society. In the long run he might be described as an egalitarian democrat.

His best known work, the series of *Sermons to Asses, Ministers of State, Doctors of Divinity and Lords Spiritual,* [44] is scathing satire of statesmen and divines and the present state of society. He judged according to absolute ethics independent of legal precedent, which held good for all circumstances and all times. According to this standard Britain was only comparatively free. Those who submit to any "human yoke", let alone sacrifice spiritual to material welfare or public weal to private gain, are no better than atheists.

He was a believer in the Millenium, "when all dominion shall be put down and God shall be all in all". No law or government will then be necessary since all men will be perfectly righteous. The kingdom of God is not of this world but a spiritual state. It comes about entirely as the work of God and not through any effort or merit on the part of man. Before the Second Coming it serves as an ideal standard by which to measure the good and evil of this world, in which the chief aim of State and Government is to create more opportunities for greed and power. For if the rule "Do unto others" etc. were observed, men would govern themselves and there would be perfect liberty. This was one variety of eighteenth-century concepts of liberty ranging from government as a necessary evil to something more like anarchism.

Such teachings prepared Jeremiah Spence the younger and others to accept the stricter discipline of the Glassites, who not only left salvation entirely to God's election but considered that this world was so hopelessly depraved that it should be left to its own damnation and that the tiny number of Christians should hold aloof as much as possible from its affairs and not even discuss the matter with the unregenerate. Their idea of the coming Kingdom of God on Earth was more concrete and material perhaps than Murray's. In Spence possible Glassite tendencies were reflected in the millenial metaphor of Spensonia, the simplification of law and administration, the absence of a penal code, the belief that unanimity can be reached through honest discussion, as the Glassites claimed to practise.[45]

Murray was near the Glassites also in regarding surplus wealth as sinful. "No man has a right to call anything his own when his brethren have need thereof and he can spare it". [46] Wordly success was at the price of conscience; under a corrupt system no honest man can expect to be successful. The public crimes of statesmen and clergy pressupose personal depravity; *vice versa,* private vice produces public evil. Nations cannot be both great and virtuous. They become great only by plundering others. What most people regarded as national prosperity was the path to destruction. Commercial progress depending on the increasing luxury consumption of the few and the permanent degradation of the majority could never be anything but a general evil. Murray's *Kingdom of the Ants* was an answer to *The Fable of the Bees.* In the Ants' happy, unmercantile commonwealth, all work and all have leisure to cultivate the arts; everything is decided by reason; the king is elected by popular vote; all functionaries are frequently changed. Bewick contributed a beautiful engraving of the Ants' Theban Harp, symbol of their pastoral simplicity and the cheerful songs at their feastings and drinking parties.[47]

But in real life there were degrees of freedom and therefore a struggle is not only possible but the obligation of a Christian or a patriot. People may have to submit to superior force but where matters of conscience are concerned they ought to prefer martyrdom to connivance. Rogues and murderers rule. Murray gives examples and concludes "Your Graces and Lordships are guilty, sinful and vile creatures". [48] Coming retribution through the rebellion of the oppressed is the subject of many eloquent passages. The Deluge is the type of disaster which can just as well come about without divine intervention. In his enlargement of the Bible story Murray describes sinners, to whom his hearers could easily attach names, overtaken by the Flood in the midst of their daily business of oppressing the weak.[49] Spence reprinted in *Pigs Meat* part of Murray's *Fast Day Sermons*[50] which sharply contrasted the rich hypocrites who are the cause of the nation's misfortunes with the perpetual "fasting" of the masses, and warned of coming retribution. The disturbances in Murray's times were primitive and unorganised, but they increased in the sixties and may have seemed to him to pressage revolt. If he did think so, his teaching that when government is corrupt rebellion is a sacred duty, meant more than most writers who used such phrases in that period.

Murray's attitude to the common people differed distinctly from that of most of his educated contemporaries, although his concept of class went no deeper than theirs. He treats poverty neither as a misfortune nor as evidence of vice. It is rather the evidence of wronged innocence. The cause is avarice not Providence. He sometimes preached patience, but never resignation. In the poor he saw some possibility of virtue; in the rich none at all.

All men can tell right from wrong. All can judge of public policy.—

> "But if there are any principles of state that plain men cannot understand, they are far too deep to be practised and must have their foundation laid more upon the lusts of corrupt ministers than upon principles of reason and science. Such as cannot understand that *as they would men should do to them, so ought they to do to others,* are to be comprehended within the ranks of idiots".[51]

He gives examples of the consequences of ignoring the people's grievances or underrating their intelligence. Men in power

> "imagine that (the people) want discernment and are not judges of what pertains to their own affairs. I can assure you, my Lords, they pay you off in your own way when you judge in this manner, and say often some very shrewd things concerning the characters of men in high offices... They will often say to one another 'These are fine men indeed to direct public affairs who cannot govern their own appetites. Are these the makers and executors of our laws, who profane them openly and abominably, who neither seem to fear God nor regard man?'... Truly, my Lords, you would be surprised to hear the sarcasms which the country people throw out upon such topics against people in high rank. Would you imagine that a country hind would be able to keep a register of all the natural children of every justice of the Quorum in the county? The people are really not as stupid as you imagine... They are almost all acqainted with the story of Haman and know the height of the gallows to an inch and make some very pertinent comments on it, that would astonish you".[52]

Governments relying on coercion and penal laws not consistent with self-evident reason and natural justice will be defied and, when the people are strong enough, overthrown.

"But when you tell them that they are not judges of your manoeuvres of state, they will soon tell you that they cannot transgress what they do not understand: and that you require of them more than the Deity requires of them or even supposes... The foolish threadbare maxim of minor politicians ought to be given up—that the vulgar are not qualified to judge of matters of state... All the common people may not be qualified to understand financiering, or how to manage a sinking fund; but if the ground of government were kept clear no such thing would be wanted... And be assured, that even amongst the lowest class of the people many understand the theory of financiering as well as the First Lord of the Treasury; and with regard to practice, his wisdom cannot be much admired on some occasions".[53]

As reason and natural law are sufficient guide (equivalent to God's law in earthly affairs), savages and heathen are equally capable of establishing justice. In Spence's story Indians embrace his Plan and contribute their uncontaminated love of freedom to the foundation of Spensonia.

According to Murray inequality and eventually despotism arose because the poorer or weaker were forced or persuaded to sell their birthright or were too indolent or selfish to resist gradual encroachment. Spence put more stress on force but the "history" is essentially the same in his writings. Murray differed from most exponents of the social contract theory in his time when he said that liberty was lost when men "forgot their interests *as members of a community*" (his italics) and followed their private interests.[54] By this definition liberty only exists as a social relationship in contrast to rights inherent in the individual and qualified by the similar claims of other individuals, that is, as a compromise regulated by the state. Murray did not develop his concept theoretically, but illustrated it, particularly for instance in spelling out the role of the corrupt voter betraying his fellow-citizens. The corrupt politician intends to sell his constituents, so that in the end they pay for his election expenses and more, including their own bribes. Those few who could command a higher price are none the less his asses whom the great man rides to further fame and fortune. Thus institutions meant to preserve liberty become organs of oppression and men make their own fetters.[55] But Spence enlarged on the social nature of liberty by identifying individual with collective prosperity, the key mechanism of the Plan which guaranteed stability and reconciled progress with civic virtue. He was also prepared for a repetition in France of the (bourgeois) revolution generating a new oppression so long as the economic foundation of liberty was not secured.

The polemics of the day which were preparing theoretical foundations for the Parliamentary Reform movement later, were chiefly concerned with constitutional law, government policies and party rivalries. The grievances of labouring people might be mentioned but did not provide the main argument. Here too Murray differed, for he gave political liberty an economic basis and declared that the obstruction which before all else deprived people of their rights was the taxation of the poor on the necessities of life.[56] Again he did not go more deeply into the matter, but pointed to the sufferings of the labouring poor as the glaring proof of bad government or tyranny. "Those who work not, eat all, and those who labour hard are destitute of the necessities of life" he wrote.[57] "Pinching hunger" had caused the riots of 1769—

> "What are mobs and riots in times of scarcity but hungry people fighting for their meat? The full, the rich and wealthy in whose interest it is to have the prices of the necessities of life high, may call them rebels or what names they please, but if they would change circumstances for a small season, they would soon alter their opinion".[58]

Commenting on a massacre of starving people in Dumfries:—

> "It is easy for a glutton of a minister to call their betters the scum of the earth and to hire scribblers to abuse them".

The standing army, he goes on, exists to keep the people down. The need for it is a sign of immanent "dissolution". The soldiers behave "as in an enemy country"[59] — which reminds one of Spence's description of landlords acting like foreign conquerors.[60]

It should, said Murray, be the duty of government to keep provisions within the reach of the poorest, whether by reducing taxes and prices or by making more money available to them. Manufacturers should be obliged to maintain workers displaced by machinery. "Every patent... is a privilege to destroy so many lives".[61] A similar remedy was suggested by a contemporary economist, Thomas Mortimer, who went so far as to rejoice that in spite of rewards offered for information, the men who destroyed the new sawmills at Limehouse (1769) were never found. "The cause of all the recent combinations and disturbances", he wrote, was that "the price of labour is not advanced in proportion to that of provisions: that the profits of the proprietors of considerable manufactories are too great".[62]

Whether Murray was influenced by any particular writer, his views were in line with those who opposed excessive exploitation and regarded technological innovations with uneasiness as a further cause of distress. They scorned the hunger incentive condoned by Petty, Berkeley, Arthur Young and, in milder terms, Adam Smith, and the argument that labourers were naturally lazy and vicious. Postlethwayte, for example, thought that prices were deliberately enhanced by taxation in order to force people to work six days a week.

> "To toil unceasingly in want is too hard a condition for a human creature to endure. Men will not be industrious but on the prospect of reaping some enjoyment therefrom: nay, it would be the most detestable tyranny to require it on any other terms". ... "As landlords have strove to keep down the price of labour in order to raise the value of their property, so farmers and master workmen have done the same for the enhancement of their

gains. From these partial and self-interested sources have been circulated throughout the kingdom the insidious reproaches of exorbitant demands of wages and the too general accusations of vicious extravagance in those who had it not in their power to be guilty of the offence. Such has been the effect of a prevailing rapacious spirit, so much the more to be censured as those who suffer them have been the means of giving affluence to their accusers: nay, the people to whom we are indebted . . . for the whole of our national power. Yet to them for their utility, the state indubitably owes convenience, encouragement and protection, which government should ensure to them, as their natural and social dues".63

The eighteenth-century economists knew no solution for the contradictions inherent in the agricultural and industrial revolution. Not all who thought that the labourer got a raw deal drew the conclusion that profits should be limited. The remedies suggested did not envisage the future development of social production based on new technology, but paternalistic social reforms based on individual labour.

Mortimer summarized a number of proposals. He included:—
Small farms stocked by the landlords; allotments of crown land to the poor; wages to keep pace with prices and proportionate to profits: loans to young artisans to set up in business: obligation on landlords and master builders to build a proportion of cottages and cheap dwellings; the encouragement of public holidays and leisure for recreation; medicines within reach of the poor; aid for large families, such as state provision for surplus children. All these suggestions are included by Spence to illustrate the advantages of his Plan, the small farms being stocked and artisans equipped by the collective landlord, the problem of large families solved by the universal dividend and schools. He could have thought of these arrangements for himself, but the similarity is nevertheless striking.

On the land question Murray was egalitarian. Properties and tenancies should be restricted. Large farms raised prices and caused local shortages by selling to middlemen — a common complaint at the time. He does not say how the partial confiscation of large estates was to be carried through, probably because he did not really see this as a practical possibility. Depriving the poor of their commons by enclosure was equivalent to theft and murder. The downfall of "this dirty land of Moab" was prepared by monopolizing the land.[64] "The security of the Commonwealth is best maintained by making small and numerous dividends, for thereby the greater number will be interested in the welfare of a nation". (The same argument and terminology were repeated by Spence). "Unequal dividends of the wealth of Kingdoms" are a sign of approaching revolution.[65] (It is not clear whether he is speaking of the distribution of the total product, which was the sense in which Spence used the term "dividend", or of the land itself). This was the Harringtonian doctrine that revolutions came about to restore a balance of interest in the State, but where Harrington's intention was to secure the new landed class in their possessions, Murray applied it to the claims of the lower classes.

Murray accepted a current fiction that the commons were the poor man's substitute for individual landholding, but also hinted at some redistribution.

> "The idea of a common suggests at once that it belongs to all within the district, and it cannot be divided without giving everyone his proper share. The original design of commons was that those who had no separate lands of their own, might have *a common estate* with so many others: and formerly, it is highly probable that every township had a common which was the poor man's estate... The legislators in Moab might as well have made a law for the rich to divide their estates with the poor, as to have made Acts of Parliament to oblige the poor to part with a privilege to which they had a prescriptive right. *The claims of freedom and liberty ended with the division of commons*".[66]

Here enclosure is regarded as the last phase of appropriation. Murray also speaks of "a few over-grown chiefs" already owning all the land, houses and money.[67] Spence's more precise statement that private property in land had originated from the continual appropriation of the property of others seems like a logical conclusion from Murray's vaguer suggestions. Meanwhile it might seem that the recent increased enclosures of commons by Act of Parliament had stimulated the opposite idea of the universal common. An association of the common with civil liberty was shortly to be given expression in the Newcastle Town Moor case and there can be no doubt that the above quoted statement connects Murray with the preparations for that campaign.

He avoided any conclusion that the land should be returned to the original common ownership. He defined a commonwealth as "a self-governing democracy"[68] and it is clear from many illustrations in his works, that unlike most educated democrats, he recognized the right to equality and self-determination literally of all degrees of men without distinction. But as he also regarded private property as a natural right and made no distinction between one kind of property and another, he could only fall back on the model of the Jewish Jubilee, small allotments, the obligation to provide for the needy and moderate personal consumption. The economic foundation of power may be implicit in what he writes, but he says more about the acquisitive motives of despotism, in a general way associating tyranny with monopoly.

Spence quoted another contemporary who drew similar conclusions from the Harringtonian position:—

> "An Equality of estate will give an Equality of Power, and an Equality of Power is a commonwealth or Democracy. Hence an Agrarian Law or something equivalent to it must make or find a suitable Disposition of Property".[69]

From this redistribution the writer expressly excludes "the rabble".

This was the form in which Spence inherited the problem. He did not discover the material foundations of liberty and the State but resolved the inconsistencies of his teachers by a once-for-all Jubilee and a universal equal share in the national "common", his "People's Farm".

From the point of view of the historical development of political thought, he may be said to have brought egalitarian democracy to the threshold of communism and was the first in England to introduce the concept of economic power explicitly into the political struggle, and to formulate a programme for a new economic system in the interests of the working classes.

At first glance Murray's 'Queries' to the Philosophical Society might seem to indicate full support of the Plan. Actually they only defend the Plan's consistency with natural law and Scriptural precept, and freedom of opinion in general. Murray did not commit himself here to the abolition of private property. The query form leaves the matter as a question for abstract speculation.[70]

Now Spence was about 15 or 16 years old when Murray began preaching in Newcastle. The early sermons introduced most of the favourite texts applied in support of "levelling" and condemning the oppression of the poor — the very texts which Spence was fond of quoting later. In these sermons Jewish society is divided into rich upper class and poor working people. The sins of covetousness, avarice, abuse of power, the Christian duty to share with one another and to relieve the needy are here as literally interpreted as in Glassite teachings. It may be noted in passing that one of the Newcastle Glassite elders and trustees was the author of an excellent pamphlet outlining their doctrines, not only repeating all that Glas had said on the matter, but seeming to give special importance to social obligation, the practice of charity, renunciation of wealth and the duty to give any surplus over modest needs to the community.[71]

This presentation of the social problem and the primitive class standpoint invited Spence from the outset to a critical examination of conditions which the vast majority then accepted as a matter of course.

Murray regarded all war unless in the defense of liberty as an invasion of the rights of others. The labour of the poor financed the oligarchs to find new fields of plunder and extortion, and the clergy "goes snacks with them" in return for blessing the slaughter.[72] The people are deliberately deceived as to the causes and aims of war. He gave many examples old and new but the topical case was of course America. Murray's political activity opened with a pamphlet exposing Wesley's support for the government's colonial policy.[73] He published the greater part of a three volume history of the American War.[74] He initiated a public meeting in 1775 to petition for a peaceful recognition of American independence.[75] The last phase of his agitation on the Catholic Relief Bill (1778) need not concern us here. He was one of the founders of the Protestant

Association at Newcastle on whose behalf he edited *The Protestant Packet* until a journal was started by the Association at London. His last writings celebrated Lord George Gordon's acquittal.

Murray had the courage to take risks. Having been warned that the magistrates were preparing to prosecute him, on the evidence of an informer who attended his lecture on the lawfulness of self-defense, he hastened to call on Lord Mansfield in London on the strength of the clan name. Mansfield warned him that he had barely escaped this time "with his skin between his teeth". Reassured, Murray published his lecture with a dedication to the Mayor of Newcastle.[76] One notes that he was able to get away with a great deal more than those unfortunate dissenting ministers who were imprisoned and victimised in the seventeen nineties for much milder democratic views, but as the most forceful leader of the opposition to the Newcastle establishment, he was a thorn in their flesh for many years. His activities were not confined to the pulpit as we shall see below.

The Contest and the *Freeman's Magazine* represented a remarkably high level of popular and practical political education.

It had been Blackett's custom to ride out canvassing at the head of a few hundred supporters. Now he rallied a still more imposing retinue from the gentry of three counties, all in hectic commotion for weeks in advance and in full array on Polling Day.

The Burgesses, determined to get as fair and orderly an election as possible, made their opponents agree to ban flags, music and processions on the day itself. They recalled that last time voters had had to pass between rows of men armed with cudgels when they went to the polls, and other unseemly methods of persuasion. They pledged their supporters to resist bribery, reminded voters of the shameful sale of votes at three shillings, and that one of the candidates had boasted that he could now have all he wanted for two-and-sixpence. They explained the meaning of the election oath. On principle they did not canvass but exposed the lies and scares put about by the canvassers of other parties. The greatest difficulty was to prevent the creation of freemen to provide new voters which had been the scandal in past contests. The Common Council dispensed with the usual procedure of calling candidates in open Guild, but feeling unsure of their legal position, kept their malpractices as secret as possible. When the Burgesses protested that steps had been placed behind the Town Hall so that strangers could enter the court room unobserved, the Mayor simply transferred the business to a private house.[116] As a good proportion of voters were in any case outlyers (non-residents) it was not easy to keep any check on their credentials. Several hundred new voters were added to the poll in spite of all precautions. Propaganda was distributed including an extract from one of Murray's sermons. *The Freeman's Magazine* was full of lively gossip, verses, letters, lampoons. No effort was spared. Only the candidates themselves, when they saw that they could not win, retired early from the hustings.

The results in unbought votes, about one-third of the poll, were in the circumstances no mean showing. The published report exposed all the electioneering tricks but concluded that had all the outlyers understood what was at stake and turned up to vote, they might even have won. It seemed to show that even on a restricted franchise and at such great material disadvantage opposition was possible and the report concluded "Cheer up lads! All is not lost!".[117] This was the optimism of the moment. Oldfield cited Newcastle as the prime example of "political ideotism" with half its electorate non-resident and in all less than a tenth of the population.[118]

The Town Moor affair had thus fallen between two landmarks in the struggle,the Instructions of 1769 and the General Election of 1774. This is precisely how its history is given in *The Contest.*

The local movement did not immediately die. Murray's American Petition was adopted at a meeting of burgesses, trades and general inhabitants called by the Constitutional Club, 23 October, 1775, with George Grieve in the chair, and was presented to the House of Commons by Sir George Savile with 1,210 signatures.[119] America was not made a special issue in the elections, in spite of the fact that the question had precipitated a dissolution of Parliament, but there is evidence that considerable pro-American sympathy existed. Two Newcastle editions of Paine's *Commonsense* appeared almost as soon as it was published, and Bewick's clearest impression of that period was that the majority of people decidedly opposed the war. The vigour of the campaign in 1775 may be judged by the fact that on the eve of the meeting thousands of copies of Wesley's *Calm Address* were hastily run off and thrown into every shop and house door in the town.

In the 1777 bye-election the radicals again put up a candidate. In 1780 Murray produced a new election pledge (unfortunately no copy seems to have survived) which was refused by all candidates in the General Election except Thomas Delaval. Their other man, Constantine Phipps, was returned, only to go over to the ministerial side and an appointment in the Admiralty.

The above narrative shows that what Namier calls a "new political movement" in Newcastle did not begin in 1774 and that the contested elections were not, as he and others assert, merely an incident of local "vendetta".[120] Movements cannot exist or changes operate except in particular and local forms with their local subjective motivations. The Novocastrians had their longstanding grievances but the actions and statements of their leaders show consciousness of national issues and political principles not reducible to local vendetta. As far as Newcastle is concerned the character of the movement and the relatively mature constitutional theory in *The Freeman's Magazine,* which could not have been manufactured overnight, would not support Rudé's conclusion that early radicalism spread out from London and that initially as an appendage to the Wilkes campaigns. Rudé was of course aware that the background was complex and ultimately determined by social-economic processes. Even less satisfactory is the facile statement that Newcastle reformers "embraced the Wilkite radical programme" but that the presence of the Town Moor committee leaves "no doubt that the vendetta against the town magistrates was their main concern".[121] Taking Parliamentary history as the starting point and the communication of ideas as the dynamic can never explain the genesis of radicalism.

The Town Moor

Spence said that the case of Newcastle Town Moor had been a lesson which he never forgot.[77] Evans said that his whole Plan was originally inspired by this example. There was some truth in this, but not in the simple direct sense which Evans implied.[78]

There were several similar disputes in the period, typical of the survival forms of the guild system. A few years previously the freemen of Morpeth had successfully prosecuted the Corporation for appropriating common land. After Newcastle there were similar unsuccessful actions at Alnwick and Durham. The victory at Newcastle made a deep impression. Commemorated in letters of gold in the Cordwainers' Hall, frequently recalled by local historians, the anniversary became a town's celebration. The Burgesses had united to challenge the corruption of the magistracy, the powerful mercantile and landed aristocracy, now servile upholders of the Court party and its alleged design to undermine constitutional government. Local interests and new political tendencies met in nascent radicalism. Spence was in his early twenties.

Conflict between the Mayor and Aldermen (the Common Council) and the body of middling and lesser freemen, including artisans in their incorporated Companies and Mysteries, went back at least to Tudor times. The self-perpetuating magistracy progressively excluded all semblance of democratic practice, monopolized revenue and patronage and created new lucrative concessions for its own benefit. "Acts of Usurpation" [79] increased under the last Charter granted in the late XVIIth century but it was some forty years before opposition began to become more open and united, and then to acquire a faintly political colour (probably after 1741). The small share in town government allowed to the Court of Guild under the rules of procedure and election was blatantly disregarded. The Mayor had long ceased to be elected, as a result of growing antagonism. "Nowhere had the oligarchical government by a select body been more completely established than at Newcastle".[80] Embezzlement long continued to be an open scandal, often at the expense of charitable endowments.[81]

Outside the Corporation, strikes and popular discontents increasing in this region as elsewhere in the seventeen sixties, were in practice directed against the Common Council or its individual members. The heirs to the Hostmen and Merchant Adventurers were the hereditary ruling class and the great employers direct and indirect of labour. They controlled not only coal, iron, lead, grindstones, salt, brewing and glass production and trade, but almost everything else, including banking throughout the North-East independent of the London financiers.[82] The monopolizers of great estates, shipping, harbours, roads, tolls, fishing rights, and the river in a region which already imported most of its grain, also controlled the basic food supply. The main local industries were such as had early developed capitalist relations and there must have been a relatively high proportion of wage labour, including the Scottish immigrants, in occupations which had never achieved incorporation. On the other hand grievances like the perennial struggle for river conservation, the repair of the Tyne Bridge (1771) and various obsolete restrictions, concerned progressive industrialists and the poor alike. The men regarded as responsible for shortages and high prices which produced frequent riots, and for conditions which produced large strikes, also enjoyed wider judicial powers than ordinary Justices of the Peace. In the riots of 1740 Common Council records were seized and burnt. Whether some particular intruments of oppression were sought it is not known but the action itself is significant.

In the early sixties there are signs that certain companies and their stewards, including men of the respectable class of tradesmen and merchants, began a more systematic attempt to break this autocracy, and to associate their aims with popular rights.

In 1764 the Court of Guild was able to insist on a special committee of stewards, presided over by the Mayor *ex officio,* to inspect the records of Town Moor boundaries and roads. These revealed continual encroachments and grants of valuable concessions for peppercorn rents going back to the XVIIth century, benefiting the neighbouring estates of leading families. At the same time, no doubt because of the growing number of impoverished small producers and rising prices, the burgesses petitioned that parcels of land should be let for cultivation, the rents to be used for the relief of poor freemen and their widows. This was rejected. Sir Walter Blackett, then Mayor, held that such enclosure would require an Act of Parliament. As to roads, the Common Council promptly granted a turnpike road on a 99-year lease at the rent of one shilling to a wealthy landlord whose unauthorized road building right across the Moor had been unsuccessfully contested at law.[83] In 1770, the Common Council further laid open claim to the revenue from mines, quarries and enclosures for the first time since a frustrated attempt to do so forty years earlier. In December, 1771, 89 acres of the Moor were advertised and eventually let for cultivation on easy terms with additional privileges of tenancy. The Court of Guild was not consulted and no one bothered about an Act of Parliament. A face-saving minute was recorded that after the first two years the modest rent should be made over to the stewards for distribution among their distressed brethren.[84]

Practically the whole body of freemen united in indignation. When protests failed they incited people to pull down the lessee's house and fences and to drive cattle onto the land. When there was still no reaction, the companies called meetings to choose a committee, including some well-to-do individuals. After notifying the Mayor and the lessee, they marched to the spot and committed actionable damage in the presence of numerous enthusiastic witnesses. In the summer of 1772 the lessee made written complaint of repeated depredations and desired to cancel his tenancy.[85] The Common Council offered to pay his expenses to sue the burgesses committee. While this private action went in the usual way to Common Pleas, steps were taken to negotiate. It was mutually agreed by magistrates and burgesses to submit their dispute to arbitration at the next Assizes. The magistrates, instigated, it was always said, by Sir Walter Blackett, tied up all the local legal talent and applied all their ingenuity, public funds and the pulpit to prejudice the case in advance.

George Grieve, a lawyer and a landowner of Alnwick, who had inherited from his father a vendetta against the Alnwick Common Council and the Earl of Northumberland, and was a member of the Society of the Supporters of the Bill of Rights, was approached, probably by Murray personally. Through him the burgesses briefed Serjeant John Glynn, Recorder of London, famous for his part in the recent Middlesex elections and Wilke's close associate.[86] Glynn was given a triumphal entry into Newcastle as champion of the Moor.

He opened the case for the burgesses in the best traditions of defending ancient rights and liberties before a special jury presided over by Sir Henry Gould and, what is more interesting, Sir William Blackstone. All things considered (some particular reasons will appear below) the prosecution wisely declined to contest a case so patently just and the verdict went to the burgesses with costs. An order of Assize instructed the parties to draw up jointly a bill embodying the verdict and defining the rights of all concerned.

The victory was celebrated with tumultuous and prolonged public rejoicings and all the resources of guild ceremonial, bells, guns, illuminations, processions, dinners, patriotic toasts, tavern meetings, presentations and testimonials, and the freedom of several companies to Nathaniel Bayles and Henry Gibson, both surgeons, who had risked personal liability to act as the nominal defendents, with other members of the committee. Liberty issueing from her temple proclaiming "Town Moor saved 10 August, 1773" and the inscription "vox populi vox dei" on the signet rings presented to them by the Tailors' Company, indicate what the victory appeared to symbolize.

The magistrates, having nothing to celebrate, stayed sober for once and used the interval to forward a bill of their own composition to the House of Commons, at the same time adding insult to injury by drawing up a scheme for Town Moor rents to be administered as a charity by church wardens and overseers of the poor, ignoring the stewards and treating the beneficiaries as paupers. The drafting was done by the Mayor, a leading Alderman, one of their lawyers and Glynn, thus in appearance representing both sides. It may be wondered why Glynn agreed either to the procedure or to the document. At the eleventh hour these underhand dealings leaked out. The incensed burgesses voted their own proposals and objections to the magistrates draft "almost to a man", and lost no time in sending them to London.

The resulting Town Moor Act[87] confirmed ownership of the soil in the Corporation as a whole, reserving herbage to resident freemen and their widows. It gave powers to the full Court of Guild to dispose of seven-year leases of up to 100 acres for improvement, the rents to be administered by the stewards of the companies on behalf of their poor members. Cow Hill Fair and the race grounds were to be preserved.

A committee of stewards voting according to the mandates of their companies and with their own chairman, was thereafter annually elected to watch over these rights, continuing into the XIXth century although never given legal status.[88] The Act and the report of the trial were published at the time and in several later editions, the story being revived whenever the Moor was threatened.[89]

The judge's summing up, regardless of what any of the charters had actually said or intended or how far they were even authentic, declared that the town's government could be nothing but the constitution of England in miniature, no legislative act being operative until passed by all three parts thereof, in this case Mayor, Common Council and Court of Guild. Thereafter the Town Moor Act, preserving what the Judge had called "the great Palladium of the Rights of the Burgesses of Newcastle", was to be their own Bill of Rights.

This pleasing fiction did not of course establish that democratic procedure was ever followed. The Merchants' Company firmly kept its hold on all offices. Later attempts to use the Act or to exploit the Town Moor in the majority interest came to nothing.[90]

What had been gained was a symbol, a democratic myth. The burgesses appeared as the defenders of their heritage and of civic liberty in general. The material gain went to a minority and was little enough when £20,000 annual revenue went no one knew where. The £10 per year per head mentioned by Evans was purely imaginery. But the humbling of the great was a memorable event for the unenfranchised majority of the lower classes as well as for the freemen.

The following year a popular party for the first time contested a Parliamentary election.

It is necessary now to outline the Newcastle political movement, which appears to be almost unique at that date, although modern historians regard it as negligeable, or rather have not troubled to enquire into the details. It is not only of interest as the background of Spence's political ideas, but may be compared with the role of the London Corporation opposition in the early stages of the Parliamentary Reform movement or the original purpose of the London Corresponding Society to restore the right to vote to those who had lost their freemanship through some anomaly — an aim almost immediately seen to offer too restricted a base.

The Elections of 1774

While the old struggle between the rank and file of the freemen and the Common Council was maturing and long before the protagonists moved into position to tread the stately measure of the law, an energetic political opposition had arisen. The Town Moor dispute was neither cause nor consequence, but one facet of an awakening political consciousness.

Namier's picturesque remark that the radicals "tacked their own political cries onto the milch cows on the Town Moor" has not much foundation, chronological or otherwise.[91]

The franchise within the town itself was restricted to freemen. Corporation affairs and national politics were inseperably mixed. Sir Walter Blackett for example was Governor of the Merchants' Company, five times Mayor, represented Newcastle as a fixture through seven Parliaments, and having gone over to the Tory party after the hotly contested elections of 1741, settled matters with his former rival, so that the two members managed the constituency amicably to suit themselves. The unprecedented expenses and more than usually open corruption in these elections had made several companies record their condemnation of the sale of votes.[92]

In one of his sermons Murray described the electioneering in 1768. The revolting farce showed the worthlessness of the MP's and that in reality there was no representation of the people. A riotous polling day ends with the drunken orgies of county gentlemen and town dignitaries in every tavern. — "What a sight, or rather what a smell!" The candidate himself is slumped in a pool of liquor and vomit — "his hat . . . swimming like an oyster boat down a tide of port, loaden with the supper of a Justice of the Peace . . . One of the pillars of the State! The hope of a sinking commonwealth!".[93]

Soliciting and buying of votes and the dependency of the voters ruled out any freedom of choice.

Murray was credited with reviving serious politics in the North-East.

"When corruption was about to overwhelm the state, he was the first to warn the people of their danger", wrote an admirer. "His satire was not like the keen, polished and poisonous shafts of Junius, shot secretly in the dark — No! his darts were naked and barbed — they rankled and tore the wounds they made! He scorned to remain under cover, but nobly stepped forth, the dauntless champion of liberty and fearlessly set at defiance the frowns of power and treated with contempt the fears of the weak".[94]

Junius was certainly tame compared with Murray's merciless exposures of the public and private records of the members for Newcastle in his two publications of 1774, for example, *The Contest,* which he wrote himself, and *The Freeman's Magazine,* which he edited.

Opposition politics in the period, in which early radicalism mixed with various trends of national and city faction fights, found outlet and coalesced in the issues raised by the Wilkes' campaigns. In Newcastle there were immediate protests against General Warrants in the early sixties. Awakening political consciousness was reflected in the rise of patriotic clubs. While having local motivation of its own, the movement responded to the political opposition in London in its triple form of Parliament, Corporation and popular agitation. The Constitutional Club at Newcastle might have been formed in response to the circular of the Society of the Supporters of the Bill of Rights in 1769 recommending the formation of provincial societies. But there is no evidence that this was so. This Club continued in existence until 1775 or '76 and may have covered Durham and Northumberland, or more likely simply corresponded with sympathisers in other towns.[95] There were one or two other patriotic clubs in Newcastle of which little is known.

The body formed to exert political pressure and prepare for the next general election was an organisation of the electorate, eventually known as the Burgesses Party with its own committee. According to the statement of this body, alarmed by the tendency of government, since the accession of George III, to restore arbitrary power and by such ominous signs as General Warrants, they had published warnings to the public in London newspapers repudiating the actions of the Members for Newcastle.[96] This would imply initiative from Newcastle before the establishment of the Society of the Supporters of the Bill of Rights. In 1769 the Constitutional Club and the Burgesses committee were in correspondence with that Society and thereafter with the Constitutional Society formed at London by John Horne (Horne Tooke), Sawbridge and the better part of the Bill of Rights Society when they broke with Wilkes in 1771. The roundabout procedure in approaching Glynn in 1772 may have been due to this split. Murray, a non-voter of course, worked closely with the Burgesses Party, edited their magazine and probably assisting to draft their documents. The wording of the Pledge presented to Parliamentary candidates for instance was always attributed to him.

Rudé, who has investigated the Wilkite movement, found no signs of Wilkite influence in Newcastle.[97] Later writers throw no further light on the matter. It depends on what is meant by "influence". Direct contact between Newcastle and London Wilkite circles is well documented. Sir Francis Delaval, the patron of the Burgesses Party, and George Grieve were both members of the Bill of Rights Society. Grieve was one of the committee who drafted the famous eleven-point manifesto (generally regarded as inspired by John Horne) and apparently remained with the Wilkes faction for a time. Delaval supported the new Constitutional Society. Grieve continued in close touch with Newcastle affairs and with the Constitutional Club, appearing at meetings when he was in Newcastle. He was a colourful character often reported in the local press. A few years later when he stirred up a revolt in Alnwick against the Four-and-Twenty (Common Council) and the Earl of Northumberland, he adopted the tactics of the Newcastle burgesses, though without their success.[98] The Newcastle family antecedents of Beckford, Sawbridge and Brass Crosby might also be noted. Their high standing in London may have helped to ensure that the Burgesses Party was not a group of rebels but widely representative of the freeman electorate.

As regards Wilkes himself however there is little evidence of a personal following in Newcastle or that he was built up there as a public hero. After the town's celebration of his release in 1770, which was duplicated in several northern towns, little is heard of "Wilkes and Liberty" there.[99] Glynn visited Newcastle five years after the Middlesex elections when the Wilkes movement was fading out and Wilkes himself concentrating on becoming Lord Mayor. Even before this the Newcastle movement seems to have been more concerned with policies than personalities.

Murray from the outset found it difficult to swallow Wilkes whose personal reputation conflicted with his apparent public character. In a sermon at that time he warmly congratulated the Middlesex electors on their stand in repeatedly returning Wilkes. As in earlier incidents too Wilkes appeared to have suffered for principle disinterestedly, he could be regarded as "politically righteous" so far, which was more than could be said of most MP's. "Yet whether five and forty such as him will save a nation from ruin is as yet uncertain". (The reference was to Sodom and the famous No. 45 of the *North Briton*). His private character was sadly inclined to the vices of Sodom and a family tyrant was in a weak position to complain of tyranny.[100] In the interests of the campaign this sermon was not printed in the first collection but in a set of Additional Sermons. By that time the writer was reassured that Wilkes had proved no exception to the rule that private and public morals are indivisible. In another sermon Wilkes was given the role of Mordecai waiting at the gate of the palace, appropriate enough for his exclusion from the House. But Mordecai's sole merit was as the agent of the Haman's (Lord North's) downfall and perhaps hinted that he was only waiting to jump into court favour himself.[101]

The Burgesses Party represented a majority of the rank and file. It was eventually supported by 25 companies, though not all of these gave official backing to their candidates at the elections. Nothing is known of any formal constitution or rules. The body seems to have existed as an open meeting of freemen, some possibly mandated by companies, who took decisions by the customary procedure. It must have included wealthier tradesmen and manufacturers whose interests conflicted with the great mercantile monopolies (as did the very extensive up-to-date undertakings of the Delavals), but the majority must have been small producers, masters employing a few workers, petty tradesmen, artisans and journeymen and, since freemanship no longer corresponded strictly to occupation, some of the poorer sort of wage labourers and self-employed. The Select Committee who conducted the Town Moor affair later (1774) appeared as spokesmen for the Burgesses Party, notably as the deputation to solicit the candidates' agreement to nomination. But the active leaders and perhaps initiators of the political struggle were not such substantial citizens, but obscure men, described with approval by democrats as "common mechanics" and by opponents as "mean labouring tradesmen".

In April 1769 a committee of three — Guthrie, White and Reed, were elected to draft Instructions to the Members of Parliament on the matter of the Middlesex elections and other points as proposed by the Bill of Rights Society. These three were a glazier, a mason and a house carpenter — trades in which independent small masters as often as not hired out their own labour and that of whatever workers they required to a "customer" or a contractor who supplied the materials and directed the work.[102] Guthrie owned a horse, so it may be taken that he was not a common workman. Their inferior status however allowed ill-natured Aldermen to treat them with contempt or even to abuse them for daring to approach them at all. They were deferential in addressing the great men of the companies. The Instructions were endorsed by a general meeting on April 15th. The Committee called with them on the MP's who treated their request as an unheard of impertinence, and then on the Aldermen. None agreed to sign the Instructions, but when interviewed individually were mostly evasive, some of them not wanting to condemn the motion outright. A few were even polite. One in particular very politely excused himself because, he said, being in the pay of the Government, it would embarrass him. The Instructions were then brought into the Guild meetings of various companies and received 627 signatures, something approaching half the electorate. But as the MP's had not accepted the Instructions, the Burgesses published their grievances in London newspapers.

In November they again supported the petitioning for the dissolution of Parliament started by the London body. The draft presented by the Committee was again accepted unanimously in the general meeting. It was then brought into the Michealmas Guild meeting of the Corporation and the Town Clerk, after voicing his objections to it, had to read it out. Seventeen companies sent a deputation to the Mayor requesting a Town's Meeting at which it would be put to the vote. This outward move assumed that the unenfranchised as well as the electorate were concerned as supposedly represented in Parliament. The meeting duly took place at Forthe House, but whether it actually had the sanction of a Town's Meeting or not, neither the Mayor nor any other of the notabilities attended. Some leading figure was needed for the chair and Guthrie, mounting his good horse Liberty, galloped over to Seaton Delaval to invite Sir Francis, the County Member for Northumberland, who was probably prepared for the emergency. The other MP's could not now ignore the meeting and appeared in person to explain their objections. Blackett refused categorically to have anything to do with the petition. Sir Matthew Ridley said that it was a moderate, even quite a good petition with which he might agree in part, and although he did not see how he could actually sign it himself, he offered "very politely" to present it to his Majesty on behalf of the petitioners. Not unnaturally the meeting unanimously refused the offer — if Sir Matthew did not agree with the petition it would be unfair to charge him with it. It was decided to confide it to Sir Francis Delaval. It was then taken round the various companies and 900 signatures collected. When the petition was presented and ignored, the Burgesses followed up with "a warm Remonstrance of their own", adopted with one vote against by a meeting chaired by Thomas Delaval, signed by the stewards of twenty-three companies, and presented by Sir Francis Delaval.[103] Support was growing.

The spirit of the petition meeting may be guessed from the shock to Sir Walter Blackett. His biographer connects the incident with the marked decline in his popularity and calls it a particularly painful exhibition of "ingratitude" among recent humiliations which preyed on his mind and hastened his end.[104]

The sharpest criticisms came from Murray who exposed his whole political record — his support of unpopular measures in the House, election rigging, monopolizing the representation of the town, misuse of public funds, and finally his true character displayed in scheming to rob the freemen of their last rights, down to the grass for the widow's cow. His charities far from being virtuous were only another method of bribery harmful to the public interest. He had kept his hands on the town's revenues for thirty years and that was the motive behind all his actions.[105]

The evident anxiety to preserve personal popularity seen in all these encounters explains why the prosecution gave way so readily at the hearing of the Town Moor case, preferring to counteract the judgement by backdoor methods. Political reputations were at stake. Glynn would hardly have missed the obvious opportunities in cross-examining the main witnesses, his political enemies. The Newcastle microcosm throws interesting sidelights on the relation of MP's to their constituents and the role of the masses. The Town Moor had its political significance and clearly the Burgesses horizon was not limited to the cows on the Moor. Nor were their actions simply an echo of the metropolis or manipulated by the political and business rivals of the local Tory interest.

A comparison of their Instructions, Petition and election pledges in 1774 and 1780, shows that their formulations were somewhat sharper than the London models and added points of their own.

For the general election of 1774 both factions of the London movement adopted a pledge which was circulated through the country.[106] The Newcastle pledge was noticeably more specific, in particular as to the rights of representation. The Burgesses programme as put forward in their Instructions, Petition and election test pledges, begins with the right to mandate MP's and absolute right of constituents to recall them "if they do not behave as they ought". The immediate aim is to replace "men of such dubious characters" as the present representatives. The elected members must be forced to obtain the repeal of "laws contrary to liberty". The points raised in the London pledge are sharpened; shorter Parliaments and "more equitable representation of the people" are coupled with the demand for the extension of the franchise, and in the first place the immediate enfranchisement of "the whole body of Newcastle freeholders" and their opposite numbers in York and Durham. It is interesting that the demand is made in this specific local form and not expressed as a general principle. It reflected the growth of a new middle class owning property in the town, who before the end of the century well outnumbered property-owning freemen. Civil list economies mentioned in the pledges were at Newcastle coupled with concrete grievances affecting both small employers and wage earners, such as the taxing of "the people's bread, beer, soap, candles, leather". [107]

The movement which organised the opposition in Newcastle was more consistently plebeian than the London leadership. They spoke of themselves as "the Leather Aprons" — Newcastle's sansculottes, against "the Laced Waistcoats". Objective class divisions advanced together in plebeian dress. They boasted that they had no aristocratic, civil, military, clerical or legal titles among them.[108] Sometimes their propaganda struck a new note of challenge to parvenue aristocracy:—

> "the upstart, unlettered mushrooms of yesterday assume office they were never fit for, and claim honours for which they have no merit and to which they never had any claim except what was digged out a coal pit or hauled from the bottom of a lead mine".[109]

(The lead mine belonged to Blackett). They frequently draw contrasts between wealth and honest poverty, labour and placemen. Egalitarianism goes so far as to declare

> "The nearer that the proportion of the various races of mankind are to one another, the stronger must the community be".[110]

In keeping with these general sentiments, *The Freeman's Magazine* published the "Address to the Electors of England" prefixed to Jean-Paul Marat's *Chains of Slavery,* the appearance of which in London had, according to the author, been sabotaged by the machinations of Lord North.[111] It is now understandable why Marat, who was acquainted with Wilkite circles in London, considered that the patriotic clubs of Newcastle were the "purist".[112]

The Burgesses Party therefore took on the character of a poor man's party. If universal suffrage was not yet the battle cry, the notion of universal equality had advanced a long way towards it.

Their political ideology was expounded in an historical survey looking back to "the patriots of 1641", something of a deviation from the usual reference to the Glorious Revolution, which had buried the regicide past. The Constitution, won after long struggle, resting on Magna Carta, the Petition of Right and the Bill of Rights was now threatened. *The Contest* added that the "treason" of the Septennial Act had hastened the process and demoralized the electorate. Quite in the spirit of the Puritan ancestors, the writer says that the people should have disregarded the Act, and sent their representatives to Westminster at the usual time "with swords".[113]

We note the outline of a history of progressive struggle (without any assumption of an ancient Constitution or an Alfredian legacy which had been corrupted). Such ideas came out of Old Whig tradition but their fresh formulation as the argument for new demands, in particular for the extension of the franchise, first appeared unequivocally in publications beginning in the second half of the seventies, which formulated the three basic demands of Parliamentary Reform eventually handed on to the Chartists.

National and local corruption was a key issue in the elections. Murray showed that the Tories only opposed Walpole's system and the Septennial Act in 1741 out of party interest while the Whigs, who voted for the Act and for excise and taxes to buy support, acted as Tories. Bribery no less than violence enslaves; "public liberty might be as mortally wounded with a squeeze of the hand as with the point of a dagger". "Great standing revenues" in the hands of a few were as dangerous as "great standing armies".[114] A detailed article on Walpole's "invisible agency" to pack Parliament declared that this had not been any sort of "mistake" but a policy deliberately thought out because it paid.[115] The writers did not know the secret lists compiled by the Ministers or the huge sums provided by the Crown to finance election expenses and reward key men, but these articles show that they understood the fraudulent mechanism.

The Germination of the Plan

The results of the elections had not been won without much effort and organising on the part of patriots, voters and non-voters. It is inconceivable that Spence, who was personally attached to Murray, would have been a passive observer of all this excitement. It cannot be doubted that the bold struggle to wrest power from the great landlords had its lessons for him, perhaps as a method unworthy of human reason.

But we can come closer than that to the Plan's direct connection with these events.

The Contest told the story of the Town Moor, putting it into political perspective, connecting local with national issues, illustrating the aims and characters of the political parties and demonstrating the need to struggle for civil rights and good government. The Whig "character" is an ideal not corresponding to the party label, for having achieved power, the Whig degenerates into a Tory. Power corrupts. The Town Moor case was a struggle against tyranny. The records of the MP's who join to usurp the political rights of the people and then conspire to rob them of their last property, are mercilessly exposed. Honest disinterested men had come forward to oppose them and won the day. All this was both election propaganda and a serious consideration of whether a democratic system of government can be achieved in practice.

To close the narrative Murray allowed himself to dream of a society founded on the principles of equal justice for which the Town Moor champions had contended. The Town Moor Act, Newcastle's Bill of Rights, is turned into a parable of good government.

> "Let us peep into futurity — and, for once, suppose the Mayor of Newcastle, in the Town Hall on a guild day, in the year 1800, or before — if your worships please — thus bespeaking the freemen.
>
> **Fellow Burgesses**
> Our revenue having increased this year above our expenses, the balance being two thousand pounds, now lies in the treasurer's hands, and the Common Council waits your directions how to dispose of it.
>
> Shall we apply it to the widening of our narrow streets — the supplying the town with plenty of soft palatable water —the support of our poor; or encouraging new branches of trade or manufactures; by giving bounties on their produce to the able and industrious?
>
> Shall we divide it amongst ourselves, and let every man use his share as most agreeable to himself? — Shall we bestow it on our poor, maimed and aged brethren, or their widows whom neither vice nor intemperance have made so? — Shall we assist the sober and industrious young artist, who has made a good apprentice to his master, with a loan to enable him to set up a business he is very capable of following? — Shall we present it to our unfortunate brothers in trade: to recover from a bankruptcy, which misfortune or large families have alone been the occasion of? — say — what shall we do with it? — the money is yours — dispose of it as you please!"

If the accounts were challenged these honest Aldermen would offer to make up any proven deficit from their own pockets and if they failed in office they would stand down for better men. There was nothing to prevent the great gentlemen of the Common Council acting in that way now and declaring "We wish to serve only to benefit you, and honour ourselves. We are gentlemen — we want not money and wish but for your applause".[122]

It is noticeable that the needs of the poor and of the town as a whole are put first, as though the Corporation no longer represents a privileged minority.

In Spence's Lecture the following year the Burgesses have become the whole people, the freemen's revenue the whole of the land and its resources, the Mayor and Common Council have been replaced by the Parish and its committee. But the association was verbally preserved in as much as the Lecture speaks of the people forming "corporations" and thirty-five years later the Parishes are described as "corporate bodies". Undoubtedly this fantasy contained the germ of the Plan. The Town Moor was another parable, like the Jubilee, to be interpreted by giving it universal application. It was a common way of thinking in those days that the Biblical type could refer to a future reality.

In his Lecture Spence did not mention the Town Moor or the dividend. His audience could see the analogy for themselves. Spence first actually mentioned "the dividend of rents" in his ballad of 1783, but it was assumed from the start. Rudkin was wrong in thinking that it was added later to increase the Plan's attractiveness.[123] All that Spence added later was an express provision that part of the revenue should always be distributed individually in cash as a device for securing the individual's independence and status and as a constant reminder of common rights. He gave it an organisational, educative and political function to assist the development of mutuality, and for similar reasons the dividend payment was adopted in the practice of co-operative trading and production by early socialists.

This background of the Plan suggests two possible attitudes in its author:— First, the lessons of the Elections that Parliamentary contests and reforms would not be enough; and secondly the over-optimism in thinking that the extension of the Town Moor parable would be convincing. The Philosophical Society with unerring instinct immediately drew a sharp distinction between petty bourgeois radicalism and revolutionary social change.

LONDON PERIOD

Spence settles in London

After Spence left St. Ann's School there is a gap of four or five years. John Bell, usually a reliable authority, states that Spence left Newcastle in 1792.[124] Both Francis Place and William Hone dated their acquaintance with him from that year.[125] Rudkin suggested that Saint's death in 1788 left him without a publisher and he saw no future for himself in Newcastle. But it is not known that he had done any work for Saint since 1782. Naturally if he was still in Newcastle in 1789 he would have felt moved to seek the centre of the upsurge of political unrest in response to the French Revolution. But it is improbable that he left his secure employment in 1787 without knowing what he was going to do next. It seems likely that it was during this period that he suffered from an illness described as an attack of palsy which left him with a permanent limp and possibly a speech impediment, first mentioned in 1792.[126]

Spence's *Pronouncing and Foreigner's Bible,* of which a few pages printed by Cook and Debrett survive, bears no date. It is thought to have been his first venture in London which for some reason was abandoned.[127] Similarly his Spensonian dictionary of which Hone later saw a part was also not finished.

Spence's son William accompanied him to London, helped in the shop, designed illustrations for some of the broadsides and probably the picture of Masaniello in *Pig's Meat,* but died young, perhaps about 1797.

According to Mackenzie, Spence married at Haydon Bridge.[128] It was always said that the marriage was not a happy one. It is not known when his wife died, probably before he left Newcastle. Before 1794 he married again — a pretty girl to whom he proposed at first sight when he saw her cleaning the steps of a house. Mrs. Spence is named among the wives of prisoners who received assistance from the victim fund of the London Corresponding Society in 1794. Several memoirists mention as evidence of his nobility, that Spence took her back after she had left him for her old lover and continued to support her after their final separation when life together had become unbearable and she had brought him to the verge of ruin.

Spence must have saved enough to make a fresh start in London and to set up his book and saloop stall — "the long stall in Chancery Lane at the Middle Row corner".[129] He joined the London Corresponding Society, took an active part in its affairs, sold radical pamphlets and began publishing political broadsides and eventually tracts of his own, beginning with his Newcastle Lecture with an introduction, under the title *The Rights of Man.*

Place, many years later, for a memoir which was never completed, wrote a not very flattering description of Spence with some details of his personal habits in the nineties. He was a small man, about five foot tall, spoke with a 'burr', looked older than he was, his face thin and wrinkled, his clothes old and sometimes ragged, and his face "marked him as a man soured by adverse circumstances and enmity with the world". Moreover he was extremely simple minded and unbelievably impractical.[130]

The Fear of Sedition and Rumours of Invasion

Popular political movements and pamphleteering for a class hitherto not known to read and "hardly intelligent enough to feed themselves", and the encouragement which educated enthusiasts for the French Revolution gave to the lower orders to apply the Rights of Man to themselves, presented the ruling class with unprecedented problems. William Pitt very sensibly remarked that "Being composed of the lower orders of the people, it (the Movement) has within it the means of unbounded expansion and conceals in itself the seeds of rapid increase".

"Public-house political clubs and alehouse debates on politics" were chased from one tavern to another by intimidating the landlords, but meetings continued even when the number allowed to assemble for any purpose was restricted by law, and open-air rallies could on occasion bring together 200,000 or more.

Even a modest reform of Parliament challenged vested property interests. The French Revolution had shown that "the mob" could be inspired to act with frightening energy. The British ruling class saw a privileged order overturned with unprecedented speed and completeness. They resorted to clumsy methods of repression for want of better, but to regard their fears as imaginary, as did their opponents at that time and several generations of liberal historians after them, is to distort the situation.

The new political forces then only beginning to emerge were necessarily unstable and ill-defined, and not to be judged by the verbal violence of the polemic. Hence the various attempts which have been made to assess the extent of revolutionary tendencies or the existence of conspiracies in the reform movement have generally proved inconclusive.

Following the royal proclamation against seditious writings (21 May 1792), a new type of organisation was launched, in conclusion with Ministers, at a meeting at the Crown and Anchor Tavern, on 20 November 1792, by Joseph Reeves, ex-Chief Justice of Newfoundland and holder of various lucrative official posts and sinecures. This Association for the Preserving of Liberty and Property against Republicans and Levellers, commonly called the Loyal Association or the Associators (or by a variety of ruder names) played a special part in Spence's affairs.

Masquerading as a voluntary body, it carried further Church and King riots against Jacobins and Dissenters, the burning of Paine in effigy, and acted as a spy agency. With the ostensible aim of tracking down and restraining seditious publications in the first place to stop the sensational circulation of Paine's *Rights of Man,* Loyal Associations were established widely at town, county and even-vestry level, thanks to the efforts of clergy, landowners and magistrates, legal advice and sometimes the local initiative being provided by Treasury Solicitor agents. They encouraged the formation of armed volunteers, advertised rewards for information about alleged disloyal subjects, pursued suspected Jacobins, prosecuted small printers and pamphlet sellers, secured signatures to loyal addresses by intimidation, incited riots, pressurized magistrates to issue special public warnings and to make arrests, and even staged their own trials, and generally spread panic. The war was certainly unpopular and various ways were adopted to spread fear of invasion and spies, in which the Association played its part too. They also flooded the country with the first written propaganda designed for the semi-literate, which supporters were invited to buy in bulk for free distribution.

The Association's direct connection with the Ministers and misuse of Government departments could not long remain secret.[131] The Parliamentary opposition and liberal leaders outside Parliament felt themselves threatened by a general smear campaign, exposed the illegal and terrorizing actions and demanded an enquiry.[132] The Association was a thinly disguised unconstitutional agency of Government.

Spence and the Associators

Spence looked an easy victim. "He was at that time as poor as any man could well be, and with some trifling fluctuation in his affairs he continued in this state to the day of his death."[133] In one of Reeves's first reports to the Treasury Solicitor's office, his stall was mentioned among booksellers frequented by a new class of disreputable customer. The pamphlet *The Case of Thomas Spence* states that he was repeatedly pestered by Reeves's agents, "surrounded, insulted and even threatened with his life, and the destruction of his little all . . . if he did not give up selling the *Rights of Man* and other political tracts".[134] The papers of the Association indeed show that Spence was an object of their special attention.

On the morning of December 6, 1792, a fortnight after the inauguration of the Association, two Bow Street Runners bought a copy of his *Rights of Man* in mistake for Paine's, and hauled him before the magistrate at Hatton Garden, who saw no need to detain him. One of the men afterwards told Spence that they had been sent by Reeves and complained that Reeves had never refunded the cost of the pamphlet.

A member of the Association on passing the stall on December 10th was disappointed to see seditious pamphlets still displayed there and read "with great avidity" by passing workmen and apprentices.

"The owner of the Bookstall at the top of Chancery Lane" he wrote, "has been repeatedly enjoined not to expose to sale or hire such seditious publications, but in open defiance of the various entreaties and threats of numerous well-wishers of the public he boasts that he will still vend and let them out to hire, and that the law cannot prevent him from so doing. Surely this is of all the greatest Evil which calls for the vigorous Interposition of the Association. The Parochial Association of St. Andrew's and St. George the Martyr have it also in contemplation to remove such a dangerous Nuisance and wish to have their Efforts for so doing countenanced and if necessary aided and assisted by those of the Committee at the Crown and Anchor".[135]

Supposing that this letter was delivered by hand the same morning it had immediate effect.

Between three and four o'clock that afternoon two more runners appeared, bought a copy of Paine's work, forced Spence to shut up his stall, hustled him into a hackney coach and took him to Bow Street. While waiting in a public house for the magistrate to finish his dinner, the men turned out Spence's pockets, confiscated a notebook and papers which were never returned, while a "gentleman" — perhaps the indignant letter-writer — seized him by the throat and threatened to strangle him. Spence protested to the Grand Jury against the arbitrary proceedings and violence, but was committed to Clerkenwell Prison. The runners threatened to march him through the streets in chains unless he paid the cost of a coach, but although the canny man replied that he would prefer chains, this public demonstration of martyrdom was on second thoughts denied. He was delivered to the gaoler at 11 o'clock at night, and after suffering further humiliations, his losses by way of gaol fees and "garnishings" amounted to £1. 4s. After thirty hours he was released on bail.

On return to his stall he found the shutters plastered with notices that the occupier was in prison for selling seditious books, which should be a warning to others.

In spite of feeling shaken and ill after the rough handling and a night in a damp prison bed, he reopened his stall and the very next day another of Reeves's informers came to enquire for some of his ballads — "the most seditious and inflammatory ever read" — but was told that they were sold out.

"But says he (Spence) I have something in my pocket (this he spoke very softly) pulling out a small Pamphlet which was the Plan of a Society in Holborn executed in the most Seditious language".[136]

At that date this could only have been a London Corresponding Society address. Making allowances for the conspiratorial atmosphere invented by the informer, the incident shows Spence as a dedicated propagandist missing no opportunity to encourage a possible recruit. To the letter-writer he seemed "just the kind of man to stir up sedition".

On the following day (13 December), he was attacked and threatened by some more Associators, but was rescued by the byestanders.

On December 24th, his landlord, urged by a "pious rector", sent his daughter with a notice to quit the stall on Lady Day (March 25th), evidently ashamed to come himself.[137]

Meanwhile an account of Spence's troubles and a copy of the warrant under which he had been imprisoned were published and subscriptions for his defence were invited, to be handed to Mr. Hamilton, bookseller, near Gray's Inn Gate, Holborn. Neither author's nor publisher's name appears on the pamphlet. Perhaps it was written by Hamilton for the style is certainly not Spence's. It must have been printed in December. A copy addressed to the President of the Friends of Universal Peace, Stockport, was intercepted by the Stockport Postmaster, who reported the matter to Reeves, noting the unflattering references to the Associators.[138]

Spence was re-arrested on 16 January, 1793. This was probably the occasion when William Hone, then a lad of about 16, on his way to work saw Spence arguing with the runners and a crowd collecting.[139] Possibly bail had been cancelled due to further pressure from the Association. He was held in Clerkenwell New Prison until his trial in February for selling *The Rights of Man,* when he was acquitted on a technical error in the indictment. Actually Spence's alleged offense had been committed before Paine's work had been proscribed. Paine's trial for seditious libel had been postponed from May till December 18th, when he was outlawed and his book declared seditious in his absence. But these facts would have been of less use to Spence than the clerical error.

Spence had prepared a new edition of his Newcastle Lecture, under the title *The Rights of Man as exhibited in a Lecture read at the Philosophical Society in Newcastle . . .*" containing a new dialogue and eighteen of Murray's *Queries.* The preface was dated November 19, 1792 — by coincidence the day before the Crown and Anchor Association was inaugurated. Publication was delayed. The title page states: "Printed for the author and sold at the corner of Chancery Lane, Holborn, 1793". If it came out in January it could have been the excuse for arresting him on 16 January. If it appeared after Spence's release in February, he was then under notice to quit in a few weeks.

The next edition bore the title *The Real Rights of Man,* distinguishing it from Paine's and pointing to the latter's inadequacy. Hitherto there had been confusion between Paine's book, Spence's pamphlet and his *Rights of Man in Verse.*

Spence's son, then about twelve years old, was arrested for selling the last mentioned broadside in the street. The sheets were taken away from him and he was detained for several hours in the Police Office and Spence paid a fine. Another boy who helped in the business and lodged with his mother in Spence's house was later treated in the same way. Among other harrassments a rival saloop seller had tried to get the magistrates to close Spence's stall.

For the next few months after his trial Spence had no further serious clashes. But in December 1793 a true bill was found against him. However the Middlesex Grand Jury threw out three indictments citing him for his *Rights of Man* ballad and *Pigs' Meat.*

Perhaps he was lucky in as much as the Middlesex magistrates still tried to live up to their reputation of upholding free speech ever since the famous Wilkes' affair. The Association repeatedly complained of the Middlesex Grand Jury's lack of zeal in acting against seditious propaganda.

Two letters from Spence published in *The Morning Post* (18 December 1794) and *The Morning Chronicle* (3 January 1795) and reprinted afterwards in *Pigs' Meat* give a brief summary of his experiences. The facts are supported by other news cuttings in Place's collection.[140]

So far the count for two years was:— dragged numerous times from his business, three times arrested, twice had a true bill found against him, once tried and acquitted, three times indicted, and finally in 1794 examined by the Privy Council and imprisoned for seven months without trial.

The Freedom of the Press

Prosecutions of writers and printers multiplied as never before. Prison sentences and fines resulting in financial ruin, shattered health and death of the victims became notorious and were remembered in nineteenth century radical journalism. Fox, Grey, Erskine and Sheridan had challenged the May 1792 Proclamation and called for action against the questionable activities of Reeves's Association.[141] The attack on supposed Francophils, the encouragement of informers, the threat to the freedom of the press and so on held dangers for more exalted persons than the little pamphleteers and street sellers. Grey in the House of Commons associated the Birmingham riots in particular with the incitement to attack Dissenters in the famous Bull letter. This first fruit of reactionary popular propaganda was satirized by many of the pamphleteers but none more effectively than by Spence in his *Letter to Ralph Hodge* which attacked the system of government for the benefit of the landowners and fund owners epitomised in the Association, and satirized the weak-minded workingmen who were used against their own kind.

Finally Reeves's pamphlet *Thoughts on the English Government* gave the opportunity to force the Attorney General to start proceedings on a Commons motion that it was "a malicious, scandalous and seditious libel". At the trial (20 May 1796) it was judged to be "a very improper publication". Reeves's was acquitted and rewarded with another sinecure, and so the farce ended.[142]

In December 1792 The Friends of the Liberty of the Press was established under the leadership of Erskine and Sheridan to combat the suppression of "liberal sentiments and manly freedom of discussion which forms the life and soul of the British Constitution". It was compensation for Erskine. Following his victory in Walker's trial for High Treason in Manchester, at Paine's trial the jury scornfully dismissed his eloquent defence, declaring that the Prosecution need not reply because a verdict of guilty was already agreed.

Besides Grey, Erskine and Sheridan the leading members included the cream of the Foxite Whigs and such well-known reformers as Lord Daer, Hollis, Arthur Pigott, Capel Lofft, James Mackintosh. The first meeting at the Crown and Anchor adopted resolutions endorsing Erskine's Address and accusing the Association of setting themselves above the Government as "state Inquisitors and liscensers of the Press", destroyers of domestic peace and patrons of venal informers. Ten thousand copies of the resolutions adopted as the Society's "Declaration" were ordered to be printed and distributed for the collection of signatures.

The first signatories included members of the Society for Constitutional Information and the London Corresponding Society, beginning with their respective secretaries and leading radical booksellers and writers. Among them are the names of Spence, Panther, Hodgson, Baxter, Gerrald, Eaton, Parkinson, Thelwall.[143]

From this it appears that Spence attended the meeting on 9th March and may well have attended the first meeting. At the time of the second he was in prison.

This society only lasted as long as it suited the leading personalities, but it may be said to have had its use in giving influential backing to the struggle for a free press. The arguments embodied in the resolutions were carried over into the broadly organized much more effective actions of radical publishers in the 1830's.

The Hive of Liberty

On vacating the Chancery Lane stall in March 1793 Spence opened his shop, The Hive of Liberty, at 8 Little Turnstile, Holborn. The change of address was circularized on a printed slip through the LCS divisions. Here he carried on business as a token dealer as well as bookseller and publisher, issuing his catalogue of tokens early in 1795. His purpose was perhaps more political propaganda than profit. His tokens condensed popular republican and reform slogans, the essential ideas of his Plan and the political jokes of the day in ingenious tiny pictures.[144]

The shop is mentioned on various occasions as the place where LCS reports could be obtained, petitions signed beginning with the Petition to the House of Commons in April 1793 and donations handed in.

In a report on radical booksellers recommending that they should be controlled by magistrates like public houses and that those stocking pamphlets below the price of sixpence should be required to take out a licence, the Hive of Liberty is described as second only to Eaton's shop as regards popularity.

"Another shop is Spence's in Little Turnstile where a periodical work entitled Pigs' Meat is published. This man lives in the dirtiest poverty, but his shop is decorated with Lines in prose and verse, expressing a determination to carry on this traffic in spite of Laws and Magistrates. This is one of the Houses where they train to Arms. Difficult to prosecute because witnesses are afraid for their lives due to the resentment of a great body of persons".[145]

Evidently by this time Spence had arrived at some standing and popularity.

Pigs' Meat

Pigs' Meat began to appear in 1793[146] in weekly penny parts consisting of extracts in prose and verse to form, when completed, a permanent guide to political knowledge. Old and new items by Spence himself and passages from his contemporaries are included but the many carefully chosen and varied selections from older authors could only have been collected by someone in Spence's position over a long period, as claimed on the title page. The work must have been begun in Newcastle. A number of the works used are quoted from Newcastle editions. While copying for his own use, at some time Spence must have conceived the idea of publishing a volume. The extent of this laborious work cannot otherwise be explained, nor the completeness of each item. Some of the *Pigs' Meat* extracts have been checked against originals and in all cases the meticulous accuracy of the copy even as regards punctuation is striking. The scrupulous handling of sources shows an instinctive sense of history and respect for both the author and reader. There is no commentary but the point which Spence thought important may be emphasised by the juxtaposition of the items or the follow-up of an idea in another passage.

One of the main purposes of the Society for Constitutional Information had been the re-publication of writings and speeches on democratic rights and the constitution. The volumes give a good overall summary of the main ingredients of bourgeois democratic ideology of the period. *Pigs' Meat* broke away from this formal, rather legalistic approach to documenting the history of constitutional theory and was guided by the intention to represent the rights of man in a much broader way, stressing the problems of social injustice. Spence goes further afield for his examples and aims at novelty and entertainment, including satire and sentiment. He does not argue with his authorities or examine their thought in context. His aim is to demonstrate that the poor man's grievances can and should be discussed and had not been ignored by the humane and unprejudiced. The result was a lively mixture of many different tendencies, but all bearing on the vital theme of social equality and in particular on the various proposals as regards the land question. Today it is of immense value to see what the writings of former political thinkers could offer to men at Spence's social level and how they were interpreted, and it might still be as good an introduction as any to the history of social thought. The originality and lasting freshness of *Pigs' Meat* can be seen when the work is compared with another book of selections published in 1795, perhaps inspired by Pigs' Meat. Here the extracts are grouped under abstract subject headings.[147] There is useful legal information but the material has been much more pre-digested and tailored to the editor's opinions. But Spence invites us "to amuse ourselves with distant Views of Happiness." — "Must we" he exclaims at his trial in 1801 "be debarred from the Pleasures of Imagination also?".

Spence did not own a press. Most of his pamphlets and some of his broadsides give his name and address as publisher or state "printed for T. Spence". The type was not always broken up immediately, but served for re-issues and second editions even after two or three years. It may be assumed that his publications were financed out of the retail book business. He also sometimes appeared as publisher of other people's works.

While Eaton was in difficulties Spence brought out one or two numbers of *Hogswash* (afterwards *Politics for the People)* on his behalf. Among his tokens is one celebrating Eaton's acquittal, (24 February, 1794).

Thus we see Spence at this date not as a lone prophet but in the thick of plebian agitation and one of that fraternity of small enterprising publisher-booksellers who played such an important part in the early movement.

Spence in the LCS

Spence belonged to Division 12 of the LCS which he represented on the central delegate committee, and was therefore among those who joined the society in the first months of its existence. By the summer of 1792 there were said to be some 24 divisions numbered in rotation.

Incidental references to Spence in government records show him undertaking all the day to day tasks of the rank and file activist. In addition he published ballads and tokens supporting current campaigns, in defense of

LCS members. All his work shows that he upheld genuine democratic demands, while regarding them as only fully to be realized in his Plan. The Parliamentary Reform movement, as may be seen from his attitude in *Pigs' Meat,* awakened public consciousness and made a starting point for the discussion of liberty.

As we have seen above, almost as soon as he opened his shop a copy of the LCS petition for reform (8 February 1793) was placed there for signature. A few weeks before his arrest in 1794 Spence was in charge of sixpenny tickets for an LCS meeting in "an evening Hop House where young men treat their ladies" in Store Street.[148]

Division 12 had a number of militant members who at times opposed the moderates. They were described by an observer as all "violent democrats", and Spence himself as "a very active manager" among them.

Samuel Godfrey, friend and attorney of Lord George Gordon, was also a member. He was elected delegate of Division 12 on 6 February, 1793, possibly to replace the imprisoned Spence. George Lyneham (14 February) objected to Godfrey on the Committee of Divisional Delegates on the grounds of his close connection with "a party leader" (i.e. Gordon). After heated argument with Godfrey, the Committee excluded him, and this decision was endorsed in the majority of the divisions. A proposal that the Committee should be empowered to reject unsuitable delegates at their discretion was however negatived.[149] Shortly after Baxter charged Lyneham with being a spy. An enquiry "trial" found him innocent but when he appeared as prosecution witness in the Treason Trial in 1794, Baxter's suspicions were fully born out.[150]

Then, April 4th, the LCS banned a society called British Citizens (Secretary W. Williams) which met at Godfrey's. As the LCS did not demand strict ideological conformity and admitted members of other organisations, such strong disapproval suggests fear of the Gordon connection or that the British Citizen's aims were extremist.

Gordon died that year in November in his debtors' prison and Spence struck a commemorative portrait token. In view of Murray's personal esteem and efforts on Gordon's behalf, Godfrey might have been friendly to Spence but nothing is known of any connection between them other than membership of the same Division, nor is there any trace that Spence was involved in the British Citizens.

What the LCS regarded as totally unacceptable appears from a resolution of 10 October 1793 to expel "any member who shall be found propagating levelling principles in the Society", and instructing the Constitution Committee then being formed to revise the rules, to take note of this decision.[151] There is nothing on record to connect this resolution particularly with Spence or with Division 12. It only tells us that "levelling" was being discussed and points to the existence of a distinct group of "levellers".

In a mild form, agrarian levelling, which was the most usual aspect of the problem, had been brought up in the Society as early as May 1792, when the Norwich societies called on the LCS to support their proposal that the future "People's Parliament" would annul recent enclosures of common lands and restore them to the public and "the robbed peasant". This was not an altogether new or unknown compromise proposal. Various writers on what was called "the management of the poor" had put forward schemes of a more equal redistribution of land, limiting the size of tenant farms, distributing waste land or even Church lands among the poor as the means of providing work and bringing down provision prices.[152]

When the Norwich letter was cited in the Treason Trial of 1794 the prosecution and eventually the Judge interpreted it as a bait to win the support of "the poorer sort of people". Land "under pretence of restoring the rights of the poor (would) be taken from the present proprieters and divided amongst the poor . . . For under the same pretence, the whole property in land of every person in the country might be destroyed. I cannot form a calculation of the immense quantity of land which, within even the last twenty years, was common land, and is now become separate and enclosed, upon the faith of which enclosures persons have laid out large sums of money . . . Here the expression is *'improper grants of land'* which may easily be applied to lands formerly granted by the Crown and indeed to the title of every person's estate".[153]

Spence could hardly have put the case better.

William Hodgson, hatter, another member of Spence's Division, also linked democracy with property relations. He was a friend of Charles Piggot, an enthusiast for the French Revolution. They were both charged with seditious words overheard when they were dining in a tavern in 1793. Hodgson was sentenced to two years imprisonment. In 1795 he published *The Commonwealth of Reason,* written in prison, outlining the plan of a democratic state based on the Rights of Man.[154] This included the nationalization of uncultivated and church lands for the settlement of the poor, a minimum wage, centralized stores of provisions and fuel to stabilize prices, national manufactories, old age pensions at 50 on the recommendation of 12 fellow parishioners, and the rotation of all public offices. The influence of the French Constitution (1793) may be supposed in the institutions of Government and there are similarities with French egalitarian ideas and the kind of social-economic demands represented by popular leaders in the period of the Convention. The whole scheme represents a type of radical or egalitarian democracy bordering on utopian socialism such as may be found in some contemporary French social thinkers. As the Pigott brothers had close personal connections with France, these similarities may not have been accidental, but the *Commonwealth of Reason* is based on specifically English conditions and was in fact one of the less abstract schemes of political and social reform which appeared in that period.

Perhaps nearer to Spence in his outlook was John Baxter, a journeyman silversmith, elected Chairman of the LCS for the last quarter of 1793, and one of those accused with Thomas Hardy and others and acquitted of High Treason in 1794. He is sometimes mentioned as voting with Spence and Hodgson on society business.

In what is still one of the most competent examinations of an important part of the evidence, A. Brown came to the conclusion that Baxter was one of the few who may seriously have contemplated the possibility of revolutionary action.[155] He was not however emancipated from what was basically old Whig constitutional theory.

His pamphlet *Resistance to Oppression*[156] appeared when the first reform campaigns had only met with intensifying repression, the support of moderates had dropped away, when the political societies although still numerically quite strong had to consider what was next to be done and to reorganise. The pamphlet was wholly practical in its approach, brief and straightforward in style. Starting from the constitutional right to resist oppression by arms if necessary, and the denial of political rights, it places the main emphasis on material economic grievances, first unemployment and starvation among the labouring poor, secondly the ruin of small farmers and tradesmen, due to "the infamous system of monopoly encouraged by our corrupt legislatures", monopolies of government, commerce, land and provisions. To these are now added the miseries of war — widows, orphans and the dead. This was the general situation which roused Spence's outbursts of anger.[157] In this state of common wretchedness, says Baxter, appears the danger of civil war. The alternative is representative government based on universal suffrage.

The political societies cannot achieve this alone. They must turn outwards and mobilize the masses. Every individual member of the societies can take the initiative in his own parish. In the first place open meetings of all the inhabitants should be called to discuss and petition. If the proper authorities refuse permission, such meetings, being the legal right of the people at large, should be called in spite of them. Out of these meetings an electorate will form capable of instructing its representatives and of recalling them should they fail to carry out their mandate. If the present rulers do make concessions, it will be because mass pressure convinces them that it is in their own interest to do so.

There is great similarity to Spence's ideas in this concept of all the inhabitants of the parish capable of acting together as a cohesive community, as the primary assembly in an absolute democracy and the development of political consciousness through political action, based on the sense of common interest. All this was in sharp contrast to middle class reformers who were so sure that if the common people were allowed to vote they would elect men of education and substance, or to Francis Place who frequently remarked on the incapacity of the working classes to achieve anything on their own account.

Baxter may have envisaged far reaching social reforms but apparently not a totally new social system such as Spence demanded. Certainly he proposed a revolution from below in answer to the same problems that were reflected in Spence's *End of Oppression* that year. But Baxter's programme was anchored to traditional procedures. Reforms would be the decisions of a popular government established according to the constitution inherited from the past.[158]

Differences within the LCS

According to Place the majority of the LCS were Painites or republicans but did not want any sudden great change in government. They differed as to the means of achieving reform — whether by peaceful agitation, by force, or by waiting for the present regime to collapse, the outcome which Place himself thought the most likely.[159] Thus he anticipated later distortions of popular movements by identifying all fundamental demands or revolutionary tendencies with armed intervention and confusing aims with the discussion of means. This simplification ignored the signs of more fundamental differences.

The LCS had virtually no economic policy or social programme. It was consistent in declaring that the minimum aims to which members were committed were universal suffrage, annual Parliaments, equal representation and abolition of rotten boroughs, and mentioned some of the benefits to be expected from these reforms such as the reduction of taxes and excise, the national debt, public expenditure, sinecures, obstacles to trade, and there were frequent references to restoring the purity of the constitution and the liberty and security of the individual citizen. They campaigned against the war and against new legislation to restrict the freedom of press and meeting. But the wages, strikes and poor law abuses of the time find no mention in their official policy statements.

On the other hand there were members who regarded the deteriorating economic conditions of the masses and the threatened small producers as of primary importance to be connected with political grievances. Some may be described as egalitarian-revolutionary, some as religious utopians. Discussions in these circles must have stimulated Spence's ideas too. No avowed supporters of his Plan are as yet visible, but he did find colleagues to whom the rightlessness of the working people was the urgent motive and who in one degree or another attacked monopolies of land and wealth.

A. G. Sinclair's book (also quoted in *Pigs' Meat)* was popular enough to go through five editions between 1789 and 1791. It has much in common with Spence in its formulations. For example: "Every creature which nature has formed with a mouth and digestive powers has an equal right to participate in her blessings". Wealth must be taken from the rapacious and indolent and distributed equitably among mankind at large; artificial laws which treat men as "ferocious animals" and thus made them so, must be removed in order to restore man to his natural sociability. There is no real programme for achieving this, but the criticism is specific and vigorous; the root evil is "traffic in its (the world's) productions of which every man by nature is equally and lawfully authorized to partake".[160]

James Parkinson, of Hoxton, known to medical history for identifying the disease known by his name, shows the same tendency, ridicules constitutional mythology, speaks concretely of labour conditions and wages, proposes village associations to encourage mutuality and spread political knowledge. At first a member of the SCI, he joined the LCS early in 1792 and wrote some of its official pamphlets. His own productions are among the most witty and effective of the period. In *Revolution without Bloodshed; or Reformation preferable to Revolt* (1794) he lists 24 demands which outline a broad social programme and imply a measure of Controlled economy in favour of the working people, including repeal of all Combination Laws (i.e. the separate Acts which existed before the consolidated Acts of 1799 and 1800 and made it a crime to ask for higher wages), reform of the Poor Law, Settlement Laws, and tithes, prevention of monopolies of farms and the necessities of life, repeal of the Game Laws, provision of employment for all and pensions for the aged and disabled and free universal education. He writes elsewhere, in the *Island of Contradiction* "industry is universally extolled, yet he who works most eats the least. The labourer starves whilst the idlest man in society rolls in wasteful abundance".[161] His mood became increasingly revolutionary until he uses Spence's metaphor and demands "tearing up the very roots of the tree".

Richard Lee, poet and bookseller, joined the LCS in June 1794, republished *The Rights of Swine,* and advertised particularly inflammatory tracts, in particular those by Pigott and Parkinson. He was a millenarian and perhaps influenced by Spence with whom he had personal contact. The following quotation for instance might suggest that influence. "Let us begin with **parochial** and **village associations.** No head or leader is requisite on this occasion — the measure is equally necessary for all; let us therefore use **equal exertions** to assist the indefeasable RIGHTS OF MAN with the moderation of citizens to whom **public tranquility** is the dearest object AFTER the security of **public freedom!**"[162] It was alleged by Ballard that he was several times thrown out of the LCS for quarrelling about religion, but this might simply mean that he used scriptural arguments for levelling and the revolutionary change of system implied in the above quotation.

Thomas Bently, who did not appear to be a member of any society but was the object of the special attention of Reeves's Association who brought him to trial before Spence (November 1792), called down the wrath of heaven on the rich, demanded the confiscation and redistribution of the land and appealed direct to the labouring poor. Once a respectable merchant in Sudbury, he had suddenly changed his whole way of life and was now to be seen with his tracts and handbills in and around Holborn. He must have been well known to Spence who published some of his writings in *Pigs' Meat* and probably sold his pamphlets.

"This land flows with human blood and is filled with murders", he exclaims. For it is murder when the wages of most workers can barely provide rent, fuel and a diet of bread for an average family, and when "men, women and children are killed by mere fatigue, and cold, and hunger, and grief", or are driven to crime to end in prison, transportation, hanging or suicide.[163]

Spence was unique in his particular scheme for solving the problem, in making the abolition of private property both the essential condition and means of social revolution, and in his clearer grasp of class relations, but he was not alone in this critique of existing conditions from the point of view of the poorer classes. All these protests reflected recent catastrophic deterioration for the labourer, the artisan and the small producer alike.

The Rules Revision Dispute

Differences in the LCS found their expression, as so often in British life, over questions of rules and procedure. On the insistence of Division 12 and other delegates, including Baxter (Division 16?), a Committee of Constitution or Committee of Revision (i.e. a rules revision sub-committee) was set up in October 1793. The Chairman was Anthony Beck, and other members were Hodgson and John Richter, and as Spence apparently was responsible for arranging meetings, he may also have been on this sub-committee.

The extent to which friction had developed is evident, for this sub-committee decided to adjourn until the General Committee paid their expenses, and this demand was unanimously supported in the Divisions (December 12).[164] Ten days after the Constitution Committee had made a report of progress in several Divisions, they were called together by Pearse, General Committee Secretary of the LCS, who proposed forming a new sub-committee. This was energetically opposed by Hodgson and Richter who maintained that a properly constituted and elected sub-committee could not be arbitrarily superseded. They then requested Spence, who was apparently not present at this meeting, to arrange the next meeting of the committee forthwith. Spence informed them that after Hardy had refused the use of his premises for a meeting when approached by Beck, Hodgson and Richter, the General Committee had consulted several Divisions with a view to appointing a fresh Committee of Constitution, and Hardy now refused to disclose which Divisions had agreed to this proposal. The existing committee objected to this high-handed attempt to ignore them.[165]

Spence printed and distributed the Committee's report, that is a draft of the revised rules. It consisted of the Society's aims and programme of constitutional reforms followed by the rules for the management of the Society. The revised rules aimed to give the delegates greater power and to ensure that published statements should distinguish clearly between those issued by the General Committee and those on behalf of the membership as a whole.

However, there was a way out. Another sub-committee was appointed to revise and abridge this report. The exact dates are not clear, but it is probable that it was this revised draft that came again into dispute in 1795, that is Baxter, Hodgson, Richter and Spence were once more at liberty, and when Ashley had succeeded Thomas Hardy as the Secretary of the Society.[166]

The Trials for High Treason 1794

These incidents began at a time of heightened agitation. The war with France, unpopular as it was and by many regarded as a war provoked by Pitt and his colleagues against the progressive French Republic, complicated matters for the Corresponding Societies and was also accompanied by distress and unemployment among the working people and decline in trade. Savage sentences of transportation passed on Muir (14 years) and Palmer (7 years) by the Scottish Court of Judiciary (1793) were followed by the forceful closure of the 'British Convention of the Delegates of the People Associated to Obtain Universal Suffrage and Annual Parliaments' (November 1793) and sentences of 14 years transportation for Skirving, Secretary of the Scottish Societies, and the London delegates, Margarott, the first Chairman of the LCS, and Joseph Gerrald — two of the most popular leaders. Protests against the conduct of the trials and agitation on behalf of this group, known as the Scottish Martyrs, proved unavailing.[167] Further repressive actions showed the Government's determination to crush all opposition.

The resolutions of the LCS became more defiant. Large public meetings took place in the first months of 1794 to protest about the transportation sentences and the war. In April it was resolved that the LCS Committee should meet daily to watch the proceedings in Parliament and that a new convention should be called immediately in the event of further threats to civil liberty.[168]

In this period Spence's address was advertised for handing in subscriptions and signing an Address to the King.

On 12/13 May, Hardy and eleven other leading members of the SCI and the LCS were lodged in the Tower on a charge of High Treason. A report based on the impounded papers of the two Societies hastily procured the consent of Parliament to the suspension of Habeas Corpus. 17 May was a memorable date as the day on which the Suspension Bill was introduced and the second volume of *Pigs' Meat* was completed. Several more persons were speedily arrested, including Spence and two other members of his Division, Franklow and Hillier, on 20 May.[169] These three were immediately brought before the Privy Council on whose warrants they were committed to Newgate. They were treated throughout as a separate group, the same form of warrants serving for all. They were first held as suspected accessories at the alleged treasonable conspiracy and as potential witnesses. Although they were all treated alike, it is interesting to note that on this occasion it was not Spence but Franklow who seems to have been regarded as the principle suspect.

It had been reported by the Home Office agent, Frederick Polydore Nodder, and also by Reeves, that Franklow and others had organised a body known as the Loyal Lambeth Association or Loyal Lambeth Volunteers, acquired arms, and met for military exercise in a room over Spence's shop.[170] This formed part of the evidence at the trial of Thomas Hardy (October - November) of an alleged intention of armed rebellion. The main facts were not disputed. The Loyal Lambeth Association had met once or twice in a small triangular room up two flights of stairs in Spence's house, where the ceiling was too low to allow them to shoulder arms. They possessed a defective musket and a manual of military drill and they exercised with broomsticks.

Neither the possession of firearms nor the formation of a voluntary corps were in themselves any offense. Hillier and Franklow insisted that the purpose was to assist in maintaining public order in the event of a riot or invasion, of which there had been repeated official warnings. The parody of Reeves's Association and its armed volunteers is obvious from the name — Loyal Lambeth Association — as well as from a flashy red and blue uniform with white breeches, imitating the military costume of the Armed

Associations, in which Franklow (who was a tailor) had appeared at a public dinner. Franklow seems to have been the only known member of his Association who actually lived in Lambeth. Franklow and Hillier admitted that such an organisation had been started but that it had never come to anything. Its rules dated 15 November, 1793 were in fact preserved in Treasury Solicitor papers.[171] This part of the prosecution evidence fell flat and was afterwards excluded.

Spy reports in April 1794 connected Spence with the Loyal Lambeth Association but gave nothing new about him.[172] John Richter's copy of the *Second Report of the Committee of Secrecy of the House of Commons respecting Seditious Practices, 6 June 1794 (5th edition)* has a margin note that two LCS Divisions trained in military drill at "Spence's".

During the trial several witnesses were questioned about Spence, but beyond admitting that that they had seen him in his shop or that he had allowed LCS members to meet there, no-one seemed to know anything particular about him.[173] But at the trial everybody denied knowing anything at all as far as that was possible. Spence when questioned had only the vaguest recollection of Franklow and knew nothing about the Loyal Lambeth Association.

He was not called as a witness at the trial. The reason is apparent from the preliminary examination before the Privy Council, the usual softening up procedure.

On 23 May he came before Pitt, Dundas, Greville and the Duke of Dorset (Lord Chamberlain), an interesting encounter for all concerned. The minutes record:

"Does not know Loyal Lambeth Association. Has heard of it at various times — does not know the members of it. Has seen Franklow at his house — does not know whether Franklow is of the Loyal Association".

So far Spence felt his way cautiously. Then he must have decided to take the lead and end the foolish questioning by coming straight to the root of the matter.

"Spence said, The Plot for the Reform of Parliament will go on, notwithstanding all these examinations of persons and seizing of papers.

He said, if the burthens and grievances were not attended to, they must look to the consequences".

Regrettably his exact words were not taken down in full. He must have said what those grievances were. Just as at his trial in 1801 he told the Court what they were really trying, so now he told the Secretary of State that not the LCS but the people's grievances were what they should be asking about.

Thus having made it clear where he stood, he would answer no more questions — neither whether Franklow had ever been in that front room up two pair of stairs, nor whether anyone had exercised with muskets, nor whether other persons named to him were ever in his house, and finally: "He declared that he would answer no questions". After one more try the Lords of the Council ordered him to withdraw and to remain in custody.[174]

He was within his rights to refuse to answer questions until brought into court. His blunt refusal was the best way to save himself trouble meanwhile.

Spence accused of High Treason

The impression has sometimes been given that Spence was merely imprisoned under the Suspension Act. The fact is that having in the first instance been detained by Privy Council warrant on suspicion, he was actually charged with High Treason no less than the more prominent twelve, of whom only Hardy, Horne Tooke and Thelwall were actually brought to trial. Spence's token recording the charge of High Treason gives no less than the fact.

On 25, October a special session of Oyez and Terminez at the Old Bailey considered a true bill of indictment found against him by the Grand Inquest of the County of Middlesex. The hearing was adjourned, and resumed on 2 November. Unfortunately no copy of the proceedings or of the indictment has so far come to light.

It is not known what evidence of High Treason could have been brought against Spence. Had Hardy and his companions been convicted, he might have been involved as an accessory. Until their acquittal his life was certainly in danger, and his fate would not have been decided on the merits of the Loyal Lambeth business alone. Hardy wrote later that he had had it on good authority that 800 warrants had been prepared to be executed immediately after the trial, that is to say any member of the LCS could have been regarded as part of the alleged conspiracy.

After the first three trials (28 October - 5 December) had resulted in acquittal and the next two abandoned, the discharge of the remaining prisoners in the case began on 18 December. In the case of Spence, Franklow and Hillier the Attorney General had already (16 December) sent down a decision of *noli prosequi* stopping all further proceedings and warrants of discharge were signed by Pitt and the other Privy Councillors on 17/18 December. Spence was ordered to appear in Court daily until finally dismissed by the Magistrate.[175] According to a note in *Pigs' Meat* he was not actually released until 22 December.

Then he returned to The Hive of Liberty. The shop must have been kept going during his absence, perhaps by his wife and son. At any rate someone must have paid the rent.

The Rights of Swine

One of the documents produced in court against Hardy was a pamphlet entitled *The Rights of Swine. An Address to the Poor.* It was signed 'A Friend of the Poor' and the copy used was dated 'January 5, Stockport'. There is no indication that it was sponsored by the Stockport Society, whose correspondence with the LCS was also produced.[176] It had been read in Hardy's Division (No. 2) and the Committee had ordered copies to be printed for distribution (20 February). Meanwhile it was published in *Pigs' Meat,* which means that either Spence had his own copy or used the one found in LCS papers. It is possible that Spence had brought it to the notice of the LCS. The interception of *The Case of Thomas Spence* at Stockport is evidence of contact with that town but the publication of this dangerous document was ignored.

The pamphlet states the sufferings of factory and domestic workers resulting from the extension of machinery and the factory system with great feeling. For years rents and prices continually rose while wages fell. At the end there is an exhortation and warning which the authorities found particularly disturbing.[177]

This is one of the earliest signs of interest among London Radicals in the state of the factory districts. It may be compared with the decay of the handicraft workers described in Pigott's *Political Dictionary,* "the miserable huts which abound in every one of these **flourishing** towns" — "Nothing but misery and wretchedness and everywhere piles of discarded shuttles, weavers' beams, looms and other implements of a lost occupation".[178] It was a new theme for Spence too, whose references to industry generally fitted small producers or the old capitalist non-factory industries with relatively large workforces and sometimes survivals of patriarchal relations in the employer's dealings with a local community. Hence, perhaps, while Spence was aware of a new type of manufacturing capitalist — bitterly attacked in *The Rights of Swine* — he often does not clearly distinguish between 'landlord' and 'capitalist'.

Thelwall as a result of his travels also became aware of the position in the factory districts and saw in their development the larger concentrations of labour which should in his opinion lead to the spread of enlightenment and organization.

The importance attached to the recent disturbances in these counties seen in the Secrecy Committee Report of 1801 was another symptom of new forces breaking into the political struggle. Their progress is to be traced in strikes and organized Luddism in the first decades of the 19th century and the mass based political agitations in the textile counties which developed rapidly after 1814 and were landmarked by Peterloo.

After the Triumph of the "Honest Jury"

Spence's first care on regaining his freedom was for *Pigs' Meat.* The title page of Volume III explains its interruption —

> The Pigs to Starve, bad Men in pow'r,
> Their Feeder sent to doleful Goal.

In his two letters to the press he appealed to the public to support *Pigs' Meat.*[179] In one of them he mentions his sufferings as an added reason (see above). It is a restrained statement considering what he had gone through and what seven months in prison meant for a man who lived hand to mouth from the uncertain sale of cheap pamphlets. These letters were an advertisement for *Pigs' Meat* rather than an appeal for aid.

Place said that Spence was resentful because he received no help from the Society when he came out of prison. Seeing that Place had got the LCS victim fund into his own hands and stopped further payments in the interests of economy, he was himself somewhat responsible. He went on to ascribe Spence's ballad on the falling off of the Whigs and moderates to his personal vexation.

The upper class friends of Reform inside and outside Parliament, after celebrating the acquittal of Hardy and the others and singing the praises of the 'honest Jury' and of Juries in general, with grand dinners and speeches, made no further effort in the cause of Reform. Even the SCI only met once more to disband (10 January. 1795), abandoning the plebian and working class supporters to the mercies of a vengeful reaction. Spence only recorded the facts.

On the late barren Patriotic Meetings; particularly that on the 4th of February, 1795

> The People's friends see how they meet,
> All in the dumps with nought to eat,
> And prudently give up reform,
> To bend their force against the storm;
> But nought afford to give relief
> To patriot woe, or patr'ot grief.

The Foxites next lo meet to dine,
And sing and toast o'er good port wine,
Extol their chief up to the sky,
Nay, they almost him deify;
But nought afford to give relief
To patr'ot woe, or patr'ot grief.

The Stanhopites, deficient no wise
To celebrate their recent vict'ries,
By hundreds meet to drink and feed,
To show themselves of the true breed;
That Burke them named in his ire,
Who for to feed would dig in mire;
But nought afford to give relief
To patr'ot woe, or patr'ot grief.

If half the wealth, and half the wind,
That there was spent to no great end,
Had been employed for to relieve
The wants of patr'ots that now grieve,
It would have caus'd without alloy,
For years to come, exquisite joy.

But sighs now follow prison groans,
And duns and landlords, in their turns,
The place of goalers stern supply,
And crush the heart late doom'd to die;
Though doom'd to die in freedom's cause,
Now doom'd to starve with bare applause.

Farewell, ye gorging parties, then,
Go feed like swine, ye are not men;
Whate'er your parties you may call,
You're all alike, so damn you all.

8 February, 1795.[180]

Spence was not alone in criticising this useless display. The cost of the "old English hospitality" at Stanhope's country mansion — only accessible for people with carriages — laid on for several hundred guests to drink gallons of choice wine under huge Reform slogans made out of coloured lights, could have relieved a good number of the poorer victims.[181] Hardy who was at least privileged to attend the dinners and did, after writing several begging letters to his former patrons, extract enough to re-establish himself in a profitable business, complained bitterly of these "citizens" sudden coldness and prevarications.

Spence, who had suffered under a similar charge and had to get out of the scrape as best he could without the aid of celebrated lawyers, did not even share in the public congratulations and heroifying. His ballad drew a political lesson at the right moment.

The legal victory could not hide the warning that Reform could be a hanging matter. It was in the long run more to the benefit of the reaction to lose a treason and conspiracy case than to win any number on charges of seditious propaganda. In addition to the retreat of middle and upper class support, Hardy and several other leading men retired from all activity. Thelwall held out for some time, continuing to give well attended lectures, speaking and publishing. There is no doubt that he was viciously persecuted. But at a public meeting and in his *Tribune,* he declared that he could carry on no longer. He had left the LCS because further restrictions could be expected. He wished to avoid answering for other people's ill-considered actions; he had been "abandoned by the men of property calling themselves Democrats" and left to pay the cost himself. The risk of personal safety and financial security outweighed the good he could do through the Society. Such excuses made a sorry contrast to his former revolutionary fervour and offended many who continued to risk all they had. Naturally the hounds chased the fleeing hare, and even set a press gang on him.

Spence made no allowances. On the title page of *The Meridian Sun of Liberty* he couples Thelwall with Burke as a defender of hereditary property. Burke too had once advocated Reform.

"Let Thelwall* and Burke from its splendour retire,
  A splendour too strong for their eyes;
Let Pedants and Fools, their effusions admire,
  Inwrapt in their cobwebs like flies.
Shall Frenzy and Sophistry hope to prevail,
  When Reason opposes her weight,
When the welfare of Millions is hung in the Scale
  And the balance yet trembles with Fate?
*See *Sober Reflections* or rather, *Lamentations over the Impending Fate of the Vessel of Hereditary Property* by John Thelwall".[182].

Francis Place and the LCS 1794-1798

Shortly after the arrests of the leaders, Francis Place joined the LCS in June 1794. In the absence of so many leading members he quickly rose to considerable influence, first as a Delegate for Division 27, then as a member of the General Committee, finally by a change of rule as the more or less permanent Chairman (from September 1795) and for a time (1796) as the paid Assistant Secretary. His activities continued for over three years, during which time he collaborated closely with the new Secretary, John

Ashley, his friend and eventually business partner. The two of them used LCS contacts to collect tailoring customers and in this period Place for the first time became an employer of labour.

According to him his aim was to guide the Society into safe channels and sound finance, and to work "as quietly and privately as possible".[183]

At first following the trials, the membership which had fallen off began again to increase and full meetings began again in January 1795. By the end of May according to John Binns there were 70 Divisions, with which Place agrees. But the total membership figure which Binns gives must be excessive while Place's figure of 2,000 is probably an underestimate. Up to the end of 1795 it was possible for delegate meetings to be over 100 and the large public rallies in October and November were estimated at 150,000 and 300,000. The year before, Gale Jones had estimated the total membership of all Corresponding Societies in the country to be about 40,000.[184] If this was any way near correct, it was the first time any government had been faced with such a formidable movement mostly drawn from classes hitherto politically passive, and what was more an organised and disciplined movement.

Hence militant activity if anything increased in 1795. The Acts against treason and sedition and against seditious meetings towards the end of that year, prohibited meetings of more than 50 persons for any purpose under heavy penalties, including the death penalty in certain cases.

Reorganisation was necessary to keep within the law. The scheme proposed by Place to interpose District Committees between the Divisions and the General Committee in place of the rank and file delegates committee could only make for bureaucratic authority and loss of initiative, which was seen almost immediately in the inactivity of the new committees. Further repressive measures in 1796 made more difficulties and Place's narrowness and love of managing other people could only have helped to hasten the decline.[185]

Disaffiliations

The discussion of rules was continued or renewed and dissention became acute. In the spring of 1795 two Divisions disaffiliated.

Division 12, Spence's unit, became the London Reforming Society, with John Bone a muslin cleaner as secretary. After debating the question of the Constitution of the Society for a full three months and drafting 13 amendments, their disagreement with the General Committee and criticism of its undemocratic procedures came to a head. They objected in any case to the number and complication of the rules. Their delegate (Spence?) was violently attacked and his expulsion from the Society demanded (March 1795). While they stood firmly by the original aims of Parliamentary Reform and desired to continue co-operation with the LCS and other political societies, particularly for the purpose of joint publications, they would henceforward remain a separate body with their own rules.[186] Spence's name has not so far been found as a member of the Reforming Society, although the circumstances clearly enough point to his involvement in the dispute. This Society declared itself to be opposed to levelling, but Spence himself was opposed to an agrarian law for the equal partition of the land and to the equal division of other property which was generally what was understood by levelling. Either the new society reaffiliated at some time or individual members rejoined the LCS, since Bone succeeded Ashley as Secretary in 1796. Bone himself, a Dutchman by origin who had come to England as a political fugitive from pre-Revolutionary France, was a religious man who desired the application of Christian precepts to public life and could have agreed with much of Spence's teaching. With the removal of Place and Ashley and the change of policy in the LCS, a separate society may not have seemed necessary. Hodgson too was one of the speakers with Thelwall and Gale Jones at the Copenhagen Fields meeting (26 October, 1795) which adopted a strongly worded Remonstrance, and again at the last open-air meeting in 1798 when all the speakers were arrested but not charged, and he was one of the General Committee when they were all finally rounded up together (18 April 1798).

The other breakaway in 1795, The Friends of Liberty, located in Spitalfields and East London, was much more intransigent and refused any further dealings with the LCS or with any societies which recognized it (in spite of Place's statement that both these splinter groups remained friendly). They gave as their chief reason their disapproval of the new constitution and rules, and their grave suspicion of "their promoter" (i.e. Place).[187] Baxter, who lived in Shoreditch, was doubtless the leader of this revolt. His pamphlet quoted above was a lecture delivered to the Friends of Liberty. It outlines a new programme to widen the basis of agitation and advances a new concept of absolute democracy based on the primary assembly of the parish. While Place was attempting to turn the LCS into a select debating club to produce intelligent cadres and to meet government repression by withdrawing into itself and avoiding public appearances, Baxter's plan offered the possibility of initiative and the security that could be given by functioning within a wide stream of popular activity, for which the first impulse comes from the immediate grievances of the working population. This was what the Parliamentary Secrecy Committees later supposed that the political societies were doing in the hunger riots and demonstrations in 1799-1801 and what the later Spenceans unsuccessfully attempted to do. Baxter's proposals were far sounder than the line eventually adopted by the last LCS leaders.[188]

Dissensions in the LCS, the tendencies ranging from atheist and republican to millenial religious fanaticism and the proliferation of small societies in 1795-1798 were noted by a hostile observer claiming inside information. His special attention to the role of benefit societies and the warning example of Masaniello suggest *Pigs' Meat* as one of his sources.[189]

The Last Phase

Eventually the militants won the leadership of a shrunken and weakened LCS, ousting Ashley and Place. According to the latter, when he failed to restrain the members from their "folly", he resigned or refused re-election to all office except divisional delegate (June 1796), which he also eventually gave up (March 1797) and shortly after both he and Ashley, thoroughly disgusted with the thankless task of trying to guide the Society, left it altogether. We have only his word for it that he chose to resign office and as to the cause of his quarrel with the membership if not actually thrown out it would be unlikely that after he had so violently opposed the views of the majority he would have been re-elected. He resigned membership barely two weeks before the meeting which he so strenuously tried to prevent, was publicly announced. When it did take place, it was surrounded by large numbers of police and troops and closed by the Magistrates. All the people on the three platforms were arrested (immediately released on bail). Whether he had foreknowledge of what to expect or not, the men of the LCS did not need Place to tell them that they ran the risk of arrest.[190]

The history of this internal friction is the obvious explanation of Place's inconsistent statements about Spence and his complaint of Spence's lack of cordiality.

Place valued his past connections with the Reform tradition and with those who had since become historic figures. He says in one place that in the end nothing but "the refuse" remained in the LCS, and in another claims particular friendship and esteem for some who remained in it to the end.[191]

Spence leaves the LCS

It is not known exactly when Spence left the LCS. Possibly it was in March 1795, with the majority of Division 12. When the LCS Committee was arrested (18 April, 1798) several other people were taken in for questioning and Spence among them (19 April). No connection could be established between him and the LCS or its alleged intentions or with the United Englishmen, whose programme was found on Thomas Evans, and he was released. The LCS members were kept in prison until the expiration of the Suspension Act. Spence was one of the collectors for the fund established for these victims which was sponsored by Major Cartwright and Thomas Hardy and for a time managed by Place.

The End of Oppression

His pamphlet *The End of Oppression* published late in 1795 marks the point when Spence must have decided that his place was no longer in the LCS. Throughout that year growing unrest found expression in food riots in many parts of the country, sometimes supported by the local militia, a number of disturbances among the miners, and attacks on recruiting houses, The cry was not for Reform but for "Peace" and "Bread". "An infuriated mob" surrounded the king's coach on 29 October shouting "No Pitt — No War!" "Down with George!" "No King!" [192] The title of the first edition of *The End of Oppression* reads: *The End of Oppression, or a Quarten Loaf for Two-Pence.* It had no author's name. It appears as part of that widespread protest.

Shortly before or simultaneously with this tract, Spence published a fuller version of his basic thesis under the title *The Meridian Sun of Liberty,* consisting of his Lecture with a new prefatory dialogue. The title itself is optimistic affirmation when not only aristocratic and moderate reformers had fallen away but also deserters from among the Corresponding Societies' veterans.

It had always been clear of course that Spence never regarded the Parliamentary Reform programme as a solution for the social problem, but necessarily supported the democratic movement in as much as it attacked rank and institutions of oppression. He may have hoped that the LCS or a section of it could develop further. It was obvious that he should first try to win support among the most politically awakened working men in its ranks, and as we have seen he found among them several who felt as he did about the injustices around them even when they did not accept his solution.

The crisis in the Reform camp and the general situation in the country demanded that they should reconsider their position. Petition, Parliamentary motions, conventions, peaceful demonstrations had all been tried. The inevitable divergence of interest between progressive Whigs and lower-class reformers had appeared. The Government intensified its repressive measures. Possibly Spence was also influenced by the fall of the Jacobins in France and the loss of economic concessions won by popular pressure. He stated the choice between passive acceptance and revolutionary initiative, which would require the preparation of a revolutionary army to support a provisional government and the immediate expropriation of the landlords.

The great men have no reason to listen to the requests of wretched beggars who, having no property, quite rightly have no say in running the country. If some reform were granted no mere change of government or form of government would change anything that really matters. Property might change hands but the institution of property, the basis of political inequality, would remain. Those who demand Reform but uphold the system of private property either already have too much to lose or hope to achieve a privileged position for themselves.

"I am weary with combatting the vile sophistry of Scoundrels that are Oppressors and Scoundrels that would be Oppressors".[193]

He opens the attack on both Painite and moderate constitutional ideology which dominated in the corresponding societies. It was clearly intended for this audience being in the form of a dialogue between an old and a young mechanic, the people who formed the majority in the Societies, and it is addressed to their class interest, not to man in general. It cannot be doubted that the pamphlet came into the LCS Divisions and was discussed.

Without mentioning Spence or the pamphlet the LCS passed resolutions and issued a Declaration of Principles in much stronger terms than before (23 November, 1795).

Equality and Property

The LCS from the beginning stressed moderation, and condemned violence, insurrection and "tumults" and danger to property. The most advanced democratic movement that had so far appeared, it accepted without question the doctrines of bourgeois individualism. The *Address* of 6 August 1792 went no further than the vague prospect that reform would bring "the necessaries of life more within the reach of the poor".

The members disclaim "that visionary Equality of Property, the practical assertion of which would desolate the world and replunge it into the darkest and wildest barbarism".

In answer to slanderous attacks, particularly from Reeves's Association their denials became more and more emphatic.

But they are often vague and confused. There might even be some reservations.

"Anticipating ill-natured epithets of **Republicans** and **Levellers**" they repeat that they want only equal representation for "society was and will be composed of people in different circumstances". — "We desire to overthrow no Property but what has been raised on the RUIN OF OUR LIBERTY! We look with Reverence on the landed and commercial interests of our Country but view with Abhorrence the MONOPOLY of BURGAGE TENURES unwarranted by Law and Reason".[194]

"Difference of strength, of Talents and of Industry, (do) and ought to

afford proportional Distinctions of Property, which when acquired and confirmed by the Laws, is **sacred and inviolable".** . . . "But let us not suffer Men, who avow no Principles of Liberty, whose favourite Cry is INEQUALITY OF PROPERTY, to estrange others of our countrymen from aiding us . . . and from restoring to the Nation that share of its Sovereignty which has unhappily been sacrificed to CORRUPT COURTIERS and intriguing BOROUGHMONGERS".[195]

Typical and trite is the small tradesman attitude in the Sheffield Constitutional Society's *Address* read in the LCS, 7 April 1794: "We have ever disclaimed the foolish idea of **levelling property;** be our property the fruit of our labour, or of our talents, might by the example, be exposed to the invasion of the first intruder".[196]

Among the first LCS leaders only Joseph Gerrald, William Godwin's friend, seems to have understood that political liberty might demand more. "A spirit of enquiry has gone forth amongst men and the foundations of the rights of property will be as accurately examined as the foundations of the rights of persons".[197]

As it was always assumed that the poor must be envious, they were credited with more sense of their position than they commonly had. Any talk of equality could disturb these potentially dangerous strata "whose hopes are instigated by the prospect of the Plunder of the Rich, and the partition of landed property of the country".[198] As early as 1792 fears of a movement that appeared to be addressed to the lower orders were expressed. "Have you not encouraged those of the idle unprincipled poor, who have become your adherents, to hope for a new division of the land, and even of the property of the merchants, and manufacturers, — by which they may be enriched without industry? Have you not stirred up the workmen to demand an augumentation of their wages . . .?"[199]

A special pamphlet was felt necessary. *An Explanation of the Word Equality* was re-issued several times and copied by provincial Societies. Equality of wealth is "a dangerous doctrine" — "God and nature have forbidden it" — It is practised neither in America nor in France nor advocated by any serious modern reformer. "The inequality derived from labour and successful enterprise, the result of superior industry and good fortune, is an **inequality essential to the very existence of society** . . . Let us hear no more of Levellers or Levelling systems".[200]

The two-edged word was proving as vexatious to our 'Jacobins' as to the French. Only in England, according to the LCS, it was not being distorted by little people struggling against forestallers and monopoly prices, but by aristocratic reactionaries. The fact is of course that the long debate about property which went on through the eighteenth century as academic speculation, could not now be kept out of any discussion of practical democracy, whichever side raised it. Spence's presence in the LCS had nothing to do with the accusations. His interest in the question was also a symptom of the total development.

The new Declaration of 23 November, 1795, dropped all hint of any control or restoration of unjustly acquired property. It declares that full individual freedom to possess and accumulate is a leading principle of the Society. This time it directly attacks 'Levellers', while treating levelling theories as something so irrational that they should be entirely ignored.

As before, levelling is taken to mean the division of property, not the abolition of property, and no distinction is made between one kind of property and another, whereas contemporary agrarian reformers like Ogilvie and Paine regarded land as a special category.

It is possible that Thelwall helped to draft this document. It is reproduced in full in his wife's memoir and he is quoted as saying at an LCS meeting (26 October) that "equality of property is totally impossible". The majority of the members, including those with republican or revolutionary leanings, no doubt shared this opinion. Here levelling is represented not as the dreams of visionary philosophers or the delusion of the ignorant poor, but out and out as the invention of malicious reactionaries.

"In these ideas of equality, they (the LCS) never included, nor, till associations of alarmists (i.e. the Loyal Associations — PMA) broached the frantic notion, could they ever have conceived that so wild and detestable a sentiment could have entered the brain of a man as the equalization of property, or the invasion of personal rights and possessions. This levelling system they know, and all rational men must immediately perceive, to be equally unjust and impracticable; and they are ready, to a man, not only to protest against it, but to oppose, with their lives, every attempt of that description — attempts which they are well aware, instead of equalizing the condition of mankind, could only transfer property from its present possessors to plunderers and assassins, and subject the nation to the brutal and ferocious tyranny of the most ignorant and worthless of mankind".[201]

The rest of the Declaration insists on peaceful and legal means only.

There had been no new allegations of levelling of any importance. The intention seems to be to impress these points on members and to close discussion. Levelling is here only defined as the equal distribution of wealth. The pledge to resist any change in property relations would equally apply of course to common property, also commonly called 'levelling'.

Spence's Recantation of "The End of Oppression"

Spence's *Recantation* obviously is an answer to particular criticism, "to many well meaning Democrats and Friends of Reform" to whom his book "has given great cause of uneasiness and alarm". He gives a solemn undertaking in mockery of the LCS declaration. He briefly restates that equality means an equal share of the rents produced by common property and ridicules the pride and the humble subservience of his critics, the individualism that outlasted the declassing process in the pre-proletariat. Everybody knows that the property owners are the only people fit to manage property. The common people wouldn't know what to do with the rents. If it did strike them to divide them "The idle, I mean the poor of society, would be claiming as large dividends as the more wealthy, which would be insufferable". He repents that the proposal to abolish the right to sell land has "deprived many poor families of sleep . . . though seldom possessed of a shilling of their own property". People evidently do not want to end oppression. "End of Oppression!" say the people, "What would this world be good for without Oppression? Why thousands of gentlemanlike callings and professions . . . would either cease or be very much reduced, with the End of Oppression".

It had been hinted to him that he could do much better for himself if he gave up these foolish ideas. "So here goes, my boys, for an estate and vassals to bow to me! Who would not be a gentleman and live without care! Especially a Democratic gentleman without a king. Avaunt! Rights of Man! I am henceforth a Democrat but no Leveller".

Now Spence never wrote anything about himself which was not literally true and as these last remarks were not essential to his argument it may be safe to conclude that they were in reply to some such suggestion.

This was his farewell to the LCS. He could not remain in a Society now explicitly pledged to defend private property with their lives.

Henceforth he fought on both fronts — landlords and capitalists, or half-way reformers. He now saw more clearly the dangers of demagogy and gave this special emphasis in the fourth part of *The End of Oppression.*

He deliberately distanced himself. At his trial in 1801 he could declare that he belonged to no party and had no support. "Even the proffest friends of Liberty keep aloof and would rather, if they could consistently, join in the Suppression than the Support of my System".[202] He repeated that public opinion treated him and his opinions with contempt "as has been hitherto done with so much success, and this manner has been particularly practiced by the most professed Champions of Liberty".[203]

"The End of Oppression" in Parliament

A marked-up copy of the pamphlet is preserved in Treasury Solicitor records suggesting that prosecution may have been considered. Lord Mornington quoted it at length during the debate on the Seditious Meetings Bill, November 1795, describing the author as "a bookseller and printer at whose house the Copenhagen House petition of 12 November lay to be signed". Mornington associated Spence with Richard Lee, whose "treason rank and foul" is still more extensively quoted.[204] Lee was prosecuted. In Spence's case there was the technical difficulty of proving authorship.

Systematising his work

The End of Oppression was finally advertised as a work in four parts. *The Meridian Sun of Liberty* would fit the sequence as the first part, but no copy of it is known nor any other pamphlet which so describes it. The idea that these pamphlets formed a logical sequence may have occured to Spence late and it is possible that there once existed a one-volume edition of all four. If this was what was meant the following analysis can be made:—

1. *The Meridian Sun* — Exposition of existing oppression in conflict with natural rights and the general theoretical solution of Spence's Plan.
2. *The End of Oppression* — The fallacy of other remedies and the revolutionary means of regaining the land and establishing true liberty.
3. *Spence's Recantation* — The deviousness of false democrats.
4. *A Fragment of an Ancient Prophecy* — The lessons of the French Revolution show that when equality is not extended to property, the landlords, 'more irritated than hurt', rise again. Nevertheless the French Army bore the banner of the Rights of Man and encouraged the democrats in other countries to throw off their feudal fetters. An age of ceaseless revolutions has begun and will last until through bitter experience of errors and disillusionment the correct solution is reached.

Move to Oxford Street

After publishing *The End of Oppression* Spence moved to 9 Oxford Street. The title page of *The Rights of Infants* (1797) gives this address, adding "lately removed from Little Turnstile". The Preface is dated 19 March 1797. Leases normally ran between quarter days. It is therefore more likely that the move was made shortly after finishing the pamphlet when the lease fell in at the end of March, than that "lately" would refer to the previous Christmas.

He also had a street pitch near the Pantheon in Oxford Street, wither he wheeled his vehicle each day, a closed handcart like a baker's van. The pamphlets were displayed on the outside and customers supplied with clean copies from within. Spence would recommend other pamphlets, talk with all who would stop to listen and describe "the prospects of what would happen to the whole race of landlords".[205]

Whenever anybody remembered Spence it was to mention this unflagging persistence.

He now produced two admirable specimens of pamphleteering art. These are not directly connected to any immediate event but add important details about the intention of the Plan and its operation. They both express irreconcilable antagonism to the propertied classes and each takes a particularly atrocious aspect of heartless crime against humanity in the interests of property.

In *The Rights of Infants* 'Aristocracy' argues hopelessly against the Mother. The maternal instinct of nature to provide for her creatures appears in the form of the real down-trodden woman who in the end will simply take the food she is denied for her child — like the woman who so often led the crowds that forced market traders to sell at reasonable prices.

The proposals of Paine's *Agrarian Justice* to return 10% of the total land revenue to the people in the form of state insurance and pensions, are contrasted point by point with the Plan. It is a powerful attack on Paine's compromise and on the theory of social contract. To suggest that infants give up their right to their mothers' milk, is to treat them as "excrescences and abortions of nature". No one at any time ever gave up the right to life and the human mother never gave up the right to eat and to nourish her young, any more than the she-bear or the she-otter. This unquestionable fact is what natural right is, and therefore cannot be superseded.

In the pamphlet the women shame their passive menfolk by taking matters into their own hands and set about taking over the land and managing the parish economy. Women's rights is not the main purpose of the pamphlet but it foreshadows the *Constitution of Spensonia* which provides for political, social and economic sex equality in all respects, except that women are not allowed to fill public offices.

The Reign of Felicity deals with the combination of savage liberty with civilized amenities, first stated in the Lecture. The cruelty, hypocrisy and avarice of the private property system are contrasted with the original nature of man, what man could or should be, symbolized in the propertyless American Indian whom colonizers propose to civilize. There are three possibilities — the aristocratic method of civilizing by conquest and turning the inhabitants into slaves or serfs, with religion to console them; the introduction of private property and free enterprise favoured by the representative of the middle class; or finally the establishment of real freedom and equality on the basis of common property. Spence did not understand these forms as historically conditioned social formations but he was able to see the class character of three types of property relations and the corresponding position of labour.

The theme of the Indians robbed of their lands, which had already appeared in *The Marine Republic* and *The Description of Spensonia* (in *Pigs' Meat),* was more than picturesque allegory. It contained concrete criticism of colonialism. The Indians complain that the colonizers compel them to work, to extract the wealth of their country for the benefit of foreign masters and to pay rent for living in their native land, just as the dispossessed in Europe were compelled to work and pay rent.

Thus Spence brought together the case of the landless labourer and poor tenant with the exploitation of the colonies as parts of one system. He treats foreign conquest as a real extension of the motive inherent in the private property system "to lay field to field". As he expressed it elsewhere, the internal monopoly gave rise to the external. This was very different from a common radical opinion at that time, that colonies were undesirable because Indian 'Nabobs' and West-Indian slave owners used their immense profits to buy Parliamentary seats and ministers, and imported habits of despotism.

The pamphlet reinforced the argument that conquest was the origin of private property. "All our boasted civilization is founded alone in Conquest" he exclaims later in *The Restorer.* Consequently *The Constitution of Spensonia* stated briefly that the Spensonians renounce foreign possessions acquired by their former rulers and declare them independent as soon as the inhabitants adopt the Spensonian system, that is, as soon as the land is fully restored to the people. This can only be understood to mean that the Spensonians assist the peoples to throw out the colonial landlords and to carry through their own Spensonian revolution. The hypothetical situation was extremely remote, but the solution recognized that conquered peoples could not simply revert to a pre-conquest state of primitive liberty, if that had existed, and yet should not be left to the mercy either of the colonizing landlords or of such rulers as the Europeans had displaced. Spence's belief that his Plan only had to be known to be accepted in any country was naive, but it had certainly led him to a problem which the development of colonial empires would eventually force on all working class parties.

Murray based the rights of nations on the natural right of the inhabitants to the territory. It was appropriate that the burdened Ass appeared on a cartoon advertising *The Reign of Felicity.* It was signed by Spence's son, William. This is the last known trace of the boy.

The universality of the Rights of Man was for most an abstraction remote from practice. It may have been little more than a convention when Hodgson depicted Indian, African and European fraternizing round a tree of liberty on the frontispiece of his book. A broadside ballad of the period which sounds more purposeful was perhaps by Spence. —

"May Afric's injured coast
Soon have of this to boast,

The Rights of Man!
Those Rights from Heav'n sent down
Where no Distinction's known
Where Black, or Fair, or Brown
Have equal claim".[206]

The Future

Having dealt with past and present in *The End of Oppression* series, Spence depicted the future in two complementary works — *The Constitution of a Perfect Commonwealth* (later *The Constitution of Spensonia),* and *The Restorer of Society to its Natural State.*

The Constitution (1798) was derived from the French Jacobin constitution (1793) which had already been published in *Pigs' Meat,* taking over almost unchanged many of the French forms and institutions and egalitarian features. The adaptation shows acceptance of that part of the bourgeois revolution which Spence regarded as permanent gain, or a basis from which true democracy might have been developed, but for its conservation of private property. In France it had first been put on ice and had now been totally abandoned.

The Restorer (1801) gives examples of what could or should happen after the removal of private property and monopolies, peacefully or otherwise, contrasting these possibilities with existing hardship and destitution. The economy will develop to create plenty and lead to the full identity of individual with social interests. People will change their attitude to life and to one another. These changes are presented as possibilities to be worked out in practice. Both *The Constitution* and *The Restorer* foresee future adjustments in applying the essential laws. Spence always claimed that the flexibility of his Plan was its great merit and that correct solutions of practical problems would be found through consultation as they arose. Many details take care of themselves but new situations may offer more than one choice. This open-ended idea of social development distinguished Spence's Plan from all the early utopian systems which laid down precise laws for regulating social life and so often mixed fundamentals with quite secondary details and regimentation.

Spence believed that scarcities were artificial, brought about by speculation and merciless private gain. He did not plan to share out scanty resources but to release powers to create plenty. The incentive of reward according to production remains, but the minor differences of income will not mean hardship for anybody. People enjoy a margin well over necessities. Universal education will raise standards and instead of scrambling for a bare existence people will work better than they have ever done to obtain the refinements and even luxuries which an enlightened society expects.

The Restorer writes feelingly of these famine years, of the increasing hours of work and effort, of masses deprived of every comfort to satisfy the luxury "of a few unfeeling monsters". It was calculated about 1803 that nearly one-seventh of the population were receiving poor relief. Secrecy Committee reports (1799-1801) give some of the facts of disturbances, noting the new factor of acute trouble among industrial workers and prolonged strikes in Lancashire and other parts. These conditions, it was said, gave opportunity to subsversive agitators, but Parliamentary debates on finding substitutes for bread, show that it was realized that suppressing seditious meetings would not still the cry of hunger.

One observer optimistically thought that politics might be starved out. ". . . The beerhouses which previous to the late rise in the necessaries of life, used, in working neighbourhoods, to be filled three evenings out of the six, have been gradually deserted. The passengers who, in the piping days of peace, were frequently obstructed, can now pass unmolested by ballad singers and drunken squabbles in the streets . . .; and this accidental alteration of circumstances, by compelling mechanics and others to share their porter with their families, has prevented many of them from being introduced to the Infidel or Political Societies at the public houses".[207]

Angry crowds in many places protested against corn monopolies, millers, farmers, taxes, low wages in 1800. Instead of public meetings petitioning for Reform, there were large gatherings to petition against low wages and dear food. For example a handbill appealed to "every journeyman, artisan, mechanic or tradesman, every manufacturer, and Labourer" to assemble on Kennington Common for this purpose.[208] The records of the LCS and other political organisations give no clue to the initiative behind these actions, although their previous petition campaigns may have suggested a model. We know that self-appointed committees of trade club members or other people could give temporary leadership in local crises and trade depressions.

The Restorer pays increased attention to monopolizers who dig millions of graves, continually lay heavier burdens on workers, crying "Work, work, ye are idle". These are not the signs of a passing crisis, but of a steady intensification reducing more and more working people to abject dependency and chronic destitution.

This situation led him beyond the old Natural Right claim to the land. It must be claimed as "a Right of Policy" for it is too dangerous to leave the source of life in the hands of tyrants. Necessity dictates the act of expropriation. He considers the essential first steps. The ground must be cleared for a glorious new republic; every vestige of landlordism that might grow again must be rooted out. The revolutionary tactics of *The End of Oppression* are expanded. Recent great actions carried out by mass unity — such as the naval mutinies or the French Revolution — inspire confidence in the ability of the people to act resolutely and in a disciplined way. Here Spence introduces his concept of "the Mutiny on Land", the general strike, of which more later.

In the Preface to *The Constitution of a Perfect Commonwealth* the motivation goes no further than a vague statement about the unanimous will of the People. In *The Restorer* he explains that the will to change and clear purpose will not come through moral teachings but through "interest" and necessity and as the result of experience through an epoch of continual upheavals and unrest and increasing hardship and insecurity. When one parish is prepared to act, then thousands of others will have reached that stage. It cannot be predicted where or when the Plan will be adopted. The fact that he happened to think of it means that it could occur to millions of others. At his trial he attempted to explain that his Plan was the result of a "Concatenation of ideas" produced by a series of experiences and impressions outside his control, that it was the discovery of something that had an objective reality and was not a voluntary construction. Once it had been communicated he could not recall it nor control what would become of it.[209] Was he only saying that a man cannot help what he thinks or that theories are the product of objective circumstances, of history? This attempt, however crude, to form a realistic prognosis approached a concept of social process in place of spontaneity or voluntary act through altruistic conviction, and is the most striking feature of *The Restorer.* And where Paine saw the age of revolutions as a chain reaction of the victorious bourgeoisie, Spence saw the prospect of intensifying struggle from below provoked by the ruthless oppression of whatever new masters arose.

Arrest in 1798

The LCS committee were all arrested at a meeting in 1798 and Thomas Evans in his home, 18 April, 1798, on suspicion of conspiratorial involvement with the United Irishmen. Spence and a miscellaneous group of other suspects were arrested the next day (19 April). After questioning him once or twice the Privy Council ordered his detention until the end of April. However it would appear that he and several others were bailed to give evidence and discharged after a week (26 April).[210] Cold Bath Fields Prison where Spence was confined had a particularly evil reputation, being known as the English Bastille. It shortly after attracted the attention of Alderman Sir Richard Phillips who demanded an investigation.

As no trial ever took place no witnesses were called and nothing further happened to Spence.

The twenty-eight LCS members suffered particularly rigorous confinement in various prisons until the expiration of the Suspension Act (March 1801).[211]

Trial for Seditious Libel, 1801

Thus Spence had twice escaped involvement in High Treason, only to be arrested on a charge of seditious libel immediately on the appearance of his *Restorer*. The preface is dated 5th February 1801, but from the indictment it appears that it was not published until 10 April. This prompt action suggests that the authorities were on the watch for a pretext. By this time nearly a full set of Spence's pamphlets had been collected and annotated in the Treasury Solicitor's office.

He came up for trial before Chief Justice Lord Kenyon and a Special Jury at Westminster Hall on 27 May 1801.

Kenyon must have been well known to Spence. He had sentenced more than one patriot as well as presiding over Reeves's trial.

The first hearing was reported in *The Times* (23 April 1801) announcing the coming trial for "the publication of a malicious and seditious libel respecting the right to property in land".[212] George Cullen of Knightsbridge noted in his copy of *The Important Trial of Thomas Spence,* that he had been proud to stand bail for Spence's appearance and had told the judge that he would have pledged himself in thousands if he had been worth so much.[213] On the day of the trial Spence took the precaution to go to Westminster Hall early by 8 o'clock in the morning, presumably accompanied by Cullen, and found that although his case stood fourth on the list for the day, it had already started.

Between his first appearance in court and the trial itself, the second part of the Secrecy Committee reports to both Houses setting forth the reasons for seeking an extension of the Suspension Act (13 April — 15 May) had been published. The first part dealt with rebellion and conspiracy in Ireland, the second with subversive activities in England, implying that they were all connected and responsible for recent unrest, riots and possible disaffection in the army and navy. Everything is suspect, including "dangerous meetings" disguised as benefit societies. The poor are incited by promises of plundering the rich and dividing the land. A new much more insidious kind of society recruited from the lowest strata has appeared calling themselves Spensonians who discuss "the complete **extermination** of royalty, nobility and property". The only evidence offered in the Report are the copy of a handbill announcing the meeting of a Free-and-Easy to discuss Spence's Plan and copious quotations from *The Restorer of Society*. All this is presented in such a way as to connect Spence and his pamphlet with a sinister network of secret societies and multifarious conspiracies plotting insurrection. The passages from *The Restorer* quoted in the Report coincide with those given in full in the three points of the indictment as the substance of seditious libel.

Neither Report nor indictment distorted the literal meaning of the words. The Report was more correct than some who have written about Spence's Plan, describing the aim as "an equal parochial division of the profits of lands as the basis of 'a beautiful and powerful new Republic'". The object was to make such statements seem a widespread call to immediate insurrection. For the purpose of proving seditious content it was immaterial whether Spence had the means or the intentions to lead a revolution.

Radicals discredited the general allegations in the Report and minimised the danger to avoid the smear spreading to themselves. Many historians followed them. Maccoby for example called the reports "unbalanced" and "alarmist", and the persecution of Spence — "this penniless and eccentric unfortunate" — seemed to him in particular a measure of their hysteria.[214]

Hone on the contrary said that Spence "was well known to the Secretary of State as a man who never concealed his political opinions", — and well he might be, in view of the personal encounters at Privy Council examinations and the many confidential reports at the Minister's disposal. There was reason for alarm and to make an example of Spence if he was typical of the agitators and ideas circulating in the dark haunts and darker minds of the poor, hitherto manageable by local magistrates with occasional help from regular troops.

Considering the crude means available, the authors of the Reports had gathered much factual information in spite of their distorted analysis and exaggerated generalizations. Of course they were intended to mislead and alarm both Parliament and public. Later generations always ridiculed their forefathers' credulity, but successive governments have used similar methods whenever they needed them.

Spence, conducting his own defence, first protested against the prejudging of his case in the Report, which had named him and made him responsible for nationwide disaffection. It could only be a deliberate intention to destroy him. But he consoled himself, "If the Government will persuade the People that they are Spensonians, whether they are or no, why should I make Objections! It is perhaps the most effectual way to make them such".

He retracted nothing. His proposals should be judged as abstract speculations for discussion, as a Bill to introduce a new law is debated and put to the vote. His ideas of social justice cannot be harmful, based as they are on reason in a spirit of disinterested benevolence and honest enquiry. It is "a foolish trial". His arguments are based on known facts. Commonsense cannot be tried or extinguished, nor can his treatise, which belongs to political science. "It is like trying Trigonometry or Multiplication Table". From another point of view it is not **his** trial "but the Trial of the Rights of the whole species . . . of the Widow and the Fatherless, the infant and the hoary

Head, the Blind and the Lame, the Dumb and all who have no Helper" — "There never was since the Creation of the World, a Trial of such Magnitude". (Which was his reason for publishing it later under the title *The Important Trial of Thomas Spence).*

To prove that this was the proper interpretation of the passages in the indictment when seen in context, he read out the whole pamphlet, complete with title page and motto, omitting only secondary items not included in the accusations and adding a few brief explanations to assist the Jury. This took about three hours.[215]

No evidence was submitted, no witness called (other than the formality of an agent's statement about buying the offending book). Spence was not questioned nor his defence answered. No point of law was raised. Lord Kenyon said that no comment of his could make the case any clearer,[216] and the Jury immediately brought in a verdict of guilty.

Spence's sarcasms did make the proceedings ludicrous. The third count in the indictment — incitement to disaffection in time of war — was entirely based on his "little sylvan joke". Four-and-twenty years ago a forester had stopped him gathering nuts in Hexham Wood. Spence objected that he would not be treated with less respect than a monkey or a squirrel, adding that if the Duke of Portland wanted to claim exclusive rights to Nature's free gifts, let him shoulder a musket himself, for he, Spence, would not fight for a country where he could not pick a nut.

After trial Spence came up for judgement on 13 June, was again remanded for a week, when sentence was finally pronounced (20 June) — one year in Shrewbury Prison and a fine of £20, about the maximum under the Newspaper Acts (1798, 1799).

In support of his last Defence before sentence, a friend in court volunteered to vouch for his character and the fact that he belonged to no party or society. "It appeared that this man was a crack-brained, half-witted organist, and the Court accordingly ordered him to be silent and mind his own business".[217] (There is no reason to identify this friend with Cullen as suggested by Rudkin). Spence himself in this report was described as "a poor insane though mischevious bookseller".

The usual comment at the time was that Spence was mad — a convenient excuse for doing nothing in his behalf. "The people without (i.e. outside the prison — P.M.A.) treat me with the contempt due to a Lunatic" he said, "for it is only the Government that wishes to make me appear of consequence, and the people within (i.e. inside the prison — P.M.A.) treat me as bad or worse than the most notorious Felons among them".[218]

The trial drew many spectators. Brief reports in *The Morning Chronicle*

(13 June 1801), the *Annual Register,* the *Newcastle Magazine* and others were not markedly unsympathetic to Spence but ridiculed the authorities for taking him seriously. In the debate on the Suspension Indemnity Bill 27 May 1801 (to clear Ministers from responsibility for detaining the reformers in 1798), a member referred to the trial as an example of unjustified severity on unsubstantiated suspicion. He challenged the Attorney General: "Whether he did not seriously think the man completely deranged? Whether any individual of the numerous audience upon that occasion did not feel a sort of indignation at a man's being put upon his trial who was a fitter object of confinement in Bedlam?"[219]

Cobbett, then a Tory, was present. Later when he had become a leading Radical agitator, at the height of Spencean popularity, he gave his impressions:—

"I was present in the Court of King's Bench. He (Spence — P.M.A.) had no counsel but defended himself and insisted that his views were **pure** and **benevolent,** in proof of which, in spite of all exhortations to the contrary, he read his pamphlet through. He was found **guilty** and sentenced to be imprisoned for I forget how long. He was a plain, unaffected, inoffensive looking creature. He did not seem at all afraid of any punishment, and appeared much more anxious about the success of his **plan** than about the preservation of his life. After he came out of prison, he pursued the inculcation of his **plan,** appearing to have no other care; and this he did, I am assured, to the day of his death, always having been a most virtuous and inoffensive man, and always very much beloved by those who knew him".[220]

"Throughout the trial" wrote another contemporary, "He maintained an openness and honesty which all who knew him know well to have been peculiar to his character".[221]

Little is known of Spence's time in Shrewsbury Gaol, except from a letter to Jonathan Panther, coachmaker, dated 20 November, 1801. He asks that friends should send a little relief if only to buy a little tea and sugar as he has been reduced to the bare prison allowance of one small loaf and an ounce of butter a day. He could eat twice the amount if he had it.[222] He is in good health but has gone very thin. He recalled that situation in one of his songs.

One Poor Man in England as loud as he could
Warned all against Judases, saying they would
Destroy all our Freedom is they had the Lands,
Proposing to take them into our own hands . . .
But alackaday! this poor Man was not hear'd,
But shut up and from every Comfort debarr'd;
Whilst all the good Democrats wink't at the Matter;
Philosopher-like, he liv'd on Bread and water.[223]

"The Important Trial of Thomas Spence"

Spence could hardly have hoped to convert the Jury by reading his pamphlet to them. He probably expected to be sentenced in any case. His aim was to save the pamphlet from extinction. Incorporated in a report of the trial he was able to republish it in its entirety, with the addition of the indictment and his introductory and concluding defense speeches. To this he added a revised fourth edition of his *Constitution* under a new title *The Constitution of Spensonia, a country in Fairy-Land, situated between Utopia and Oceana.* A note inside the title page states that Lord Kenyon had repeatedly asked to see this work "for the sake of Illustration" but unfortunately no copy was available as the second edition had been sold out. At the back of the first edition of *The Restorer* there is a note announcing that the third revised edition of the *Constitution* was being reprinted. Its appearance was obviously prevented by Spence's trial and imprisonment.

The Important Trial of Thomas Spence (1803), including the *Constitution of Spensonia* was first published in the phonetic or Spensonian script and copies presented to the friends who had helped Spence pay the fine. An edition in normal spelling was published in 1807.

In spite of the excuse that this was a report of a legal case, Spence probably felt some anxiety in case this too was suppressed, and he printed the following note at the back of the book:—

A Serious Caution

> If this Book should be suppressed, when may the World expect to see such another? Therefore, let it be taken care of; especially the former Edition printed in natural, or philosophical Orthography, which will soon be esteemed a scarce, curious, and valuable Book. And as it is no Party-serving or Time-serving Work, but meant to promote the general happiness of mankind through all ages, the Author earnestly takes his leave in the expressive words of Scripture, saying, "Consider of it, take advice, and speak your minds".

How the work was continued

The second edition of the *Constitution* was published from 9 Oxford Street. On the first edition of *The Restorer* Spence's address is given as 3 Great Castle Street, Oxford Market. After his release from prison Spence earned a living as a number carrier or book pedlar and seems to have lived at various addresses in the same neighbourhood. *Something to the Purpose,* a penny sheet giving extracts from *The Constitution of Spensonia* and the *Jubilee Hymn,* dating probably after 1807, gives his business as number carrier and bookbinder and his address as No. 15 Princes Street, Soho. This could have been a bookbinding workshop or an accommodation address for receiving orders. A letter to Spence is addressed 29 Castle Street and the last address recorded in *The Giant-Killer* (1814) is 71 Castle Street. He was evidently unable to open another shop and all accounts show that he was wretchedly poor.

After *The Important Trial of Thomas Spence* he did not publish anything except some cheap songbooks and small single sheets. A sheet entitled "*A New and Infallible Way to make Peace at any Time*" is headed *Spence's Miscellanies.* A similar sheet *A New and Infallible Way to make Trade* does not have the general heading. There are a few broadside ballads which appear to belong to this period.

The three main Acts against treasonable practices and seditious meetings passed in 1795 and 1796 had made organisation much more difficult but had not succeeded in killing the political societies. The series of repressive laws was completed by the comprehensive Act against seditious societies in 1799 and the consolidated Combination Acts (1799 and 1800). The Secrecy Committee Report of 1799 recapitulated the history of the societies and seditious movements to date, giving Spence's edition of the draft rules of the LCS in the Appendix. The resulting Act prohibited the LCS and four other societies by name, all corresponding societies or such as were organised in branches, administered oaths, had secret committees, did not keep lists of members. (39 George III, cap. 79). There were penalties for allowing "unlawful meetings" in public or private houses: lecture rooms charging admission were classed as disorderly houses. The definition of seditious libel was made more elastic and sixteen clauses reinforced the Newspaper Act of 1798, by requiring not only the registration of presses but of types and of letter founders.

Many provincial societies had already dropped out by 1797, and LCS activity and membership greatly declined. It was now extinguished and its leaders in prison. No new organisation was attempted when they came out.

What chance had Spence?

How he functioned in the next ten years is indicated in the handbill to which the Secrecy Committee Report of 1801 had attached such sinister meanings. It was dated London, 18 March, 1801.

> "At a meeting of
> REAL FRIENDS TO TRUTH, JUSTICE
> and
> HUMAN HAPPINESS
>
> It was Resolved, That the Principles of Citizen Spence's Theory of Society, are immutable and unchangeable, as Truth and Nature on which they are built, and therefore only require universal Investigation to be universally acknowledged.

Resolved — therefore, That it be recommended to all the well-wishers to that System, to meet frequently, though in ever so small Numbers, in their respective Neighbourhoods, after a free and easy Manner, without incumbering themselves with Rules, to converse on the Subject, provoke investigation, and answer such Objections as may be stated, and to promote the circulation of Citizen Spence's Pamphlets.

Resolved also, that such Convivial, or Free and Easy Meetings should assume some Appellation, indicative of their Principles, as Restorers of Society to its Natural State,* Spensonians &c".

*Aluding to a new publication, which all Men for their own sakes ought to read".[224]

Thus the Plan was spread through informal gatherings, without any programme of public activity. There was no society to be suppressed and as not even a name was necessary, we hear of none after 1801. "He appears to have been more anxious that his writings should have their effect upon society in general than that he should be the head of a party — that what he thought the truth should prevail, than that he should be eminent".[225]

Spence often pointed out in his writings that the poor having no resources must improvise as best they can with whatever lies to hand. So Goliath was slain with a common pebble. Spence turned to the crudest, simplest methods.

One night in his Bed,
It came into his Head,
    While locked up in Shrewsbury Jail;
To send out Field Preachers,
And Peaceable Teachers,
    With Doctrines that can never fail.[226]

His poem *The Propagation of Spensonianism* could be the verse version of *The Restorer.* It begins —

"One night as slumb'ring I lay on my bed,
A notable Vision came into my Head:
Methought I saw numbers forth going to teach . . ."

It ends with the Spencean revolution —

"I beheld till these Preachers were well understood,
When the People in all Places arose like a Flood;
All ancient Oppressions were then swept away . . ."

Meeting he regarded as the first essential and singing as the means of communication which could reach all and yet be the least easy to suppress.

"Do not men when they meet encourage each other and resolve each other's Doubts and thus build one another up in their Opinion? And cannot small meetings be effected where larger Ones durst not be attempted? If but two or three meet together in so good a cause, a blessing will attend them. Even under the modern tyrannies of China, France, Turkey &c. what could hinder small Companies from meeting, in a free and easy Manner, and singing their Rights and instructing each other in Songs? Can Tyrants hinder People from singing at their Work, or in their Families? If not despair no longer but begin immediately, too much time has already been lost. Sing and meet and meet and sing, and your Chains will drop off like burnt Thread.

Let's hear no more of Despair,
But sing your dear Rights to each other,
Till all think alike every where,
Even from one Land's end to the other".[227]

Evan's *Humorous Catalogue of Spence's Songs* advertised Spence's Free and Easy at the Sign of the Fleece, Little Windmill Street, every Tuesday at 8 o'clock. A copy of this slip has a handwritten correction of the day to Monday.

"At the Sign of the Fleece
For a triffle a-Piece
Spence treats all the Swine to a Book;
But not for vile pelf:
Tis all wrote by himself,
To instruct you by Hook or by Crook".[228]

According to Mr. Porter's song, *Spence's Plan,* he met his friends at the Swan in New Street Square on Mondays. Perhaps there was more than one group meeting at different public houses.

Hone recalled that about 1808 or 9 Spence gave him a ticket to admit the bearer to a meeting of this club or society, but Hone did not go to it. An unsigned note in Place's collection says that a regular society was formed in 1812.[229] It was probably not new but the continuation of the club known to Hone, and still an informal discussion circle or convivial meeting serving as a centre for distributing literature; and leaving it to individuals to further the cause in whatever way they could. The admission ticket does not imply any regular organisation, but was a safeguard against unwanted visitors. Spence would reserve a room in the pub for a social evening with friends like any other convivial club and take care to give tickets outside the regular circle only to individuals whom he trusted. Even such a modest club ran some danger as can be seen from the suppression of Gale Jones's debating club in 1810. It is possible that local societies may have continued to keep contact and reappeared later, adopting the name of Cartwright's aristocratic Hampden Club or known as Reform Clubs or Unions when the membership shows a much more proletarian character. It is possible that the Spencean Free and Easy had a continuous if muted existence the whole time from

1801 to 1814. It shows remarkable tenacity. There was no conspiracy — just bread and cheese and porter and cheerful songs.

The history of popular political organisation and public propaganda has yet to be written, for everything had its beginning.

Wall propaganda by poster or writing on walls had been extensively used by the LCS in its early years. The case of their arrested bill-poster is told in Hardy's Memoirs. "Every wall in London has been covered with inflammatory and seditious writings" wrote a contemporary in 1793.[230] Reeves's people frequently complained that their posters were defaced or torn down as fast as they went up.

Spence's friends used the cheaper method of chalking which was one of the few means of communication not expressly restricted by the Newspaper Act. It required no name or address and could not be traced unless the writer were caught red handed. They did not write up anything in itself seditious so far as one knows.

Several contemporaries record seeing their inscriptions and the Home Secretary drew the attention of the police to sayings like "Spence's Plan and full Bellies" which had appeared "on every wall in London". "His Spence's disciples chalked them (the words 'Spence's Plan' P.M.A.) on every wall in London".[231] — "We have all seen for years past written on walls in and near London the words 'Spence's Plan' and I never knew what it meant until . . . I received a pamphlet from Mr. Evans . . . detailing the Plan very fully".[232] This was the subject of Porter's song, mentioned above.

SPENCE'S PLAN

By Mr Porter

As I went forth one Morn
For some Recreation,
My thoughts did quickly turn,
Upon a Reformation,
But far I had not gone,
Or could my thoughts recall, sir,
Ere I spied Spence's Plan
Wrote up against a wall sir.

I star'd with open Eyes,
And wonder'd what it meant sir,
But found with great surprise
As farther on I went, sir,
Dispute it if you can,
I spied within a Lane sir,
Spence's Rights of Man,
Wrote boldly up again sir.

Determin'd in my mind,
For to read his Plan, sir,
I quickly went to find
This enterprising man, sir,
To the Swan I took my flight,
Down in New-Street-Square sir,
Where every Monday night,
Friend Tommy Spence comes there sir.

I purchased there a book,
And by the powers above sir,
When in it I did look,
I quickly did approve sir. [233]

Porter turns up again in spy reports of Spencean activities. He frequented the Bull's Head, Clerkenwell, where he used to sing seditious songs, and he was present at inner meetings of the Spencean leaders at the White Lion, Wych Street. In April 1820 he was active on behalf of the Cato Street prisoners under sentence of death, when all organs of press, Parliament and pulpit were pouring out hysterical execrations.[234]

Spence attended public meetings and took any opportunity to talk about the Plan. Hone did not cultivate closer contact with him, because he "disliked his manner" but "was a frequent observer of him on account of his fearless thinking and printing. About 1808 he came to the Stand for one of Sir Francis Burdett's speeches, and talked away about his 'Plan' and the landlords, against whom he was inveterate. On leaving he gave me a card (long since lost) admitting the bearer to a meeting at the **something** and Lamb in or near Windmill Street, where he said he met his friends to talk over and co-operate towards his 'Plan''.[235]

Friends and Supporters

Among Spence's friends were some whom he had known for a long time in the LCS. Two of these, Jonathon Panther and Arthur Seale, ran into trouble for publishing protests against the renewal of war with France in 1803. We do not know how far they shared all Spence's theories but the incident shows that they possessed a fearless independence and feeling for the working classes similar to his.

Spence knew Panther at least since 1792-3 when the latter appears among the Friends of Liberty of the Press. He was a faithful member of the LCS and his donations towards the liquidation of its debts in 1797 were more than the average subscription, no doubt because he was in a better position, which would be why Spence chose to write to him from prison.

Seale was a Divisional delegate in 1794[236] and sometimes printed for the LCS. He printed or published all Spence's writings after 1797. The imprint conforms to the recent Newspaper Act, but he may have printed earlier Spence tracts which have no printer's name. He risked prosecution as the printer of *The Restorer* and *The Important Trial,* and published and possibly financed *The Giant-Killer.* Imprints show that Seale was at one time in partnership with Bates (of whom nothing is known). He cannot have been very prosperous for in the 1830's Place traced his widow to St. Pancras Workhouse.

Panther was prosecuted for a somewhat incoherently worded statement that the war "is a war of the rich man against the most sober and industrious part of the people of this nation who have always been the principle support of the rich", and that hardships already too much to be born will ensure that the war is lost. "I am positively sure that the King, Lords and Commons which is the Church and State have long since lost the goodwill and affection of a very great majority of the People of this nation as such I am sure the men you want most will not fight for the present government for the greatest part of this people hate and detest the conduct of the government and as to the Blackguard Papers which have been published by Reeves's Committee at the Crown and Anchor and stuck all over the town I say they are an insult to commonsense and there is not one word of truth in them . . . I again declare that no power shall force me to take up arms neither will I pay any fine whatever imposed by this Act for I will sooner lose my life than submit to assist in destroying my country. 2, White Lyon Yard, Oxford Street. Aug. 5, 1803. Jon. Panther".[237]

Seale's offence was the publication of a pamphlet dated Nottingham July 30th, declaring that the people have nothing to fight for and that "government has no right to our assistance till it redress our wrongs".[238]

Spence must also have known Thomas Evans for several years but it is not certain when Evans joined the LCS. He became secretary in 1797. The policy which he pursued with Crossfield in 1798 and the plan for the United Englishmen, modelled on the United Irishmen, which he sponsored were far removed from Spence's ideas. But he must have formed a closer connection with Spence soon after his release from prison. He contributed one item to *Spence's Songs,* four to *Spence's Songs, Part Second* and one to *Spence's Songs, Part Third,* but the dates of publication are not precisely known.

Allen Davenport is said to have met Spence in 1804. In 1810 he became a delegate of the Shoemakers' Union, which in spite of the Combination Laws was strong enough to keep up correspondence with all shoemakers' clubs in every place of any importance in the country, and was involved in the unsuccessful general strike of the trade in 1813. After disappointing experience of the co-operative and trades unions movements in the 1820's and

30's, he reaffirmed his adherence to Spence's theories and perceived that common ownership should be extended to means of production that had developed since Spence's time. However his attempt to form a general social theory in the forties was an unoriginal and for that date even reactionary egalitarian utopia. Before that he had done more than anyone else to preserve Spence's memory and was the main living link between Spence and the Chartists.[239]

Thomas Preston met Spence in 1811. He described him as "an eccentric but hearty and sincere man". — "He had been reduced by persecution . . . and he remained the lingering victim of publishing what he thought **right**".[240] After taking a prominent place in the Spencean Radical Reform movement, he too lived to influence the Chartist generation and in extreme old age was courted by representatives of the Anti-Corn Law League.

James Wedderburn came to know Spence about nine months before his death and followed his teachings with great attention.[241] He liked to sign himself "Wedderburn, the Deluded Spencean" and of all Spence's immediate disciples he was the one who most accurately and literally interpreted his doctrines.

The son of a West Indian slave by her white master, he found in Spence not merely an opponent of slavery on moral grounds but the only thinker of that time who offered what seemed to be a practical way to national liberation and international relations based on equality. This new contact may have had something to do with the attention to the question of slavery in *The Giant-Killer*. Wedderburn sent information about Spence's Plan to Jamaica in the hope that it would inspire and guide a slave rebellion and thus took the first step towards Spence's playful fantasy —

"For who can tell but the Millenium
May take its rise from my poor cranium?
And who knows but it God may please
It should come by the West Indies?"[242]

W. Tilly, the author of *The Spencean Jubilee* in the Songbook, was undoubtedly William Tilly, grocer, of 23 Castle Street, Oxford Market, not far from Spence's last addresses. He had belonged to The General Association of Householders, a reform club active in 1796/97.[243] The name is not very common and it seems likely that this was the same Tilly to whom the Public Receiver made over Paine's skeleton when the auctioneer of Cobett's effects objected to its inclusion in the sale, for surely only someone with special feeling for the democratic struggles of the past would have wanted it.[244]

Alexander Galloway, Thomas Evans's brother-in-law, an engineering mechanic and one of the LCS committee imprisoned in 1798, and his friend

Robert Moggridge were also in contact with Spence's circle. Galloway blossomed into a successful businessman and friend of Francis Place. Already in 1816 he was contemptuous of the Spencean movement and leaders, although chiefly responsible for managing young Watson's escape to America after the Spafields Riots.[245]

It must also be assumed that the foundation members of the Society of Spencean Philanthropists were people who had known Spence personally, but nothing is known about them until after his death.

Last Days

The leaflet *A New and Infallible Way to Make Peace at any Time* proposes buying over the opposing army by offering double pay for life. "No Army on Earth (except the British and their Allies) could resist the temptation". But only a country freed from the burden of landlordism could afford such generous terms. What is meant here is that the prospect of liberty and prosperity will defeat the enemies of Spensonian revolution. It is added that once Spensonia is established it will need no standing army; all armies will die out.[246]

From this it may be concluded that revolutionary tactics was one of the problems discussed among Spence's friends. His further reflections on the matter in the light of the experience of the war, are the most important addition to the new version of *The Marine Republic* published in *The Giant-Killer.*[247]

Two or three numbers of *The Giant-Killer; or Anti-Landlord* were published in 1814. The paper now begins to look like the organ of a group and contains outside contributions and readers' letters. It responded to the new situation at the end of the war.

Meetings to petition against the Corn Bill early that year, threatening demonstrations, "violent speeches and ballad singing", when in London troops were called out to protect the precincts of Parliament, marked the beginning of a powerful wave of popular protest against food prices and low wages in many towns and country districts. The following year large numbers of destitute unemployed and disbanded soldiers added to renewed and more serious machine breaking led to a more broad-based agitation for political reform, and lent fresh significance to Spence's teachings.

On the eve of this new period, Spence died suddenly of a stomach attack on 1 September, 1814. He was buried on 8 September from his address in Castle Street, Oxford Street, in St. James's Burial Ground, Hampstead Road, with his favourite tokens, the Cat and the Meridian Sun, placed in the coffin.[248]

About forty persons walked behind the coffin, preceded by a pair of scales containing equal weights of earth and adorned with white ribbons, symbolizing the justice and purity of his aims and his conduct in life. The oration at the graveside was delivered by William Snow. Quantities of his tokens were distributed to mourners and onlookers, so that he literally went to his grave still spreading his immortal message.

The Courier (12 September 1814) announced: "Died on Thursday Thomas Spence, Author of several political tracts &c. He devised and published a plan by which all human kind could be provided with sustenance without pauperism. His writings are truly singular and uncomplimentary, and evince a most disinterested desire to serve mankind". This is similar to a longer account in *The Morning Post* (10 September 1814) and other notices occur in *The Monthly Magazine* (September 1814), Cobbett's *Register* (September 1814), *The Annual Register* for 1815 *The Gentleman's Magazine* (September 1814 and March 1815), which copy one another. There are probably other such obituaries if one looked for them.[249]

One of the most sympathetic memories of Spence by a non-Spencean came from William Hone in spite of not finding him personally congenial.

"Spence was a native of Newcastle, small in stature, of grave countenance and deportment, serious in speech and with a broad burr in his accent. He would sometimes relax at little evening parties where his plan was discussed. On these occasions he sang a song highly characteristic of himself and his plan, in which is a sentiment denoting the pleasing state of being "free as a cat" and indeed his love of personal independence was as great as any Man's, or greater, with a fierce impatience of oppression and rigidly pertinacious of his plan, which was ever first in his thoughts and foremost in his purpose, it is not surprising that in his humble walk in life he lived with difficulty and died poor, leaving nothing to his friends but an injunction to promote his "Plan" and the remembrance of his inflexible integrity".[250]

Many people who had known Spence in the nineties, such as Thomas Hardy, Thelwell and John Binns did not mention him in their writings. Place did not begin collecting information about his life until the thirties and his own recollections of Spence so far as he committed them to paper are scanty, showing that during Spence's lifetime he had not thought it worthwhile to keep any record, that he really did not know very much about him, and that what he did know, for example about Spence's relations with the LCS, he did not choose to record.

Among later notices the all-time record of nonsense biography is Cushing's:— "An English schoolmaster, on the Quayside, Newcastle, and born in that city; he came to London and died there".[251]

The Spencean Philanthropists

Preston says that the Society of Spencean Philanthropists was founded shortly after Spence's death. He mentions no earlier organisation. He was one of the most active members of the new society.

The name of Spencean Philanthropist does not seem to have been used during Spence's lifetime. When the Society published its *Address* to the public (1814/15), complete with elaborate rules, programme and the meeting places of four sections, there was no hint that this was the continuation of one already existing or that the rules amended any earlier rules. It appears as a completely new organisation.

The approach and style must strike one immediately as very different from Spence's but closely similar to Evans's *Christian Policy. The Salvation of the Empire,* published about the same time. The *Address* makes the Society sound very important. It also claims to have international connections and invites correspondence from other countries.

The rules complicate what Spence would have kept as simple as possible even when there was no need for caution. The institutions and procedures in his *Constitution of Spensonia* show that he endeavoured to discard non-essentials and anything that might foster disunity or sectarianism. His model was the customary benefit society, meeting ground for people of different views but common interest.

Evans reserved for himself the permanent office of Librarian, which amounted in practice to permanent Secretary, other officers being frequently re-elected. The sectarian tendency visible in the first *Addresses* developed as sectarian practice, authoritarianism and eventually Evans's isolation. For once Place was not far wrong in calling him "a high priest under the title of Librarian".

Spence was given a minor role in these new formulations. He is not mentioned in a passing remark and bracketed with Moses and Lycurgus as marized under his name. In *Christian Policy in full practice* he is only mentioned in a passing remark and bracketed with Moses and Lycurgus as an exponent of the Agrarian Law which he so expressly repudiated. The Rappist community even in the version which Evans offers as the ideal of social equality and fraternity, was far indeed from Spence's idea.[252]

In several important points Evans changed Spencean theory.

1. Evans not only gives the Plan a religious basis but a specifically Christian one. He insists that Christianity is the essential foundation of civilization and that only if a country is already Christian can the Spencean system be immediately operated. "Pagan" in Evans's vocabulary is equivalent to

"feudal", "barbarous", "tyrannical". Contrary to Spence's universalism, Evans imports a chauvenistic tone with this religious bias. (Granted he had his own peculiar notions of Christianity, possibly excluding a creator or a personal god).

2. Evans did not give a class interpretation of the origins and character of landlordism, but adopted the well-worn theory of Norman Conquest opposed to Saxon liberty. The English Constitution and the laws of Alfred are adequate and legitimate basis of equality, grounded on a social contract. None of these concepts will be found in Spence who envisaged no resurrection of supposed ancient rights or contract but an entirely new system to restore natural rights adapted to modern conditions. Certainly Spence's notion of the British constitution was derived from republican theory, regarding the Bill of Rights as an advance.

Variants of this theory, far from claiming that an earlier constitution had been destroyed by the Conqueror, explained that public apathy had allowed an oligarchy to whittle away the citizen's rights recognized in 1688. The other version identified the true constitution not with 1688 but with Alfred the Great. The official theories of the LCS, which Spence repudiated, were influenced by both these traditions. Thelwall was one of the exponents of Saxon liberties and his later writings show how they could be harmonized with sentimental patriotism.

Popular ideas were even more influenced by this Alfredism in the second decade of the 19th. century. The Spencean radicals for instance called their newspaper *The London Alfred.* The Constitutional mythology of the late eighteenth century was not a simple continuation of an earlier "Norman Yoke" argument against the monarchy. It contained the new elements of incipient radicalism on the one hand, and on the other the desire of enthusiasts like Major Cartwright and Sir William Jones to restore the status and patriarchal virtues of the nobility and gentry who were becoming increasingly subordinated to merchant capital and bureaucracy. These tendencies were gaining ground in the nineties and inspired one of James Parkinson's clever satires. In the LCS several of Paine's admirers regretted his contempt for the British constitution and his often misunderstood remark that no such thing existed. Paine was in fact closer to real history in stating that the basis of Parliament had not been derived from the people's rights but granted as a boon, and that the concessions forced from the monarch at various times had been mistaken for a constitution.

Spence was acquainted with these theories and disposed of them briefly with the remark that all conquerors, be they Roman, Saxon, Israelite or Norman, merely exchanged one set of tyrants for another.[253]

3. The new proposal was that the nobility and landowners were to become salaried state officials to manage the land. The social system, it is stated, would remain unchanged. Hence the land would not be returned to the people in any real sense, large estates would not be broken up and the ruling class would still be a ruling class although the land would be nominally nationalized. There is no scope here for the initiative of the parish collective from which Spence had anticipated mutualism and self-government to develop. Evans in fact formulated something like nationalization of land and single tax under capitalism without that possibility of socialisation which appeared in Spence's conception of universal participation in decision and administration, not to mention that officials would not be elected and recallable but appointed from an hereditary elite.

Comment shows that the suggestion of reducing landowners to paid functionaries was considered particularly insulting, but that did not make Evans's scheme any more progressive.

It cannot be imagined that Spence would have made such a concession to class superiority even as a joke. In Spensonia not a trace of aristocracy remains. All representatives and executives must be chosen from among the people themselves, who may be trusted to act honestly by them. He would have thought it foolish to give public responsibility to those who had always been "useless drones", "public robbers", "the hardest set of masters that ever existed", who "cannot bear to see us endeavouring to act for ourselves". They had never shown mercy to those beneath them — whether they inherited property through no merit of their own or were "monopolizers and forestallers, Plundering Nabobs, Slave Traders, and all sorts of griping miscreants, who like Judas, come with the reward of Iniquity in their hands to buy a field of Blood".[254] If these obstructed the new order, their movables as well as their lands would be confiscated. The best prospect was that this class should die out as painlessly as possible and ex-landlords become "as harmless as other men", indistinguishable from the rest. This cannot in any way be reconciled with Evans's proposal that the people should continue to pay £20 million for the monarchy and Establishment, £5 million for the Church (apparently to remain part of the political state) and pensions of up to £30,000 p.a. to members of the nobility.

4. When Evans said that no change in the existing order of society was necessary except as regards the land, he had clearly failed to grasp that important part of Spence's teaching, the relationship between property and power. He assumed that social rank and class relations could be separated from property relations. Spence did not fall into any such absurdity, but attempted to work out the changes in all social relation-

ships and all conditions of life which he thought should result from abolishing private property in the means of livelihood and hence the abolition of the power of any man to compel and profit by the labour of others.

It was Evans's version of Spence's Plan that attracted Southey and he picked out religious revivalist elements in Evans's writings which seemed akin to his own reactionary ideology.[255] He therefore thought that Spence was not without his merits.

The real purpose of Southey's article, to discredit the reform movement in the service of the reactionary government, was exposed angrily by Sir Richard Phillips, who was himself sometimes called a Spencean and was certainly influenced by Spence in the matter of land reform.

Spence's name however was known and necessary. The Society carried on the earlier activity of chalking and added posters explaining the Plan. According to Cobbett:—

"We have all seen for years past, written on the walls, in and near London, these words "SPENCE'S PLAN"; and I never knew what it meant, until a little while ago I received a pamphlet from Mr. Evans, Newcastle Street, Strand, detailing the Plan very fully. This Mr. Evans, I understand to be a very worthy man, and his pamphlet, though I do not agree with it in opinion as to many of its propositions, contains interesting observations, and breathes a spirit of benevolence throughout the whole".

Handbills posted up "everywhere" had "excited much apprehension" and were reproduced in newspapers. Cobbett's example is an extract from the Society's *Address* and is headed "Spence's Plan". It states that "The Landholders are not the Proprietors in chief, they are but the **Stewards** of the Public; For the Land is the PEOPLE'S FARM. The Expenses of Government do not cause the Misery that surrounds us, but the enormous exactions of these **"Unjust Stewards".** Landed Monopoly is indeed equally contrary to the benign Spirit of Christianity, and destructive of the Independence and Morality of all Mankind. "The Profit of the Earth is for all"; Yet how deplorably destitute are the great Mass of the People! Nor is it possible for this situation to be radically mended, but by the Establishment of a system Founded on the immutable basis of Nature and Justice. Experience demonstrates its necessity; and the rights of mankind require it for their preservation".[256] Then follows a general invitation to the public to attend meetings of the four sections.

This woolly statement is very different from the decisiveness and vigour which is found in Spence's briefest arguments and Spence would never have overlooked the close relation between "expenses of Government" and

Landlord vested interests. How the other Spenceans came to accept this new interpretation of the Plan is hard to understand.

The Spencean Philanthropists came into prominence in the post-war crisis with petitioning, mass meetings, allegedly riotous, addressed by a new type of popular plebeian and working class speakers, and the trial for High Treason of four leading members of their Society in 1816.

The Secrecy Committee reports on these fresh manifestations (February - June 1817) and debates on the Seditious Meetings Bill and the Suspension Bill (February - March 1817) reviewed past history. It was said that the long-forgotten teachings "of a visionary of the name of Spence" had lately been revived "with some variations" and spread throughout the country in the Hampden Clubs and Union Clubs. Middle-class politicians were once more showing interest in Parliamentary Reform and Castlereagh in particular took the opportunity to hint at the hidden hand of "men distinguished in station and ability" behind the disturbances.[257]

The working classes in the industrial districts had begun for the first time to take a leading part in popular political agitation. The Reports and Ministerial statements, while insisting that distress "is the instrument rather than the cause of dissatisfaction", reflected this development. They exaggerated the extent to which the Spenceans had been able to influence Reform Societies but quoted some of their propaganda quite correctly, for instance that they regarded Parliamentary Reform as a half-measure "unworthy of their attention" and called for the take-over of the land in parochial partnership, as the People's farm, and spoke of "overturning what they call 'the privileged class' as distinguished from the People, who are described as consisting of Labourers, Artizans, Tradesmen and every profession useful to society".[258]

The Unlawful Societies Act of 1799 (39 George III c.79) which had illegalised societies organised in branches or corresponding with affiliated bodies, needed now to be completed by prohibiting all societies communicating by means of delegates or missionaries. The Spenceans however should be expressly prohibited by name and description regardless of their mode of organisation or their numerical strength and influence, purely on account of their doctrines "which are utterly subversive of every well regulated state, subversive of all property, order and good government".[259]

For the first time there was no attempt to justify suppression on alleged facts of seditious conspiracy, but simply on account of the opinions which they openly propagated. As no one wanted to defend attacks on private property, the opposition could not make much of the usual argument that a trivial case was being made an excuse to curtail public liberties.

The resulting "Act for more effectively preventing seditious meetings and assemblies" (57 George III c.19) prohibited: "All societies or clubs calling themselves Spencean or Spencean Philanthropists, and all other societies or clubs, by whatever name or description the same are called or known, who hold and profess or shall hold and profess their objects and doctrines".

Davenport remarked that the impression on the Government "must have been very deep or it would not have enacted transportation for meeting under the name of Spenceans!"[260]

The Spenceans had already split. At first there appears to have been a kind of division of labour. The Evans group devoted itself entirely to discussion and the majority were active in immediate political organising and agitation, some of them also attending the meetings of the original society. They all met to commemorate Spence's birthday, for the last time in 1819 at the Navy Coffee House, Catherine Street, Soho.

After the banning of the Society, Evans, his son and a few followers set up the Christian Philanthropists. The majority formed no new Spencean body but for a few years became the most forceful leadership of the open Radical Reform movement campaigning for the old Parliamentary Reform demands, while maintaining a secret Spencean Committee and provincial contacts by means of visiting delegates. It is not very clear to what extent they regarded the possible achievement of the universal franchise as the means to their ends, but there can be no doubt that the Spencean Radical Reformers looked on Spence's plan as the ultimate objective, and certainly discussed and possibly attempted to prepare for revolutionary action along the lines laid down in *The End of Oppression* and *The Marine Republic*.

Evans meanwhile strongly opposed both intervention in the immediate political struggle and any kind of revolutionary action. His society soon became a tiny isolated semi-religious sect, and eventually he quarrelled violently with his former colleagues. He still enjoyed considerable personal respect for the sake of his long devotion to the cause and particularly his recent sufferings when again imprisoned for a considerable period without trial. Attempts were made to draw him into the political campaign in the crisis of 1819.

The fate of Spence's teachings in the complicated history of these years cannot be dealt with here. The Cato Street case in 1820 ending in the execution of five leading Spenceans, for the alleged conspiracy to assassinate the Cabinet, did not bring in any issue of Spencean doctrine or organisation. The friends of the accused always maintained that their comrades had been led into a trap by the notorious spy, Edwards, as did many other contemporaries, and this has generally been the view of later historians. Neither the motives of the Cato Street men who acted on their own initiative, nor the credibility of the evidence can be discussed here. There exists some spy statements which would suggest that the Spencean leaders had shortly before reviewed the situation and decided that their forces were insufficient for any decisive action. It is perfectly clear that Spence himself had never contemplated a revolution led by a minority or starting from an act of terrorism.

The Cato Street victims' memory was honoured; they were regarded as less mistaken than betrayed. That was the opinion of Preston who promised further revelations, and was even more strongly stated by Benbow.

While the Gagging Acts of 1819 destroyed the Spencean press and introduced even more restrictions, the indecision of the Peterloo protest campaign and the effect of the Cato Street broke up the remains of the Spencean organisation and served as an excuse for the strong measures particularly associated with Castlereagh and Sidmouth to stifle all Radical Reform activity for a number of years.

Former Spenceans appeared in the movements that developed later and a few veterans were among the Chartists, but the name was avoided. Sufficient reason was the Act outlawing organisations propagating Spence's theories and the Cato Street affair which had been exploited to the full.

NOTES

1. Place MSS. British Library. Add. 27808, 27809; also scattered in other MS volumes, particularly Add. 27789, and in Place Collection of newspaper cuttings.

   Evans, Thomas: *A Brief Sketch of the Life of Mr. Thomas Spence, Author of the Spencean System of Agrarian Fellowship or Partnership in Land &c.* Manchester. May 1st, 1821.

   Mackenzie, Eneas: *A descriptive and historical account of the Town and County of Newcastle upon Tyne, including the Borough of Gateshead.* Newcastle-upon-Tyne, 1827; vol. 1. p. 339, 340. The same account was published as a separate tract — Mackenzie, E.: *Memoir of Thomas Spence of Newcastle-upon-Tyne.* Newcastle-upon-Tyne, 1826.

   Bewick, Thomas: *Memoir of Thomas Bewick written by himself 1822-1828.* Ed. Selwyn Image, London, 1924. p.p. 61-63, 70.

   Davenport, Allen: *Life, Writings and Principles of Thomas Spence, Author of the Spencean System, or Agrarian Equality.* London n.d. (c. 1836).

2. Davidson, John Morrison: *Scotia Rediviva.* London 1890, p.p. 86-95; *Concerning four precursors of Henry George and the Single Tax as also the Land Gospel according to Winstanley 'The Digger'.* London, 1899, p.p. 25-47.

3. Welford, Richard: *Men of Mark 'twixt Tyne and Tweed,* 3 vols. London 1895; p.p. 212-219, 429-433.

4. Rudkin, Olive: *Thomas Spence and his connections.* London, 1927. (Reprint. New York, 1966).

5. Waters, A.W.: *The Trial of Thomas Spence in 1801.* Privately printed. Leamington Spa, 1917.

6. *Catalogue of a scarce and curious collection of books and engravings formerly belonging to Thomas Bewick . . . To be sold at auction on Tuesday, Wednesday and Thursday, February 5th, 6th and 7th, 1884.* Newcastle-on-Tyne (1884).

7. Bewick, Thomas: op. cit. pp. 61-62.

8. Oliver Thomas: *A new picture of Newcastle-upon-Tyne or an historical and descriptive view of the town and county of Newcastle-upon-Tyne, Gateshead and Environs.* Newcastle-upon-Tyne, 1831; pp. 215-216.

9. *Newcastle Weekly Chronicle.* 4 November, 1888.

10. Add. 27808, ff. 151, 204; Add. 27789 f. 61; Wallas, Graham: *The Life of Francis Place.* London 1898, p. 165.

11. Mackenzie, op. cit. vol. 1. pp. 168, 383. Before Spence's birth Sandhill, Quayside and the Close were described as poor, crowded and dirty, the Quayside itself very narrow and no wealthier residents remained. The old walls and gates along the waterfront began to be pulled down in the sixties. .— Bourne, Henry: *The History of Newcastle-upon-Tyne or the Ancient and Present State of that Town.* Newcastle-upon-Tyne, 1736; p. 133; Middlebrook, S.: *Newcastle upon Tyne. Its growth and achievement.* Newcastle upon Tyne, 1950; p. 144.

12. Mackenzie, op. cit. vol. 1. p. 339.

13. *Directory for the year 1801 of the Town and County of Newcastle-upon-Tyne, Gateshead and Places Adjacent.* Newcastle-upon-Tyne, 1801; p. 37.

14. Spence, Thomas: *A Supplement to the History of Robinson Crusoe.* Newcastle, 1782. p. 3. — Dalton, R. and Hamer, S. H.: *The Provincial Token Coinage of the Eighteenth Century.* London, 1914. vol. 2, p. 217; Waters, A. W.: *Notes of Eighteenth Century Tokens.* London, 1954, p. 17.

15. *Register of the Ballast Hills Cemetery. Grave Books.* Transcribed by C. E. Whitney, Newcastle-on-Tyne, 1930; vol. 1. p.185.

16. *Register of Freemen chiefly of the Eighteenth Century.* Ed. A. M. Oliver. *Publications of the Newcastle-upon-Tyne Records Committee.* vol. VI, 1926, pp. 104, 121.

17. Spence was not "chiefly instrumental" in its formation as stated in *Newcastle Weekly Chronicle,* 11 December, 1880. The presence of Rev. John Baillie and similar people indicates a much more "respectable" circle. Richardson in *Local Historian's Tablebook.* Newcastle upon Tyne, 1842, vol. II, p. 235, wrongly included Bewick, who denied that he had any connection with the Society. It should not be confused with the debating club meeting in Spence's Castlegarth schoolroom, described by Bewick.

18. "At the Philosophical Society on Wednesday night, the question 'What is virtue', was debated . . . At the same time they expelled Mr. Tho. Spence, for publishing, without and against the approbation of the society, a lecture with the title of 'property in Land, every Man's Right', which he had delivered at a former meeting, of which they disclaim all patronage; being informed that he had previous to the delivery of the lecture, read it in different public houses; and became a member, apparently, for the purpose of obtruding upon the world, the ERRONEOUS **and dangerous levelling principles,** with which the lecture is replete, under sanction of the society. —" *Newcastle Chronicle* 25 November, 1775.

19. Place. Add. 27808 f. 235. Bewick had recently completed his apprenticeship with Beilby.

20. *Reports, papers, catalogues etc. of the Literary and Society of Newcastle collected by Anthony Hedly 1820-1821;* Watson, R. S.: *History of the Literary and Philosophical Society of Newcastle upon Tyne.* Newcastle upon Tyne, 1897, pp. 16-20.

21. *Newcastle Magazine,* 21 March, 1821.
Presumably the first print of the Lecture had the formal opening addressed to the President given in the later editions, which identified it with the society.

22. Evans, Thomas: op. cit. p. 2.

23. The allegation had been circulated by the new Literary and Philosophical Society founded in 1793, quite a different kind of society mainly interested in natural science with a strong bias towards industrial technology. Possibly warned by its predecessor's fate, this society ruled from the outset to prohibit discussion of "Religion, British politics and all politics of the day". — See: *Law of the Literary and Philosophical Society of Newcastle-upon-Tyne with a list of members,* 1794.

In reply to a reference to Spence's Lecture in *The Annual Register* of 1797, a letter was sent to this and other journals disclaiming any connection with the old Philosophical Society and the Lecture. Again, alarmed by a remark in a review of Evans's *Christian Policy. The Salvation of the Empire,* a more detailed disclaimer that Spence's theory had originated in their society, was sent to the *Quarterly Review* (23 February, 1817) and to the Newcastle Members of Parliament.

"There did exist a Debating Club in Newcastle more than forty years ago . . . Of this

Society or Club Spence . . . was a member and there produced his strange paper, which was heard with very little attention. Spence however got it printed and hawked about the town, as an Essay read at the Philosophical Society of Newcastle, upon which a respectable member of the Club moved at the next meeting, that Spence should be expelled, and was unanimously expelled accordingly. He soon after removed from Newcastle and was entirely lost sight of there". — Watson, R. S. op.cit. p. 25.

This anxiety to disassociate themselves even from the society that had expelled Spence, is understandable. The Spenceans had been chosen as the main excuse for proposing further restrictions on organisation and meeting, and it was by no means clear how far non-political bodies might be endangered. In order to play down the Spenceans as a lunatic fringe, the opponents of the Seditious Meetings Bill recalled that Southey, whose recent article in the *Quarterly* sympathetic to the Spenceans which had started all this, was at once the hired mouthpiece of the Government and the author of much more dangerous sedition in his *Wat Tylor.* Spence and his doctrines were spoken of as long dead and only revived now to suit the Government's ends. The many references to Spence in earlier Government reports were conveniently forgotten. He had died little more than two years before at the age of 57 as reported in London newspapers, but Lord Albermarle referred to him as "an old gentleman" who had lived a long while ago and was "very mad". Hence Sir Matthew White Ridley, member for Newcastle, in the debate on 14 March, 1817, desiring to clear his loyal fellow-townsmen and the Literary and Philosophical Society of the impression created by the *Quarterly,* gave the House a more highly coloured version of the Society's explanation. "His (Spence's P.M.A.) conduct was so generally reprehended that he was ultimately obliged to leave Newcastle. Nothing was heard of his Plan for many years until some months ago". — *Hansard* vol. xxxv. February 19 and March 14, 1817; *Quarterly Review* vol. xvi, Nos. xxxi, xxxii, 1816; Southey, R.: *Essays Moral and Political,* London, 1832, vol. I, p. 96. fn.

24. *Newcastle Courant,* 10 and 16 March, 1776.

25. Oliver, Thomas: op.cit. p. 117; Mackenzie: op.cit. p. 451. There were some 100 pupils of parents able to pay eightpence a month (sixpence extra for arithmetic); Dendy, F. W.: *Extracts from the records of the Company of Hostmen of Newcastle upon Tyne.* Surtees Society, 1901, p. li.

26. *Common Council Books.* Transcripts. Newcastle City Records Office. *179,* pp. 303, 307, 313, 314, 319; *1780,* p. 342; Sykes, J.: *Local Records.* Newcastle, 1866; vol. 1. p. 294.

27. *Newcastle Courant,* 12 June, 1782.

28. *Common Council Books,* 1779, f. 303; 1787 ff. 54, 61.

29. Gray, Gilbert: *The Complete Fabulist . . . Designed for the instruction of both sexes as well as the use of English schools.* Newcastle-upon-Tyne, 1753, p. 275.

30. Law, A. R.: *Schola Novocastrensis,* vol. 2, p. 99.

31. Gray, Gilbert: *The Pleasing History or Impartial History of England . . .* (1st edition), London, n.d.; *Epitome of the Annals of Great Britain, or a succinct impartial History of England from the remotest period of Intelligence to the conclusion of the last war . . . with an introduction on the Constitution of Great Britain. Useful for youth at school as well as all those who are desirous of relating what they read to the history of their country.* Newcastle, 1773; *Epitome . . . Second edition enlarged and corrected.* Newcastle, 1777.

32. E.g. Historical examples of Agrarian Law; dividend = share in rent or profit from joint estate, equivalent to the share in Nature. Symbolism of Millenium, Jubilee, Deluge, Giants and Spence's MS. History of the pre-Diluvian giants, origin of the Nobility, usurpation of the land, coincides with Murray's *Lectures on Genesis* with additions from

Sprigge. See Place Add. 27809. f. 232. Spence's song *Men of Renown* = third *Lecture on Genesis.* Folklore Giant/Ogre in Murray's *Lectures to Lords Spiritual* p. 11 (Bishops' palaces surrounded by mangled limbs of their victims): Spence exhorts workers to be giant-killers, like Jack or Hercules: his paper is called *The Giant Killer, or the Anti-Landlord:* name of John Gast's trade society is The Philanthropic Hercules. Cf. Marx, *Capital,* Moscow, 1959. vol I p. 692; Buckle, H. T.: *History of Civilisation in England.* London, 1908, vol. I. p. 335.

33. Hone, William: *Biographical sketch of the Rev. James Murray* in Murray, James: *Sermons to Asses.* Ed. Hone. London, 1819. p.V; *Newcastle Magazine.* September, 1826.
Murray is not included even in Caroline Robbin's nearly exhaustive catalogue *The Eighteenth Century Commonwealthman,* Harvard University Press, 1959) although such a staunch admirer of the Cromwellian republic fitted the description better than some of her examples.

34. Short biographical notices in: Scott, Hew: *Fasti Ecclesiae Scoticanae.* Edinburgh, 1928, vol VII. pp. 513-514; anonymous *Memoir* in Murray, James: *Travels of the Imagination.* Newcastle-on-Tyne, 1828; Mackenzie, op.cit. vol. I 385, 388; Mackenzie: *History of Northumberland.* Vol. I p. 439; Tate, George: *The History of the Burgh, Castle and Barony of Alnwick.* London, 1866, 1869. Vol. II. pp. 172-173. Hone, William: op.cit. pp. iii-xiii; Skelly, George: *Alnwick in the past.* Alnwick, 1896. p. 68; Sykes: op.cit. I. p. 321; Welford, R.: *Men of note 'twixt Tyne and Tweed.* London, 1895. pp. 212-219; *Newcastle Weekly Chronicle,* 10 April, 1886; *Dictionary of National Biography.* Later notices add little to earlier ones and are sometimes less accurate. Little is known of Murray's early life, except the bare facts of his Edinburgh degree, employment as a tutor in the Weddell family (Yorkshire gentry) and marriage to one of the daughters. No publications are recorded before he settled in Northumberland.

35. Sever, John: *Morrison of the 'Pioneer'. Notes on his life and background.* (Unpublished typescript). Oxford, 1963. pp. 2, 4, 5.

36. Thirteen congregations formed the first Newcastle Presbytery in 1781-1783 and signed the Confession of Westminster, i.e. immediately after Murray's death. High Bridge did not apply for admission until 1785 when membership seems to have declined. See Mackenzie, op.cit. vol. I. pp. 388-389; Oliver: op.cit. pp. 86, 90; (J. G. Bell): *Historical memorials of Presbyterianism in Newcastle-upon-Tyne. By an Episcopalian.* 2nd edition. London, 1847. p. 110.

37. Letter of Administration granted to Sarah Murray 15 March, 1783. University of Durham, Department of Palaeography and Diplomatic Probate, 1783. A 29.

38. Bewick, Thomas: op.cit. p. 105.

39. *Judges* iii. 22. See Murray, James: *Sermons to men, women and children.* Newcastle-upon-Tyne, 1768. Sermon I; *New Sermons to Asses.* London, 1773 (all on this text): *Eikon Basilike. Or the character of Eglon, King of Moab and his ministry.* Newcastle-upon-Tyne, 1773 (Enlarged version of the earlier sermon in two lectures).

40. Murray, James: *Eikon Basilike,* p. 13.

41. Lincoln, Anthony: *Some political and social ideas of English Dissent. 1763-1800.* Cambridge, 1938. p. 43.

42. Murray, James: *Sermons to Asses.* London, 1768. Another edition published at Newcastle in the same year. These are described as a second edition, apparently a revised edition of *Sermons to men, women and children.* The second edition carries the Ass vignette, a striking example of animal portraiture by an unknown artist.

43. Spence, Thomas: *Restorer of Society to its Natural State,* London 1807. p. 56.

44. I.e. *Sermons to Asses* (v.supra); *New Sermons to Asses: Sermons to Doctors in Divinity.* London, 1771; *Lectures to Lords Spiritual. Or an Advice to the Bishops concerning religious articles, tithes, and Church power. With a discourse on ridicule.* London, 1774; *Sermons to Ministers of State.* Newcastle-upon-Tyne (1780). The whole series was reprinted by Hone as *Sermons to Asses, to Doctors in Divinity, to Lords Spiritual and to Ministers of State.* London, 1817-1819. All quotations from this edition. Murray prepared a third, enlarged edition, which friends dissuaded him from publishing as too obviously seditious libel.

    Murray continued the tradition of popular preachers of the late 17th. century characterized by choice of texts with a topical application, avoidance of high-flown, literary style and difficult language, short sentences often terse and epigrammatic, graphic imagery, illustrations from common life, logical order and division of subject. — Cf. Cragg, G. R.: *Puritanism in the period of the Great Persecution 1660-1688.* Cambridge, 1957. pp. 209-212.

45. Glassites or Sandemanians. The largest congregations in England and the last to survive were at London and Newcastle. Murray's respect for Glas and sympathy for the sect, in contrast to marked hostility of most other religious writers, can be seen in (Murray, James): *A history of the Churches in England and Scotland. By a Clergyman.* Newcastle-upon-Tyne, 1771/72. pp. 518-519. Murray's theological views were on several matters close to Glassite doctrine. Other points in common were informality, plain language and literal interpretation of scripture, tolerance of all forms of recreation and customs not expressly prohibited. A major difference was that the Glassites demanded strict conformity to majority decisions as to theory and practice and disciplined or eventually expelled transgressors.

46. Murray, James: *Sermons to Doctors in Divinity,* p. 96.

47. Murray, James: *The Magazine of the Ants. Or the Pismires' Journal.* Newcastle-upon-Tyne, 1777.

48. Murray, James: *Sermons to Ministers of State.* p. 13.

49. Murray, James: *Lectures on the most remarkable characters and transactions recorded in the Book of Genesis.* Newcastle-upon-Tyne. 1771. III.

50. Murray, James: *Sermons for the General Fast Day.* London, 1781; *Pigs' Meat* vol. I. pp. 165, 201; vol. II. p. 23, p. 74.

51. Murray James: *Sermons to Ministers of State.* pp. 32-33.

52. Ibid. pp. 53-54.

53. Ibid. pp. 56-57.

54. Murray, James: *New Sermons to Asses.* p. 26.

55. Ibid. p. 2; *Sermons to Asses.* p. 24, pp. 25-26.

56. Murray, James: *Sermons to Asses.* p. 14 — 15.

57. Murray, James: *The travels of the imagination. A true journey from Newcastle to London.* (1773) Newcastle-upon-Tyne, 1828. pp. 47-48.

58. Ibid p. 15.

59. Ibid pp. 51-52.

60. Spence, T.: *The end of oppression.* 2nd. ed. p. 7.

61. Murray, James: *New Sermons to Asses. p. 22.*

62. Mortimer, Thomas: *The elements of commerce, politics and finance.* London, 1772. p. 86, p. 105. On laws to protect workers from the "oppressive weight of cruelty and avarice" and employers from "unwarrantable extortion", i.e. a legal maximum and minimum wage, see pp. 71-72.

63. Ibid. pp. 85-86. Marx notes Vanderlint, Forster, Price and Postlethwayte on the workers' side of the question. — *Capital.* Moscow, 1959. Vol. I. pp. 274-275.

64. Murray, James: *New Sermons to Asses.* p. 20.

65. Ibid. p. 19.

66. Ibid. p. 22.

67. Ibid. p. 22, p. 37.

68. Murray, James: *The magazine of the ants.* p. 18.

69. *Pigs' Meat.* Vol. II. No. 85.

70. Place MSS. Add. 27809 f. 235; *Pigs' Meat.* Vol. III. p. 240.

71. Handasyde, John: *A practical essay on the Lord's Prayer.* 2nd. ed. Whitehaven, 1799. pp. 31-36.

72. Murray, James: *Sermons to Ministers of State.* Nos. V, VI, particularly pp. 34-38, p. 39.

73. Murray, James: *A grave answer to Mr. Wesley's Calm Address to our American colonies. By a Gentleman of Northumberland.* n.d., n.l.; *An old fox tarr'd and feathered, occasioned by what is called Mr. John Wesley's Calm Address to our American colonies. 'In politics I dabbled too, Brave Jack of all trades!'. By an Hanoverian.* Printed for the Author. n.l., 1775 (exposing Wesley's plagiarism of Dr. Johnson's *Taxation no tyranny;* Murray, James: *The finishing stroke to Mr. Wesley's Calm Address to the people of England. Newcastle-upon-Tyne, 1777.*

74. Murray, James: *An impartial history of the war in America.* 2 volumes. Newcastle-upon-Tyne, 1778-1781. The third volume was completed after Murray's death and published by William Graham, Minister of the Close Meeting House (United Seceders) and Secretary of the Protestant Association, Newcastle. Also a London edition of the whole work. For Murray's pro-American sympathies see his *Travels of the Imagination,* p. XVI and 'Ahab Salem': *The new Maid of the Oaks. A tragedy.* London, 1778. Cf. Baker: *Biographia Dramatica.* London, 1812. vol. iii. p. 79; Inglis, Ralston: *The dramatic writers of Scotland.* Glasgow, 1868. p. 89.

75. *Newcastle Chronicle,* 28 October, 1775.

76. *Newcastle Magazine,* September, 1826; Mackenzie: op.cit. Vol. I. p. 387, where the incident is connected to the wrong occasion; Welford, R.: op.cit. vol. I, p. 215.
Murray, James: *An alarm without cause; or the administration of peace supported by the sword of the spirit: An evening lecture delivered in the High Bridge Meeting, Newcastle.*

'He that hath no sword let him sell his garment and buy one'. — Luke xxii. 36. Published on behalf of the Protestant Association. Newcastle-upon-Tyne, n.d.; 'Clerus'. *The lawfulness of self-defence explained and vindicated on Scripture principles. An evening lecture.* Glasgow, 1780.

77. Spence, T.: *Restorer* — p. 27.

78. Evans, T.: *Brief Sketch of the Life of Mr. Thomas Spence.* Manchester, 1821. p.l..

79. *Report of the Proceedings of the Town Council of Newcastle-upon-Tyne on the Freeman's Quarry.* October 10, 1842. p. 6.

80. Gibson, T. F.: *The Borough History of Newcastle-upon-Tyne.* Newcastle-upon-Tyne (1875?). pp. 41, 43, 44 cf. pp. 30, 36, 38.
Clarke, Joseph: *A friendly address to the Free Burgesses and other inhabitants of Newcastle-upon-Tyne.* Gateshead, 1809. pp. 14-17.
Clarke, Joseph: *Newcastle Freeman's Pocket Companion.* Gateshead, 1808. p. vi.
Neff, J. U.: *The Rise of the British Coal Trade.* London, 1932. vol. I, p. 400.

81. Clark, J.: *A friendly Address.* p. 6 seq; pp. 16-17.
Clarke, J.: *The Newcastle Freeman's Pocket Companion.* pp. 81-83.
Clarke, J.: *Newcastle Remembrancer and Freeman's Pocket Companion. A new edition.* Newcastle, 1817. pp. 82-88.
Report on the Proceedings of the Audit of the Accounts of the Corporation of Newcastle-upon-Tyne. Published agreeably to a resolution of the Court in Guildhall, on Michaelmas Monday in the year 1809. Gateshead, 1809. p. 5 seq.

82. Neff: op.cit. vol. II, pp. 121, 133.

83. *Proceedings of the Stewards of the several companies of Newcastle respecting an Enquiry into the Rights by which any Roads over the Town Moor &c. are enjoyed with the Report of the Committee by them appointed for the Purpose. n.l., n.d. (Newcastle-on-Tyne, 1771).*

84. *Common Council Books.* Transcripts. pp. 132-136.

85. Ibid. pp. 156-157.

86. (Murray, James): *The Contest,* 1774. p. 121.

87. 14. George III c. 105.

88. *Newcastle Weekly Magazine.* 2 October, 1776; *Town Moor Act 1774.* Newcastle-upon-Tyne, 1811. p. 12; (Clarke, Joseph); *The Newcastle Freeman's Pocket Companion.* Gateshead, 1808. p. 73.

89. —*The Town Moor Case.* (Newcastle-on-Tyne) 4 October, 1773; Brown, John. Attorney-at-Law and Secretary to the Body of Stewards: *A short account of the customs and franchises of the Freemen of Newcastle.* Newcastle-upon-Tyne, 1823. pp. 82-90: *The Act of Parliament obtained in the year 1774 for confirming the resident Freemen of Newcastle and their widows their full Right and Benefit to the Herbage of the Town Moor, Castle Leazes and Nuns' Moor. By a Burgess.* Newcastle-upon-Tyne, 1811 (1810); (Clarke, Joseph): *Newcastle Freeman's Pocket Companion.* Gateshead, 1808. pp. 58 seq.; Ibid.: *Newcastle Remembrancer and Freeman's Pocket Companion.* Newcastle-upon-Tyne, 1817; Newcastle Journal. 12 January, 1861; Watson, Roger Cradock: *Newcastle-upon-Tyne,* Newcastle-upon-Tyne, 1869 pp. 7-14. *The Town Moor Common of*

Newcastle-upon-Tyne. History and State in 1935. Issued by the Ratepayers' Union. Newcastle and Northumberland. January 1936.

90. *Town Moor Case.* pp. 52 seq; *Freeman's Magazine.* 1774, pp. 2-8; (Clarke, Joseph): *The Newcastle Freeman's Pocket Companion.* Gateshead, 1808. pp. 74, 92-93; (Clarke, Joseph): *Newcastle Remembrancer and Freeman's Pocket Companion.* Newcastle-upon-Tyne, 1817 pp. 63-66. *Report of the Proceedings of the Auditors of the Accounts of the Corporation of Newcastle-upon-Tyne . . .* Gateshead 1809. p. 5; A. Burgess (i.e. Joseph Clarke): *The Town Moor Act 1774 . . . with a full and interesting Detail of the public and private proceedings for obtaining a New Act &c. &c.* Newcastle-upon-Tyne, 1811. p. 28; Brown, John: *A short account of the customs and franchises of the Freemen of Newcastle.* Newcastle, 1823; *Report of the Investigation of the case of Messrs. Brunel, Walker and Angus before the Mayor, Aldermen and Common Council of Newcastle-upon-Tyne.* Newcastle-upon-Tyne, 1835. p. iii; *A full Report of the Evidence and Discussion during the official investigations into the affairs of the Municipal Corporation of Newcastle-upon-Tyne before His Majesty's Commissioners &c. &c.* Newcastle-upon-Tyne, 1939. p. 115; *Report of the Town Council of Newcastle-upon-Tyne on the Freeman's Quarry. October 10, 1842.* Newcastle-upon-Tyne, 1842; *Newcastle Journal.* 15 October, 1842..

91. Namier, L. B.: *The Structure of Politics on the Accession of George III.* London, 1929. p. 121. f.n.

92. (Murray, James): *The Contest. Being an account of the matters in dispute between the Magistrates and the Burgesses and an examination of the merits and conduct of the candidates in the present Election for Newcastle-upon-Tyne. 'Give the Devil his due'.* (Newcastle-on-Tyne), 1774. p. 15. (Listed among Murray's works by reliable near-contemporaries and so catalogued in Newcastle City Reference Library; opinions and style, consistent with Murray's authorship). For the character of Newcastle representation and the Blacketts' influence and political record, see: Blair, C. H. Hunter: *Members of Parliament for Northumberland and Newcastle-upon-Tyne 1539-1831. Arch. Aeliana.* 4th series, vol. xxii, 1945. pp. 102-103; 148-149; 132..

93. Murray, James: *Sermons to Asses.* p. 68.

94. *Northern John Bull.* No. 1. July 1829.

95. Maccoby, S.: *English Radicalism 1762-1785.* London, 1955. p. 113.

96. *Freeman's Magazine or The Constitutional Repository.* 1774. p.v.

97. Rudé, George: *Wilkes and Liberty.* Oxford, 1962. pp. 103-104.

98. Tate, George: *A descriptive and historical view of Alnwick,* 2nd edition. *Alnwick.* 1822. vol. 1. p. 476, vol. 2. pp. 328-332; *History of Northumberland.* vol. vii. p. 399.
Grieve eventually sold up and went to America, later to France where he was a member of the Jacobin Club. After the fall of Robespierre with whom he was personally associated, he retired to Brussels.

99. Mackenzie: op.cit. vol. 1 p. 60; Sykes: op.cit. pp. 271-272.
Similar celebrations at Darlington, Sunderland, Shields, Morpeth, Hexham etc. on a scale which shows the interest of well-to-do tradesmen — flags, processions, guns, dinners, illuminations and public entertainment with play on the slogan "No. 45" such as a 45 lb. sheep turned on the spit by 45 men from 6.45 a.m. to 11.45 p.m. served to 45 guests with 45 potatoes, 45 biscuits, 45 quarts of ale, 45-inch clay pipes. It seems an excuse for a holiday and display of protest and self-assertion among the working tradesmen and middle ranks. Rude found no political motivation in Wilkite slogans heard in

popular disturbances and strikes. Vulgar history has exaggerated Wilkes's significance as a popular leader. His memory does not seem to have been preserved in popular sources. Word-play in a Newcastle contemporary bawdy ballad, *Wilkes's Riggle,* shows that his career was common gossip and the political implications understood, but hardly that he was personally much respected.

Wilkes's Riggle

Last week I rambl'd to the Strand
  To have a roling shine O,
A Damsel then did seize my hand,
  All dress'd so neat and fine O;
My Hand she pressed my lips she kiss'd,
  So cunningly did wheedle,
My Dear, said she, come, go with me,
  And I'll give you **Wilkes's** Riggle.

Then she took me up to the Ken,
  And I called for a Bottle.
Her Mistress quickly brought it in,
  I made the Glasses rattle.
I flash'd my day and to Moll say,
  Did smile and tip the Giggle.
I'm sure I can please any Man,
  With Wilkes's pleasant Riggle.

My Girl and I then fell to Work,
  We rowl'd it both together
And every move and every jerk
  She called out **Wilkes** for ever:
See here's a skin that's sound within
  You see I want no Doctor,
Then tipped the giggle with Wilkes's riggle
  And hollowed out no Proctor.*

**Name of the candidate run against Wilkes at the Middlesex Elections.*

Of all the riggles then said I,
  I ne'er knew such another.
My dear, said she, we'll come to it again,
  As soon as you do recover:
With all my heart I will not start,
  Said I, I've no objection,
Then with each shove she cry'd my Love
  Wilkes, and a free Election.

Then gently down she put one Hand
  The t'other was o'er my Shoulders,
Now Liberty he soon shall stand
  And I'll back him with two Freeholders
For I the Country am you know
  And you do well content me,
Therefore be true, for none but you,
  Shall ever represent me.

There's many Riggles as I have heard,
  Some people say there's twenty;
There's Maggy's Riggle, and Boots* it's true,
  Three Million Riggles is dainty,
But Wilkes's Riggle doe beat them all
  The motion is so clever,
For it makes your Eye squint with surprise
  So Wilkes's Riggle for ever.

Lord Bute

From: "The Sons' of Tyne's Garland, composed of six new songs". n.l.; n.d.

100. Murray, James: *Sermons to Asses.* p. 62. The allusion is to Wilkes's application to annul the Deed of Separation from his wife.

101. Murray, James: *Sermons to Ministers of State.* Sermon VII.

102. Alternatively described as a surgeon, a tailor and a glazier.

103. *Freeman's Magazine,* pp. 137-141; p. V.

104. J.S. (i.e. John Sykes): *Memoirs of the public life of Sir Walter Blackett.* Newcastle-upon-Tyne, 1819. pp. xxviii-xxix. At the Election he had to face "all the virulence of the most raucous opposition and terms of the most naked and insufferable contempt". — (Baillie, John): *History of the Town and County of Newcastle-upon-Tyne and its vicinity.* Newcastle-upon-Tyne, 1801. p. 180.

105. (Murray, James): *The Contest,* pp. 2, 5, 6.

106. Maccoby, S.: op.cit. pp. 192-194. On significance of the Instructions and Pledges cf. Rudé, op.cit. p. 195; Christie, Ian R.: *Wilkes, Wyvill and Reform.* London, 1962. p. 48.

107. For the Burgesses programme see *Freeman's Magazine* pp. 3-4, 93; (Murray): *Contest.* p. 30.

108. *The Burgesses Poll at the late Elections of Members for Newcastle-on-Tyne.* n.l. (1774) 1775. p. 23.

109. *Freeman's Magazine,* p. 77.

110. *Freeman's Magazine,* p. 8.

111. *"To the Electors of Great Britain"* in *Freeman's Magazine,* pp. 95-98. Cf. (Marat, Jean-Paul): *Chains of Slavery.* London, 1774; Marat, Jean-Paul: *Les Chaines de l'Esclavage.* Paris, 1793. Copies of the book reached Newcastle 27 May, 1774, addressed to three incorporated companies by "an unknown person". — See Newcastle Chronicle, 28 May, 1774 i.e. months before the London printer released it for distribution. Marat believed that his life was threatened by North's spies, which could explain the anonymity, but his personal contacts at Newcastle whoever they were must have known the source, otherwise the Address would not have been printed in the *Magazine.* By itself it was simply a very generalised appeal to voters to return honest representatives. A Newcastle edition of *Chains* under Marat's name, said to have been financed by the patriotic clubs, appeared in December. — See *Newcastle Chronicle,* 4 November, 1774; Merivale, Herman: *Historical Studies,* 1865. Copies survive in the Literary and Philosophical Society and King's College libraries. — See P. M. Horsley: *Some Frenchmen in Newcastle in the*

Eighteenth Century. Heaton Works Journal. Summer 1957, p. 33. *Chains* shows no specific connection with Newcastle. Possibly the Burgesses movement misled Marat as to the nature of the guild system which he later defended in opposing the anti-combination law of Le Chapelier.

112. Bax, E. Belfort: *Jean-Paul Marat. The Friend of the People.* London 1908, p. 38. It is now agreed that Marat exaggerated his prestige in English Radical circles — cf. Manfred, Albert: *Essai d'Histoire de France du XXIIe au XXe siecle.* Moscow 1969. p. 58 Some modern writers exaggerated his connection to the proletariat. See for example Manfred's criticism in his introduction to Ts. Fridljand: *Jean-Paul Marat i grazdanskaja Vojna.* Moscow, 1959. p. IX, p. XII, and Fridljand's confusion of companies with trade societies. — op.cit. pp. 50, 60. There is no evidence that *Chains* created any sensation as claimed by Marat (in his *Lettre aux Presidents des Etats Generaux.* 23 aout 1789, included in the French edition). — See for example — *Marat. Textes Choisis.* Editions Sociales. Paris, 1963, p. 10. Certainly no Newcastle club ever sent anybody any certificate in a golden casket and it is difficult to credit that any company would have bestowed its freedom on account of the book, although they might have recognized medical services to the town in some way. Marat's criticism of the English Parliamentary system and proposed reforms in *Chains* (1774) repeated the main points of SSBR, (only adding a reference back of new laws to the constituencies — a device of direct democracy which seldom interested English reformers except Spence who took it over from the French (1793) Constitution). The formulations of the early seventies remained the basis of Marat's critique when English Parliamentary reformers had reached a more advanced position. Murray as a leading democrat at the time of Marat's residence in Newcastle must have been known to him. Because of the Newcastle connection some similarity of their ideas about the origins of despotism, mechanism of corruption, acquiescence of the people might invite closer comparison. Volgin's reference to similarities with English Radical views is vague — Volgin, V.: *Le Developpment de la Pensee sociale en France au XVIIe siecle.* Moscow, 1973. p. 272. Nothing connects Spence with Marat except the coincidence that these two remarkable historic documents — the *Lecture* pointing to critical utopian socialism and *Chains* to bourgeois democratic revolution — appeared almost simultaneously in Newcastle. Spence never mentions Marat, who offered nothing to his purpose on property, but may have taken something from the most important aspect of *Chains,* the necessity of popular insurrection and in particular its tactics. Marat's thesis is said to contain the germ of revolutionary dictatorship (Manfred, op.cit. p. 56; Volgin, op.cit. p. 271) while actively involving the masses.

113. *Contest.* p. 9.

114. Ibid. p.7.

115. *Freeman's Magazine.* p. 100.

116. *The Burgesses Poll,* p. 12, p. 22.

117. Ibid. pp. 23-24.

118. Oldfield, T. H. B.: *The History of the original constitution of Parliaments.* London, 1797. p. 331: *The representative history of Great Britain and Ireland.* London, 1816. vol. LV, p. 304-305.

119. Sykes: op.cit. p. 141: *Newcastle Chronicle,* 28 October, 1775.

120. Namier: loc. cit.; Christie, Ian R.: *Myth and Reality in Eighteenth Century British politics.* London, 1976. pp. 258, 260.

121. Rudé: op.cit. pp. 174, 176; Christie: op.cit. p. 257.

122. *Contest.* pp. 26-27.

123. Rudkin: op.cit. p. 66.

124. Bell, John: *Gatherings of scarce books locally printed in the counties of Northumberland and Durham or relative thereto* n.l.; n.d.

125. Place Add. 27789 f. 61.

126. *The Case of Thomas Spence.* London, 1793(?) (Second edition).

127. Place. Add. 27808, 249-252.

128. According to Mackenzie this was partly the reason for leaving Newcastle.

129. Place Add. 27808 f. 314.

130. Place Add. 27808 ff. 151 204; Add 27789 f. 61.

131. A recent monograph quotes abundant evidence for this but illogically treats the Association as a prototype of a modern extra-parliamentary pressure group. See Black, Eugene Charlton, *The Association. British Extra-Parliamentary Political Organisation 1769-1793.* Harvard Univ. Press, 1963; pp. 233-236.

132. *Parliamentary History* XXX December, 1792, 15, 28 February, 1793. e.g. "The Friends of Peace in the country were in the same manner denounced as leagued with foreign invaders, and this was the real secret of Messrs, Reeves, Burke and Co. for **levelling the levellers,** at the source of which, considering the men, many people have been so much surprised. The nation was panic-struck and apprehension and credulity go hand in hand". — Wilson, Jasper, *A Letter commercial and political addressed to The Right Hon. William Pitt* . . . London, 1793, p. 49.

133. Place Add. 27808. ff. 152-3; Wallas op.cit. p. 61.

134. *The Case of Thomas Spence,* London, 1792, p. 4.

135. BL. Add. 16922 f. 133 (Association Papers).

136. Add. 16922 f. 33.

137. *Case of Thomas Spence,* p. 5.

138. BL. Add. 16923 f. 90.

139. Place. Add 27808 f. 314.

140. Place. Add 27808 ff. 254/5.

141. *Parliamentary History* XXX 20 December, 1792.

142. *Parliamentary History* XXXII — Proceedings in the Commons respecting Mr. Reeve's Libel on the British Constitution. 23 November; Howell, *State Trials.* XXXII.

143. *Proceedings of the Friends of the Liberty of the Press on December the 22nd 1792; January 19th and March 9th 1793.* Printed by Order of the Committee. London, 1793, pp. 5, 11, 12.

144. Rudkin, op.cit. pp. 91-94. For the most comprehensive discussion of Spence's political tokens and their symbolism see Thompson, R. H.: *The Dies of Thomas Spence (1750 – 1814). The British Numismatics Journal* vol. XXXVIII, 1969 (1970); — *Additions and Corrections. The British Numismatic Journal* vol. XL, 1971 (1973); *Jacobin Grotesques: the deliberate Muling of Dies in late Eighteenth-century England. Actes du 8 eme Congres International de Numismatique. New York – Washington. Septembre 1973.* Paris-Bale, 1976. pp. 671-679.

145. PRO. Treasury Solicitor. 11/965.

146. Editions and dates of publication in Rudkin op.cit.

147. *The Manual of Liberty,* London, 1795.

148. PRO. T. S. 965 (2) 3510 A.

149. Place 27814 ff. 105-108. What exactly happened is not quite clear.

150. Place, Add 27814. ff. 120, 121.

151. Ibid. f. 144.

152. *Public Advertiser,* 26 May 1792. Cf. Hall, W. P.: *British Radicalism 1791-1797. Studies in history, economics and public law.* Columbia Univ. vol. 49, No. 11, 1912, p. 170.

153. Gurney, Joseph: *The Trial of Thomas Hardy for High Treason . . . Transcribed in short-hand by Joseph Gurney.* London, 1795. vol. IV p. 256-257.

154. Hodgson, W.: *The Commonwealth of Reason.* London, 1795.

155. Brown, P. A.: *The French Revolution in English History.* London, 1918 (reprint 1923); pp. 142, 143; 47.

156. Baxter, John: *Resistance to oppression; The constitutional Right of Britons . . .,* London, 1795.

157. E.g. Spence, *Restorer,* Letter VII.

158. See: Baxter, J.: *A new and impartial history of England.* London (1795). pp. i-x.

159. Place. Add. 27814 f. 113.

160. Sinclair, A. G.: *The Critic Philosopher, or Truth Discovered.* 5th edition. London, 1791; p. 2.

161. (Parkinson, James): *An account of some peculiar manners and customs of the people of Bull-land or the Island of Contradictions: faithfully detailed by Old Hubert.* London, 1795, p. 70.

162. Lee, Richard: *The Happy Reign of George the Last.* London, 1794.

163. Bently, Thomas: *The Poor Man's answer to the rich Associators.* London, 1793.

164. Place, Add. 27814 f. 152.

165. John Richter's notebook, confiscated 1794, contains memoranda on the constitution of

the society and the committee of revision — TS. 11 p. 90. LCS Constitution included in *Report of the Committee of Secrecy to the House of Commons, 1794.* Appendix 2.

166. *The Report of the Committee of the Constitution of the London Corresponding Society. Printed for the use of the Members. Sold by Thomas Spence, No. 8 Little Turnstile, High Holborn;*
Report of the Committee appointed to revise and abridge a former Report of the Constitution of the London Corresponding Society. Printed by order of the General Committee. nl.; nd.

167. Many references to and articles about the Scottish Martyrs in nineteenth-century Radical and working class press and in verse, particularly for example poems by Ebeneezer Elliott, evidence the lasting impression.

168. London Corresponding Society. *Address to the Friends of Peace and Parliamentary Reform.* London, 1794.

169. *An account of the Seizure of Citizen Thomas Hardy, Secretary to the London Corresponding Society; with some remarks on the Suspension of the Habeas Corpus Act.* Printed by order of the London Corresponding Society (distributed gratis). (1794); p. 8.

170. *Second Report of the Committee of Secrecy of the House of Commons respecting seditious practices. 6 June, 1794;* col. 693; PRO: PC 168/78; 206/13; TS 3505.

171. PRO: TS11.964 H 33; 3510 B; PC 1/22 A 36 (a); Gurney: *Trial of Thomas Hardy* vol. I p. 311; vol. IV p. 121.

172. PRO. TS 11. J 28 and 965.

173. *Gurney:* vol. I. p. 311, 327, 329; vol. III p. 315; vol. IV pp. 315, 347, 352, 398.

174. PRO: PC 1/22 A 36-37. A published report of this examination has not so far come to light. Its existence is in doubt as it appears in no contemporary advertisement.

175. PRO: PC 11/22 A 36-37.

176. I.e. The Society of Friends of Universal Peace and of the Rights of Man.

177. *Pigs' Meat.* vol. ii. pp. 97-102; *Second Report of the Committee of Secrecy* . . . May, 1794. Appendix E; Howell, *State Trials* XXIV, 745-748; TS 11/965 (2); 3510A; Gurney: vol. I, 215, vol. II 392-398; vol. IV, 365.

"Open your eyes, O ye poor of the land! in vain are your hands and your mouths open! . . . Ye poor, take a further look into your rights, and you will see, that, upon the principles of reason and justice, every peaceable and useful person has a right, yea, a **divine right** to be satisfied with the good of the land! If the benevolent father of the universe did not send amongst mankind provision enough, and more than enough and running over, such is the waste of the great and the gluttonous, that many of you poor, would get none at all! Say not, therefore, ye oppressed, **'there is a famine, or scarcity of provisions in this land!'** It would be false. The land contains plenty; and if provisions were (as they ought to be) reduced to your wages, you would enjoy your unquestionable right; a comfortable sufficiency. . . .

Hearken! O ye poor of the land! Do you fret and whine at oppression — 'yes', — Then, as ye do, so did your fathers before you — and, if you **do no more,** your children may whine after you! Awake! Arise! arm yourselves — with truth, justice and reason — lay siege to corruption; and your unity and invincibility shall teach your oppressors terrible things — Purge the representation of your country — claim, as your inalienable right, universal suffrage and annual parliaments. And whenever you have the gratification to chuse a representative, let him be from among the lower order of men, and he will know how to sympathize with you and represent you in character . . .".

In the *Pigs' Meat* copy there is a footnote: "See Spence's Rights of Man". It is not impossible that the pamphlet was written by Spence in the first place and passed off as a Stockport production.

178. *The Rights of Man. Extracts from Pigott's Political Dictionary.* (Ed. R. Lee). London n.d. p. 6.

179. Republished in *Pigs' Meat,* III, pp. 3, 4.

From the Morning Post
of December 18, 1794.
To the Editor.

Sir,

My second volume of Pigs' Meat was finished on that memorable day, the 17th of May, 1794, the day on which the Commons passed the Suspension of the Habeas Corpus Act; and terror being the order of the day, you declined inserting my advertisement.

On the Tuesday following, May 20, I was dragged to the Secretary of State's Office, under pretence of being charged with treasonable practices, and from thence in a few days committed to Newgate, where I yet,* to the honour of the government, remained untried. But, finding, that on account of my long imprisonment, the business of my shop is much decayed, I have essayed once more to get my book advertised, hoping that now you will not be afraid.

I need not but to remind the public of a well known truth, namely that many thousands have read, and as many thousands have approved this incomparable political instructor; wherefore, being conscious that those who shall purchase this my publication, will receive no less than value in full for their money, I the more confidently hope, in this time of my distress, for the countenance and assistance of the Friends of Freedom and Political Truth, in the vending of a work so eminently calculated to enlighten mankind.

I am Sir, &c.

T. Spence

Newgate,
High Treason Side,
December 17, 1794

**T. Spence was discharged from Newgate, December 22.*

From the Morning Chronicle
Of January 3, 1795

FELLOW CITIZENS TO THE PUBLIC

I am again restored to my shop, after a tedious confinement of more than seven months, but change of circumstances renders my return productive of but small joy. But though the **public enemy,** has acquired the satisfaction of reducing me to the inability of carrying on my little business, with my wonted alacrity; yet, I trust I shall not be overlooked by the patrons of the **Martyrs of Freedom** in the dispensation of their favours. I beg leave therefore to observe to the friends of freedom and political truth, that by assisting me in the sale of my book, called

PIGS' MEAT;

they will not only essentially serve me, but will also contribute greatly towards the enlightening of mankind.

That I have been a considerable sufferer in the Cause of Liberty, is evident from the following facts; since the prosecutions began in 1792, I have been four times dragged from my business by runners and messengers — Three times have I been indicted before Grand Juries, and twice have they found true bills: — Thrice have I been lodged in prison for different periods of time, and once have I been put to the **bar,** but never once convicted. — Neither did my son, (a boy of twelve years of age) escape a prison, for selling in the street, *the Rights of Man in verse,* (price only One Halfpenny), the poems which he had were confiscated, and I paid a **fine,** and thus the mighty affair ended.

And for what has all this been? Why, for doing those things which my own rights, and the rights of mankind would not suffer me to dispense with, and which to decline, would have been to betray the liberties of my country.

I am, &c.

T. SPENCE

No. 8, Little Turnstile.
December 22, 1794.

It may be noticed that there was no mention of the Privy Council examination or the adjourned trial for High Treason. The reader would assume that Spence had been persecuted only on account of publishing or bookselling. In view of the *Morning Post's* nervousness he may have thought it better not to emphasise the gravity of the charge which had in effect been withdrawn.

180. *Pigs' Meat* vol. III p. 56.

181. Joyce, Jeremiah: *Sermon preached on Sunday February 23rd 1794 by Jeremiah Joyce. Twenty-three weeks a close Prisoner in the TOWER OF LONDON.* 2nd edition. London, 1795; Appendix, p. 24 f.n.

182. The original by William Roscoe reads "Let Burke like bat". It had long been in circulation. Spence printed it under the heading *"A Song sung by Mr. Meredith at Liverpool on the Anniversary of the French Revolution",* without naming the author. — For Thelwall's explanations see: Thelwall, John: *Peaceful Discussion and not Tumultuary Violence the means of Redressing National Grievance, The Speech of John Thelwall, at the General Meeting of the Friends of Parliamentary Reform, called by the London Corresponding Society and held in the Neighbourhood of Copenhagen House; on Monday October 26, 1795.* London, 1795; *The Tribune* No. XV, 1796, pp. 332-334; also reprinted as a separate leaflet in reply to further "malignant" or "mistaken" misrepresentations of his conduct. The pamphlet to which Spence refers is *Sober Reflections on the Seditious and Inflammatory Letter of the Right Hon. Edmund Burke to a Noble Lord.* 1796.
1796.

183. Place. Add. 27808 f.28 and 27810 f.91.

184. Binns, J.: *Recollections of the Life of John Binns.* Philadelphia, 1854, p. 45; Jones, John Gale: *A sketch of a speech delivered at the Westminster Tavern on the 9th, 10th, 23rd and 30th December, 1794 on the following question . . .* London, 1795, p. 11.

185. Place. Add. 27808 ff. 68-69; 27817 f. 41.

186. *Report of the Committee to the London Reforming Society (June 18).* London, 1795, p. 15.

187. Ibid. Loc.cit. Both these groups were closely watched. Cf. House of Commons debate for 17 November, 1795. *Parliamentary History.* XXXII.

188. Reid, William Hamilton: *The Rise and Decline of Infidel Societies in this Metropolis.* London, 1800, pp. 6, 9, 11, 108.

189. Ibid. p. 14.

190. Place Add. 27808 ff. 67, 75-76. There were contemporary accusations that Place was an informer. He appears to have enjoyed a strange immunity while most other LCS leaders were repeatedly arrested. Inconsistencies in his own narrative are obvious, so that even Maccoby remarks that Place "protests too much". Such a complex personality could have thought that his ends justified his means, while conscious that he should not leave it on record. Bourgeois historians have long taken Place at his own evaluation, and no critical analysis has been carried out to compare his own statements and other documentation in order to clear up this point. Cf. Maccoby, S.: *English Radicalism 1760 - 1832*. London, 1935; p. 98.

191. E.g. Galloway and Hodgson. See Add. 27808 f. 106.

192. *Annual Register,* 1796; Binns op.cit. pp. 54-57, 62.

193. *Spence, Thomas: The End of Oppression.* Second edition. London, n.d. p. 7.

194. London Corresponding Society. *Address to the Nation from the London Corresponding Society on the subject of Parliamentary Reform. Together with resolutions which were passed at a General Meeting of the Society. Held on Monday the 8th July 1793 at the Crown and Anchor Tavern, Strand. Printed by Order of the Society and distributed (gratis);* London Corresponding Society. *Address to the Friends of Peace and Parliamentary Reform. November 15, 1793. p. 4 ff.*

195. *Address of the London Corresponding Society to the Other Societies of Great Britain united for obtaining a Reform of Parliament.* (London, 1793); also *State Trials* XXIV.

196. *Address to the British Nation.* 8 July, 1793. See Gurney op.cit. Vol. I, pp. 206, 208.

197. Gerrald, Joseph: *A Convention the only means of saving us from ruin.* London, 1793; p. 60.

198. *Second Report of the Committee to the House of Commons . . . presented May 15th, 1801; p. 4.*

199. *Facts, Reflections and Queries submitted to the consideration of the Associated Friends of the People.* Edinburgh, 1792; p. 39.

200. Examples in Place. Add 27814 f.49 and BL 1389d. 27/4.

201. *To the Parliament and People of Great Britain. An explicit declaration of the Principles and Views of the London Corresponding Society.* Committee Room, Beaufort Buildings. November 23rd, 1795. (London, 1795). Separate prints, one in Place. Add. 27814 f.80. Full text also in Mrs. Thelwall: *Life of John Thelwall,* London, 1837.

202. Spence, Thomas: *The important trial of Thomas Spence.* London, 1807, p. 9.

203. Ibid. p. 67.

204. *Parliamentary History.* XXXII col. 332.

205. Hone, William. Letter to Place, 1830. Add. 27808. f.315; Wallas, op.cit. p. 61.

206. Broadside, BL. 648 c.26/57. No author or imprint but type and style similar to Spence ballads in same collection. Spence broadsides are found with and without imprint.

207. Reid: op.cit. p. 109.

208. *Second Report of the Committee to the House of Commons.* 1801. Appendix A. On general unrest see Maccoby op.cit. p. 141.

209. Spence: *Important Trial* p. 57.

210. PRO: PC 1/42 A 144; PC 1/41 A 138.

211. Twenty-eight were imprisoned without trial for up to a little over two years. For some particulars of their hardships see: Binns, op.cit. pp. 78-91; Place Add 35143. ff. 59-65. Several refused to give sureties and demanded trial, and were released only after an Act of Indemnity had been passed to protect ministers from proceedings for wrongful arrest.

212. *Times,* April 23, 1801. . . . "The object of this publication was to show that all the oppression and distress which at present prevailed in the country were owing to the proprietors of land, and that in order to remedy these evils, it was indispensably necessary that the present system of landed property should be completely exterminated, and that all the land in the kingdom should be equally divided among all the inhabitants of the island, without distinction. This the author considers as the only effectual cure of Monopolies, Forestalling, Regrating &c. Although at first sight it appeared difficult to be accomplished, yet in fact nothing was so easy. It might be effected in the course of a single day. As the Almighty said 'Let there be Light and there was light', so the Public had only to say 'Let the Land be ours and it would be so'. . . .

213. Marginalia on a copy of a book (Boulanger, M. A.: *Christianity Unveiled.* Translated by W. M. Johnson. New York, 1795) bound up with Spence's pamphlets in BL show that Cullen was a self-educated man, the child of poor Catholic parents and now the bitter enemy of the church and of religion. Charles Hall in one of his letters to Spence in 1807 asks to be remembered to Cullen. Spence had sent Hall a copy of his *Important Trial* in phonetic script, perhaps at Cullen's suggestion.

214. Maccoby, op.cit. p. 148.

215. Spence: *Important Trial* p. 59.

216. Kenyon was not perhaps the right man to appreciate Spence's notion of science in framing laws, nor his references to the Bible backed by quotations from Harrington, Priestley and Lauderdale. According to his biographer:— "Narrow, coarse, uncultured, he practised the common law without discovering it to be a science", and "commended to a jury the example of 'the Emperor Julian, a prince so celebrated for the practice of every Christian virtue that he was called Julian the Apostle ". — W. C. Townsend, *Life of Lord Kenyon.* 1846. Quoted in Fifoot, C. H. S.: *Lord Mansfield,* Oxford, 1936.

217. *Annual Register* 13 June, 1801.

218. Spence: *Important Trial* p. 67.

219. *Parliamentary History.* XXXIV col. 1512.

220. Cobbett's *Weekly Political Register.* vol. XXXI, No. 24. 14 December, 1816; col. 748-9.

221. *Newcastle Magazine.* January, 1821, p. 5.

222. Place. Add. 27809 f.252.

223. *"An Address to Posterity"* in *Spence's Songs, Part First.* n.l.; n.d.

224. Printed in Appendix to *Second Report of the Committee to the House of Commons,* 1801.

225. *Newcastle Magazine,* January, 1821.

226. Evans, Thomas: *A Humorous Catalogue of Spence's Songs,* undated slip bound in with the collections of *Spence's Songs* in the Goldsmith Library, Univ. of London.

227. *"An Address to all Mankind"* in *Spence's Songs. Part Second.* The verse is from the Song *"Spence and the Barber".*

228. In the Goldsmith Library volume of Spence's pamphlets.

229. Place. Add 27808 f.227.

230. Anon.: *Opinions delivered at a numerous and respectable meeting in the country, lately held for the purpose of signing a declaration for the support of the Government in the present alarming crisis.* London, 1793.

231. Place. Add. 27808 f.229; HO. 65, 1, 2, 187; *Cobbett's Weekly Political Register* 14 December, 1816, col. 749.

232. Letter from Cobbett to Henry Hunt in: Hunt, H.: *Memoirs of Henry Hunt written by himself.* London, 1820-1822, vol. III, p. 381.

233. *"Spence's Plan"* by Mr. Porter. Slip bound up with *Spence's Songs.*

234. PRO. HO 42, 195 HO 44, I - various entries.

235. Letter from Hone to Place, 23 September, 1830. Add. 27808 f.315.

236. PRO: TS 965 (2) 3510A.

237. PRO: TS 11/939.

238. PRO: TS 11/939 3362.

239. *National Co-operative Leader,* 8 March, 1861, p. 196; *Bronterre's National Reformer,* 1846, No. 78; *Northern Star,* 3 October, 1846.

240. Preston, Thomas: *The Life and Opinions of Thomas Preston, Patriot and Shoemaker.* London, 1817, pp. 22-23.

241. Letter from Robert Wedderburn to Place 22 March 1831 in Add. 27808 f.322. On Wedderburn see: Ashraf, P. M.: *Africans among Reformers.* (Russian translation). Moscow, 1960, pp. 326-537.

242. Transcribed from *Epilogue* to the *Constitution of Spensonia* in *Dhé Import'ant Tri'al ŏv To'mis Sp'ens.* London, 1803, p. 37.

243. *The Origin and Plan of the General Association of Householders within the Kingdom of Great Britain united and uniting to procure A Reform in Parliament upon the Plan of their full and equal Representation in the House of Commons . . . digested by the Present Head Committee.* London, Clerkenwell, 1796.

244. *Newcastle Weekly Chronicle,* 25 September, 1886.

245. Letter from Alexander Galloway to Francis Place, undated, (1817) in Place (Newspaper) Collection, vol. 39. Copy of *Restorer,* 1st edition, with 'R. Moggridge' written on title page and Spence's signature to the Introduction, was possibly a presentation copy. Cf. Place. Add. 27808 ff. 257-277.

246. Spence, Thomas: *A new and infallible way to make peace at any Time.* Handbill, N.d.

247. *The Giant-Killer,* 6 and 13. August, 1814.

248. For particulars regarding burial and entry in Register of burials in the Parish of St. James's, Piccadilly, see: Waters, op.cit. p. 240. On St. James's New Burialground and the Act of 1788 see: Miller, F.: *St. Pancras Past and Present,* London, 1874, pp. 184-5.

249. Also: Sykes, op.cit. vol. 2, p. 85, and *Newcastle Magazine,* January, 1821.

250. Hone, W.: *(Memoir of Spence)* appended to *Riots in London.* Part 2. London (1816), Copy in Place Collection vol. 39.

251. Cushing, W.: *Initials and Pseudonyms.* London, 1886, p. 556.

252. *Address and Regulations of the Society of Spencean Philanthropists.* London (1815). Second edition, *Address of the Spencean Philanthropists to all Mankind* (1816), omits this summary but embodies a variant of the Plan and a tribute to Spence in the *Address.* In his *Christian Policy. The Salvation of the Empire.* London, 1816, Evans claims what he takes from Spence's Plan as his own without mentioning Spence at all. 'A Christian Philanthropist' (i.e. Thomas Evans): *Christian Policy in full Practice among the people of Harmony.* (London) November 1818, mentions Spence only as an example like Moses and Lycurgus.

253. For a different opinion see: Hill, Christopher: *Puritanism and Revolution.* London, 1962. pp. 105-107. — "Spence's views of the origin of property . . . had a strong affinity to the Norman Yoke theory". He "drew on the traditions expressed by the demand for a restoration of Saxon freedom". The strongest evidence for this distortion of Spence's thought and its "affinities" Hill finds in the role of the parish, as though the parish were not the obvious local unit for any purpose in the eighteenth century and as though Spence's federated parishes might not also be compared with Rousseau's ideas. Hill identifies Evan's programme with Spence:— "What was implicit in Spence became startlingly explicit in Thomas Evans". But as this 'Norman Yoke' is also laid on Paine, the phrase ceases to have any precise boundary.

254. Spence, Thomas: *The Restorer of Society to its Natural State.* London, 1801, p. 14.

255. Southey, Robert: *Quarterly Review.* October 1816.

256. Cobbett's *Weekly Political Register.* 14 December 1816, col. 749-751. The poster is also found in *Morning Chronicle* and other papers, and in the above quoted article by Southey.

257. *Hansard* XXXV col. 431, 444. 608, 611.

258. *Hansard* 24 February 1817, XXXV col. 591, 593.

259. *Hansard* XXXII col. 852-854.

260. Davenport, Allen: op.cit. p. 22.

2. Teachings

Spence's Plan, first announced in 1775 and elaborated over the next nearly forty years, was simple and his writings were not intended for scholars. Natural right gives to all men an equal claim to use what nature provides during their lifetime. As no system of division can maintain this right of use in every generation, all land with all thereon and therein should be the common property of the people who live on it. The inhabitants of each parish or other small territory shall constitute a corporation to lease or otherwise exploit the land, mines, forests, waters and fisheries and use the revenue for their common needs, sharing the surplus equally among all.

Although Spence may not have foreseen the nature of the changes in preparation in his day, he saw society in flux and to this extent departed greatly from former inventors of ideal systems. His working life began at that date which the majority of historians assign to the beginning of the industrial revolution. His constant theme is the intensified exploitation of tenant and worker alike, and he uses the word 'rent' in the sense of 'profit'.[2]

Hence any study of Spence in relation to his times ought to start from the transition to industrial capitalism in England with all that that implied. When primitive accumulation is passing over to reproductive capital every available means to increase productivity is sought and there appears a particularly sharp conflict between survivals of very old institutions and the new commercial methods and mechanisms, for which people have not yet found a terminology. It is characteristic of this phase that Spence repeatedly refers not only to the iniquity of traffic in land, but to the baneful extension of commercial avarice generally. Everything, he says, down to religion, has become vendible, a commodity, and nothing is sacred. Hence a changing attitude to land itself is visible in his writings. Land represents to him not only the bounty of nature and subsistence economy, as it did to the old peasant leaders or to the seventeenth-century Diggers. It is "the means of industry",[3] for the husbandman has already become a wage worker; and he speaks more often of 'labourers' than of tenants.

The definition of 'Land'

"All that appertains" to land and water in Spence's definition is not limited to the soil in the usual sense or to its agricultural use. The concept, in addition to all natural resources, includes all man-made improvements and permanent structures. The intention is to make the sources of wealth, as well as of primary subsistence, common property. Naturally cultivation takes first place in Spence's calculations and is considered to be an inexhaustible outlet for surplus labour (the Chartists and Robert Owen also thought that land settlement would keep up wages in industry). But unlike most land reformers, Spence's scheme confiscated all industrial establishments and their major equipment.

Since his Plan was conceived first in Newcastle, and he did not come south till he was about forty years of age, it might be remembered that he had before him a particularly striking example of the complex alliance of the landed interest with city merchants and large industries already run on capitalist lines.[4] The real masters even of the keelmen were now the coalowners. The bulk of capital investment in the coalfields, on which the prosperity of Newcastle was founded, went into sinking shafts (which had reached a hundred fathom by the 'sixties), drainage, prospecting, the construction of wayleaves. The latter alone in Spence's day could cost a few thousand pounds to construct (out of the timber which Spence often mentions as a profitable parish asset), and yielded far higher rents than farming tenants. When it is considered that all this by Spence's definition would become the collective property of parishes inhabited almost exclusively by miners, there is not much doubt as to what would have been the outcome. The parish might have evolved a corporation not unlike an extension of the old miners' working partnership. The keels themselves would have been of little use to the fitters deprived of the staithes. There was little of great value that the dispossessed owner could have removed from the iron works, which would fall to the share of similar nearly homogeneous populations; nor in the case of the shipyards, breweries, glass houses and the shot tower which would be the portion of the town parishes. As Spensonians were certainly going to drink beer, glaze the windows of those new homes "like gentlemen's country-houses", and equip their army, navy and flourishing merchant fleet, it was not intended that hewers, puddlers, shipwrights, carters, keelmen and so on would all retire to grow cabbages. On the contrary, "shipping, Collieries, Mines and many other great Concerns" which cannot be divided "can yet be enjoyed . . . in Partnership".[5] We are also told that the Parish will "engross" business on its own account *(Restorer).*

It seems clear that Spence intended large-scale industry to be public property or if not managed by the Parish as a whole, to be run by "corporations" of workers collectively. From land confiscation which included these larger industries intimately associated with land tenure but already long established on capitalist lines, there is not a great step to the concept of the workers' ownership of the means of production. The tools of production that remained individual property corresponded to the general level of industrial technology before the large scale introduction of machinery. Had Spence been able to foresee the further results of the industrial revolution which was then scarcely begun, he might well have been entitled to claim that he had already assigned all the sources of power and all the factories with their structural equipment to public ownership.[6]

What really happened was that the concept of natural right to land began to be transferred to machinery in the early eighteen-thirties. Allen Davenport, who had known Spence and regularly attended the Spencean Philanthropists' meetings, writing about 1835 or 1836, thought that under Spence's

Plan the ingenious mechanic would come into his own and "machinery would be employed for the benefit of all . . .".[7]

A number of writers in the eighteen-thirties and forties drew analogies between nature, or land, and machinery. Machinery also appears to be both indivisible and indispensable. Spence said the landowners behaved "as if they had manufactured" the land *(Meridian Sun).* The next generation asked whether the capitalists had made the machines.[8]

Spence's most comprehensive statement, however, was not derived from the natural right to land, but from labour value. It may be significant that it is in the dialogue between urban mechanics that he developed the argument that "the labourer is the first proprietor of everything" *(End of Oppression).*

It became a commonplace in the writings of Bronterre O'Brien, Peter McDouall and others that the workers had been twice robbed — of the land by the feudal barons or their successors, and of the machines by the capitalists.[9]

In addition to small independent producers and little capitalists, the Parish board or committee built and maintained buildings, roads, bridges, harbours, parks, hospitals, schools, fisheries, dwellings and workshops by direct labour. A list of separate trades paid by the Parish on Quarter Day rules out sub-contracting. Hence the bulk of the building and construction trades alone would be absorbed in public works. The Parish could also initiate and run any other enterprises it liked.

Further Spence gave the model of a co-operative enterprise in his Marine Republic. All the members of the crew are paid a wage in accordance with their grade of work, but the surplus profit of each voyage, after deducting wages and expenses, was equally divided among them as their "interest" on their indivisible property in the ship. The ship is not only an allegory for the general partnership on land, but it takes the place of "nature" and is therefore a model for organizing any enterprise involving a more complex division of labour. (It may be noted in passing that unlike his great contemporary William Godwin, Spence was not opposed to the division of labour. On the contrary, in his few remarks that bear on the subject he favours specialization. It was not division of labour that reduced the worker's personality, but the ill-division of property).

Spence, therefore, as he summed it up in a verse, distinguished between the equal right to land and the unequal reward of each man's labour. Julian Harney, influenced by Spencean ideas through Allen Davenport,[10] brought this point up in commenting on the *Communist Manifesto.*[11] It is quite clear from the whole context of Spence's ideas and the classless society of working people which he aimed at, that the reward of labour simply meant what the working man — artisan or farmer — obtained by his own labour. Spence rightly or wrongly thought that the prohibition of investment in land and its appurtenances would not only prevent extortion of rent or interest, but would check private accumulation and cut off the means of exploiting the labour of others. Charles Hall in his letter to Spence in 1807 disagreed and pointed to complexities of economic cause and effect which Spence had ignored.[12]

The Dividend of Rents

After his first outline of his Plan, Spence progressively placed more emphasis on the dividend until it seems to be regarded as an essential part of the scheme. The term in connection with the Plan first occurs in James Murray's "Questions to the Philosophical Society" in defence of Spence's lecture, and this leads back to a sermon composed by Murray in 1768.[13] The dividend stresses the conception of the Parish as a joint stock corporation which was a common enough idea later in workers' co-operatives. The dividend was not in the nature of a rent or tax rebate, since it bore no relation to rent or earnings, but seems to be simply a way of partially levelling up differences of income and of preserving the original equality of all as joint heirs to the common 'hunting park'. It may have seemed to Spence sound economics to circulate money for the good of trade, but the value of the dividend was more social than economic. It was a tangible benefit which all could grasp. It embodied and encouraged the mutuality on which Spence counted for the practical success of the Plan. It provided for the unfortunate without making them paupers or infringing on their independence, yet made the orphan and the aged welcome in the household. It undermined the patriachalism of family relations. It gave the young worker his start in life and the girl her free choice of a husband. Finally, it expressed the common people's notion of fairness. They do not condemn bad luck or even mistakes, because they themselves know what it means to be "once down always down" *(Restorer)*.

The Parish

Spence was not unaware of the alternative of nationalization but specifically rejected it in favour of parish ownership and autonomy (*Restorer,* Letter VI). Again, the reason was political rather than economic. Like other radicals he distrusted remote government and like many, particularly older political writers, he thought that small states ensured international peace.

But the real importance of the Parish system lies in the application of democratic principles. Here self-government is literally the direct participation of every grown citizen. The parish administrative function over centuries, with unpaid officers drawn from the lower ranks, was an obvious example of the people's ability to manage their local affairs.

Nationalization may seem to be logically implied in the Plan, but to call Spence a land nationalizer assumes too much. By his definition of parish autonomy and federation, the Plan was not municipalization either, although that expression has also been used to describe it. In this respect the Plan lies somewhere between Paine's democratic republic with its national agrarian law and the complete statelessness of Godwin's ideal — or "between Utopia and Oceana", as the title page of *The Constitution of Spensonia* sums it up. The state does not disappear but many of its present functions vanish. Private property is abolished, but neither the community of goods of the apost-tes nor the Godwinian version is substituted.

The concept of public property

The most radical land policy of the Chartist phase was nationalization, for the Chartists felt themselves to be a national force. But the Spencean term, the People's Farm, was still often used in its original sense, that is, the revenue farm of what was once called the Manor of England. This ancient formula is preserved by Spence ("The public then is Lord of the Manor" — *Reign of Felicity).* He held that the feudal overlordship of the Crown had passed into the hands of a new aristocracy. It is in order to stress that the land is the rightful property of the whole people, irrespective of occupation, that O'Brien accuses O'Connor of forgetting "the People's Farm". This was in 1847; but he assumed that everyone would know that he referred to a widely accepted principle.[14] Harney criticized O'Connor in the same way, actually naming Spence as the authority who had settled the matter once and for all.[15]

Every Utopian before the industrial age necessarily looked to the land. There was nothing very original in mid-eighteenth century in speaking of a natural right to the earth or of an agrarian law to redistribute the land. Instead of giving the land to the peasant or re-settling the urban poor to grow their own food, however, Spence proposed to make them landlords of property they did not occupy, the owners of land-capital and the recipients of rent-interest. "Drivellers" might talk of a return to small farms. The present system was bound to favour larger holdings. Nor could landlordism be rooted out by creating a host of petty proprietors. The least of them would have all the vices of "aristocrats". In the North-East, where lawyers made large fortunes out of conveyancing in the eighteenth century, no doubt the expulsion of the cottager was less striking than the selling up of the copyholders and the decay of the hereditary little farmers, who as a class, even in poverty, offered examples of small-proprietor individualism and respect for the gentry.

Spence shows no desire to restore the old peasantry. There was nothing to regret in the past; the journeyman and labourer "were always from hand to mouth". If he thought that a dim memory of ancient freedom lingered among the people, he did not attach it to any period of English history that could be named. The Normans served to illustrate expropriation by conquest, but Spence never spoke of Saxon liberties, like Major Cartwright, for instance, or later his own follower, Thomas Evans. The future society, although made up of small men living in a "happy mediocrity", would enjoy urban amenities in their villages and rural neighbourliness in their towns. They would have different and wider interests.

The famous Town Moor case[16] would have reminded Spence that people like his own parents and other Scottish immigrants did not share even the right to herbage on the common. The incident had been a notable victory against the city magistrates and added strength to the political opposition. The time came when the burgesses' privileges were challenged as the selfishness of a minority. Spence condemned any country or community that acted on "exclusive principles". Hence a year's residence qualified every newcomer to full citizen's rights in a Spensonian parish.

A few years after his death, one of Spence's followers dismissed Cobbett's cottage smallholders scheme with similar arguments, adding that as the peasantry was always the stronghold of reaction, they could be used as a military force to suppress the unrest in the towns.[17]

The husbandman might still be the foundation of everything, and Spence may have points in common with the physiocrats, but the urban workers were acquiring their distinctive outlook. Indeed it hardly seems possible that where none had ever been, a conscious working-class movement could have arisen in the first place out of land nostalgia. Although Spence may still be called an agrarian leveller — in his sense of the term — his theories gave the land question new content characteristic of transition towards the industrial age. Yet when Hyndman and others, including land reform leaguers, revived Spence in the eighties of the last century, it became the fashion to connect him with any kind of agrarian utopianism irrespective of period, with land reform as then understood, or with single-tax panaceas.[18]

The class character of Spence's Plan

Spence's contribution to the emergence of socialist ideas did not lie in economic theory. The solvency of Little Dalby is almost the least important aspect. He took over from Harrington direct the dependence of political powers on property, but not his balance. The relationship which was not fully explicit in Harrington and resulted in a hierarchy of benevolent country gentry in Oceana Spence conceived as cause and effect. We know, he says, that men are ranked and rated "by Property for Property" *(Restorer)*. The government is determined by economic relations. Hence he saw that a republican form of government did not necessarily correspond to any real social equality nor were its political rights ever effective for the lower classes. This has long been a commonplace of political knowledge but it was not so in Spence's time. "He alone of all the British radicals understood in its full significance the economic basis of human society".[19]

His views differed profoundly from those of the majority of his contemporaries and in particular from those "Jacobins" who concentrated their attack on monarchy and aristocracy. What he attacked was not only landlords "in all their degrees" (a wider concept than the nobility and gentry) but the system that created landlordism, and strengthened it even more under the English "mixed" government or the bourgeois republic. The feudal Normans were "fools" compared with their successors who had grown strong enough to rid themselves of royal overlords. But they took over the labour theory of value in its crude form, not in order to explore the mechanism of an economic system but to justify the comprehensive claims of labour, as well as a number of other current radical propositions.

At the same time he rejected very explicitly one of the favourite theories, the social compact, in all its forms. There can be no valid contract between those who are unequal. Ralph Hodge points out how little say a labouring man has in the matter of his employment or anything else. Natural rights, since they arise at birth and are inalienable, cannot be bartered for civil rights nor mortgaged for future generations. The official declaration of the London Corresponding Society during most of its lifetime grounded the right to representation on the contract, endorsed by the authority of Thomas Paine. Their consequent inconsistency is the theme of the introductory conversation to the *Meridian Sun;* the people work in order to pay themselves "compensation" for the rights they are supposed to have agreed to exchange.

While many republicans, not least Paine, held that hereditary government was based on conquest, Spence understood conquest as the expropriation of the people, leaving them in a state of perpetual warfare *(Rights of Infants; End of Oppression; Reign of Felicity).* This deep and bitter conflict can never be reconciled. It demands drastic measures. Hence is always an economic category in Spence, and he is not concerned whether the ruling class is composed of the nobility or not. The struggle is between "the spoiler and the spoiled". The formulation shows a sense of the dynamic connection, of the process of exploiting and oppressing, where other writers speak of "rich and poor" as distinct states among men due to their different circumstances, and in that sense static.

Spence did not define capitalism nor see its existence with the clarity of the next generation, but he certainly thought of land monopoly as the starting point from which ever new forms of monopoly and extortion were continually extended *(Felicity).* Private accumulation gave power over labour, but the working class alone was socially creative:

"Slaves and unfortunate men have cultivated the earth, adorned it with buildings and filled it with all kinds of riches. And the wealth which enabled you to set these people to work, was got by Hook or by Crook from Society . . . All Riches come from Society, I mean the Labouring Part of it. And when all these Improvements return back to Society, they will only return to the Source from whence they came".[20]

Labour gives the title not only to its products but to its means; not because it produces things but because it does so socially and is in fact the universal provider and civilizer. The claims to superiority of those who monopolize and misuse the bounty of labour or of nature are contemptible and ludicrous. Without workers the gentry would revert to savagery, like Saltykov-Shchredrin's "wild squire" *(Rights of Infants,* Conclusion).

Thus the abstraction "labour", which allowed servants to be regarded as an extension of the proprietor's person (in Locke, for example) becomes concretely "the toil of the labouring classes". It is doubtful whether anyone had ever so emphatically changed the conception of "the labouring poor" and made it the decisive social force. Economists praised industry and radicals elevated the industrious middle class, the enterprising self-made man, but only Spence drew the conclusion that what the labourers had created they alone had the power to use as it should be used.

Spence began work at his father's trade, net-making, at the age of ten. It is possible that he and his brother Jeremiah served apprenticeships and worked as journeymen.[21] Spence did not become a regular schoolmaster till he was about twenty-six.[22] The hardships suffered by his family in spite of all their honest industry first made him reflect that the cause must lie in "the bad System of the World".

It is sufficient to read any of his tracts to be quite sure to whom it is addressed. When Spence said "the people" he would add "the labouring part, I mean" or some such phrase, if this were not clear from the context. We know where we are with his readers who earn sixpence or *even* a shilling a day. When he was tried in 1801 Spence claimed he was entitled to a jury consisting at least half of labourers. Throughout his defence he pointedly identified himself with that class.

Spence defined the position of the proletariat at its birth. The working man had no property, a stranger in the land of his fathers, with less rights than caterpillars and worms who "riot in untaxed luxuries" all their days. He had no country to fight for *(Restorer)* and his allies must be the oppressed in other countries. When Spensonia was established "the slaves and disfranchised labourers of other nations would here find emancipation and ascend to the real character of man" *(Felicity).*

At home and abroad the face of nascent capitalism, "the scrambling system" *(Felicity)*, looked the same. The only healthy part of society is caught up in a blind struggle for existence:

> "... But even in England, that dunghill of Judases, the most laudably and usefully industrious are such as have no prospect or hope of purchasing land. Happy would they be if those insatiable Field-hunters above them would suffer them to procure by their labour the necessaries of life. But notwithstanding, they must pump or drown".[23]

The intensification of labour and rate of profit about the turn of the century inspired indignant comment on the gospel of hard work:

> "Instead of working only six days a week we are obliged to work at the rate of eight or nine and yet can hardly subsist . . . and still the cry is work — work — ye are idle" . . . "But we, God help us, have fallen under the hardest set of masters that ever existed" . . . "They begrudge us every comfort of life. Everything is reckoned an unbecoming luxury for such scum of the earth, to such a swinish multitude".[24]

The historical significance of Spence really was that he sought the aspirations of the lowest labouring class and the pattern of what society might become in the character and potentialities of that class. He was certainly the first political writer to do so. When Spence says "They cannot bear to see us endeavouring to act for ourselves" and means not the section whom most radicals refer to as "the People" but the lower classes, a new epoch is beginning. Spence's over-simplifications were almost an historical necessity in order to show that the business of government was not a sacred mystery, but that "a small portion of reason might suffice".

As the model for self-government and economic planning he took the well-tested experience of the common people in organizing their numerous benefit clubs and societies.[25] Everybody knew that these purely voluntary associations ran on democratic lines without friction. They could count on finding honest treasurers from among themselves and competent secretaries, and met their liabilities year after year. Newcastle seems to have been particularly rich in every type of box society and provident club, whose functions varied from permanent mutual insurance to a monthly or annual share-out of the stock.[26] All these bodies were regarded as in some way philanthropic in as much as they stood for mutual aid. Many adopted mottoes that expressed noble ideals of brotherhood, charity, humanity. The trade clubs proper were not very different in their general purposes, and non-trade benefit societies did on occasion use their organizations for entirely different purposes. A number of Newcastle box societies, for instance, broke the provision merchants' price ring by a boycott and by setting up their own corn import trade. The Boxmen, described as working men, earned the praise of grateful fellow-citizens for this public spirited endeavour.[27]

The most famous example of course was the keelmen's society whose great hospital built by their subscription was regarded as a monument to philanthropy. A mutual aid fund started in 1701 in the course of the long dispute with the Hoastmen, became a regular benefit society, not only to provide for widows and orphans but as insurance against short time and unemployment, in spite of the fact that they suffered from seasonal work and half of them came from Scotland.[28]

The benefit society embodied forms of spontaneous solidarity and mutual aid which everybody could grasp and was the best example of working-class initiative and practical fraternity before the rise of stable trade unionism. It was this aspect which Spence connected with the functions of the Parish organization.

The Parish meeting did not debate theoretical reforms and policies but practical business in which all were immediately interested; "and thus we are not mere spectators in the world, but as all men ought to be, actors".[29]

Spence had faith not only in the workers' common sense, but in their ordinary social qualities. Men will work better for themselves than for task-masters. Man is an active animal, always making work for himself, and knows that nothing is to be got without work. People will take an interest in improving parochial property because they share in the results. They will work because wives will still be wives and "spur them to industry", because they have children to care for, because no normal person either wants to be dependent himself or likes supporting parasites.

Spence repeatedly contrasts the inhumanity and vice of the upper classes with the ethics of the common man. The new, just republic will not cram even uncooperative ex-landlords into poorhouses. There will be elected magistrates and no "law of reprisals".

The "happy mediocrity" of Spensonia is a levelling up as seen from the labourer's standpoint. People will no more work all the hours that God sends. There will be a 5-day week, holidays and feasts. A man will be able to "spend his social penny", be hospitable, dress decently and no longer bring up his children "to be whores and soldiers for the quality" and die "in a ditch or a workhouse" *(Restorer).*

To Spence must go the credit of first bringing the labourer onto the scene as an active, class-conscious, political force. What the barber, the warehouse labourer, the stable boy or the mechanic has to say about public affairs is recorded alongside Locke and Puffendorf; and Spence may be believed when he says that he had discussed his proposals with people of all classes.

Spensonia was scaled to working-class standards of nearly two centuries ago. The point of view may be illustrated by the Spensonian housing laws. Private letting of unfurnished rooms, like all forms of sub-letting, was forbidden. The Parish built houses suitable for renting in single rooms and small apartments to meet all needs. Spence thought about the kind of people who lived in single rooms, but his solution of their problem would still sound utopian to those in Britain who have to contend with complicated controls or the lack of them.

This intimacy with the real needs of the working people can be seen in the social and political reforms that are mentioned only incidentally in the course of Spence's various writings. A list of nearly forty of these secondary benefits can be made, and all but two or three became concrete demands in the labour movement; sometimes they were the special aims of long campaigns and generations of agitation. Perhaps one of the most interesting of those not yet realized is the abolition of private patents and the purchase on behalf of the public of all new inventions and scientific discoveries for the benefit of the whole community. The right to work was guaranteed by the basic arrangements of the Parish partnership. Either the Parish engaged the unemployed for public works or provided tools and materials for self-employment or land with the necessary stock and implements.

Spence discarded the great legislator and based his proposals on the possibilities of life as it is. Manners and morals will improve but the men and women who build the new life are the same people they have always been. There is no waiting for them to be transformed or "perfected" by education. Spence uses the human material as he finds it, confident that the working class taken as a whole is good enough for the purpose, and in any case more promising than any other.

In speaking of motivation Spence does not rely on any change of heart. He always predicts that the landlords will continue in their iniquity until they are faced with superior forces, and that only those who have the sense to make the best of a bad job will co-operate with the new order. Society is not to be changed by preaching:

> "If religion could have any influence on Men's lives, we ought to be the most Righteous and compassionate people on Earth. Where is there a People that abounds more in preaching Men, and preaching Books in all Sects and Persuasions, and also in Books of Morality, Philosophy, Satire &c". *(Restorer,* Letter XI).

The answer is not "enlightened self-interest";

> "It is natural and universal Interest alone can cement our society when established".

This "natural and universal interest", as may be seen from many other passages, is a collective interest, solidarity or mutuality in a classless community; for unlike the social contract philosophers, Spence saw little ground for conflict between the individual and a society of equals. This, I would suggest, flows from his working-class sympathies rather than the influence of philosophical thought.

From the same source comes his realistic sarcasm at the expense of the eigtheenth-century ragged-trousered philanthropists who are "so silly good natured" in *The End of Oppression.*

Revolutionary Aims and Methods

At no time did Spence suggest that his reforms could be realized through any of the recognized constitutional procedures of petition, by Act of Parliament, or even by a struggle within Parliament. Logically the abolition of private property could hardly be expected from a House composed of landholders and fundholders, most of whom regarded their seats as part of their inheritance, returned by an electorate mainly of landlords and dependent tenants. They were not going to concede even the small reform of the franchise for which the reformers foolishly hoped *(Meridian Sun).* Godwin, the only distinguished English thinker whose criticism of the existing system was fundamental and who agreed with Spence in considering the form of government less important than property relations, saw no solution except to wait until men one by one developed to a higher stage of reason. Robert Owen, when he came, clung all his life to the extraordinary hope that royalty might be persuaded to adopt co-operative socialism. The difference between Spence and the democratic radicals was one of principle:

> "But who pray among all the Revolutionists in either America, France or England, or anywhere else, ever disputed or attempted to invalidate the rights of the landed interest?"[30]

As time went on he spoke less of the delusion of such leaders. He questioned not only their ideology but their good faith.

> "With grief I behold the indirect and suspicious modes which the professed Reformers of the World take to deliver it from Oppression . . . Who to serve some temporary purpose, perhaps to plunder, would put all things in a state of requisition and then suffer matters to end in as much, perhaps more, oppression than they began".[31]

"The Champions of the Rights of Man" would set up new monopolies *(Restorer,* Letter XII). The new rulers of France "are making Fortunes and acquiring Estates as fast as they can" *(Restorer,* Preface).

Consequently Spence considered that his Plan was aimed "at the overthrow of all Establishments" as no other had ever been. Defiant invective, for instance in *A Further Account of Spensonia,* expresses irreconcilable conflict.[32] The ruling class are "a warlike enemy quartered upon us". "The war must be eternal".[33] The rich are "insatiable as the grave" and drive the people to fight for their very existence. In *The Rights of Infants,* the Mother appears, like the personification of Nature that cannot be bribed or terrorized, to threaten Aristocracy with that hitherto undirected power of the masses which the great pretend to despise but really fear.

There is an ethical as well as an economic crisis. "The World can no longer live with innocence or the least plausible Excuse in the present monopolizing unjust state" *(Restorer,* Letter XII). "This bad system makes Good bad and the Bad worse" *(Important Trial).*

Although like Paine and others Spence felt that a great change had taken place, and like them speaks of the impossibility of stifling progress, he did not look forward to a triumphant march of freedom, but to a long and painful period of wars, revolutions and crises. He became more and more concerned with the urgency of present distress due to the growing aggressiveness of the rich. The crisis brought about by great accumulation of wealth, war and artificial famine seemed to him to be reaching a climax in the first years of the nineteenth century.

> "When I contemplate the meagre and beggarly appearance of the working people at this deplorable period and at the same time hear their deep and desparate exclamations sighed from their broken Hearts, I cannot help thinking that we are on the eve of some very great commotion".[34]

He arrived at a formulation of social revolution which extends the fight beyond landlords in the narrow sense and prepares for the conscious class struggle against capitalism.

> "You see, Citizen, we are arrived at a very serious crisis . . . We must now study for Life or Death. The question I say is no longer about what Form of Government is most favourable to Liberty . . . but which system of Society is most favourable to existence and capable of delivering us from the deadly mischief of great accumulations of wealth which enables a few unfeeling monsters to starve whole nations in spite of all the fruitful Seasons God Almighty can send".[35]

In his first writings the Plan is presented as a spontaneous decision of the people — "it is solemnly resolved by the whole nation" *(Rights of Man,* 1793). The progressive majority of the Crusonians achieve their ends simply by weight of numbers in debate. But if that sufficed for an allegory, the

I

Spence Tokens

Portrait of Thomas Spence from "Thomas Bewick His Life and Times" by Robert Robinson, 1887.

III

SERMONS
TO ASSES,
TO
DOCTORS IN DIVINITY,
TO
Lords Spiritual,
AND TO
MINISTERS OF STATE.

BY THE LATE REV. JAMES MURRAY,
Of Newcastle.

WITH AN ENGRAVED PORTRAIT OF THE AUTHOR,
AND
AN ORIGINAL SKETCH OF HIS LIFE.

"Issachar is a strong ass couching down between two burdens."
GEN. xlix. 14.

"A nation of slaves is a kingdom of asses."—SERMONS TO ASSES.

"The Articles of the Church, and the Athanasian Creed, are like the two laps of Balaam's saddle."—*Ibid.*

LONDON:
PRINTED FOR WILLIAM HONE, LUDGATE HILL.
1819.

THE

Meridian Sun of Liberty;

OR, THE

WHOLE RIGHTS of MAN DISPLAYED and most Accurately Defined,

In a LECTURE read at the PHILOSOPHICAL SOCIETY in Newcastle, on the 8th of November, 1775, for printing of which the Society did the Author the honor to expel him.

To which is now first prefixed, by way of PREFACE, a most important DIALOGUE between the CITIZEN READER, and the AUTHOR.

Th' invention all admir'd, and each, how he
To be the inventor miss'd; so easy it seem'd,
Once found, which yet unfound most would have thought
Impossible. MILTON.

" *Let Thelwall* * *and Burke from its splendour retire,*
" *A splendour too strong for their eyes;*
" *Let Pedants, and Fools, their Effusions admire,*
" *Inwrapt in their cobwebs like flies.*
" *Shall Frenzy and Sophistry hope to prevail,*
" *When Reason opposes her Weight;*
" *When the welfare of Millions is hung on the scale,*
" *And the balance yet trembles with Fate?"*

By T. SPENCE.

LONDON:

Printed for the Author at No. 8, Little Turnstile, High Holborn, Patriotic Bookseller and Publisher of that best School of Man's Rights, entitled Pigs' Meat; the End of Oppression; Grand Repository of the English Language, &c

---

* See " Sober Reflections" or rather, Lamentations over the impending Fate of " the vessel of Hereditary Property," by John Thelwall.

Price one Penny.

1796.

ROBINSON CRUSOE.

A SUPPLEMENT to the Hiſtory of

ROBINSON CRUSOE,

Being the HISTORY of

C R U S O N I A,

O R

Robinſon Cruſoe's Iſland,

Down to the preſent Time.

Copied from a Letter ſent by Mr Wiſhit, Captain of the Good-Intent, to an intelligent Friend in England, after being in a Storm in May, 1781, driven out of his Courſe to the ſaid Iſland

Publiſhed by the ſaid Gentleman, for the agreeable Peruſal of Robinſon Cruſoe's Friends of all Sizes.

A New EDITION.

Th' Invention all admir'd, and, each, how he
To be th' Inventor miſs'd; ſo eaſy it ſeem'd,
Once found, which yet unfound moſt would have (thought
Impoſſible.

MILTON.

NEWCASTLE:

Printed and Sold by T. SAINT, in 1782.

Price 6d.

THE

CASE

OF

THOMAS SPENCE,

BOOKSELLER,

THE CORNER OF

CHANCERY-LANE, LONDON;

Who was committed to

CLERKENWELL PRISON,

On MONDAY the 10th of DECEMBER, 1792,

For Selling the Second Part of

Paine's Rights of Man:

And a BILL of INDICTMENT found against him.

To which is added an extract of a Letter from

His Grace the Duke of Richmond,

To the Chairman of the Committee of the County of Sussex, convened at Lewis, January 18, 1783, for the Purpose of presenting a Petition to the House of Commons, to take into consideration the unequal State of Representation in Parliament, &c.

[PRICE THREE-PENCE.]

1792.

PIGS' MEAT;

OR,

LESSONS FOR THE PEOPLE.

Alias (According to BURKE)

THE SWINISH MULTITUDE.

PUBLISHED IN PENNY NUMBERS WEEKLY

Collected by the Poor Man's Advocate (an old perſecuted Veteran in the Cauſe of Freedom) in the Courſe of his Reading for more than Twenty Years.

INTENDED

To promote among the Labouring part of Mankind proper Ideas of their Situation, of their Importance, and of their Rights.

AND TO CONVINCE THEM

That their forlorn Condition has not been entirely overlooked and forgotten, nor their juſt Cauſe unpleaded, neither by their Maker, nor by the beſt and moſt enlightened Men of all Ages.

The Pigs to Starve, bad Men in pow'r,
Their Feeder ſent to doleful Goal,
And eager bent him to devour,
Long time the Pigs did for him wail.
But now the Storm is blown o'er,
That drove him from his bleſt Employ;
And to his Taſk return'd once more,
He feeds them with his wonted Joy.

VOLUME. III.

LONDON:

PRINTED FOR T. SPENCE, NO. 8, LITTLE TURNSTILE, HIGH HOLBORN.

The pig trampling on the symbols of Royalty. Frontispiece to Pigs' Meat
Designed by Spence.

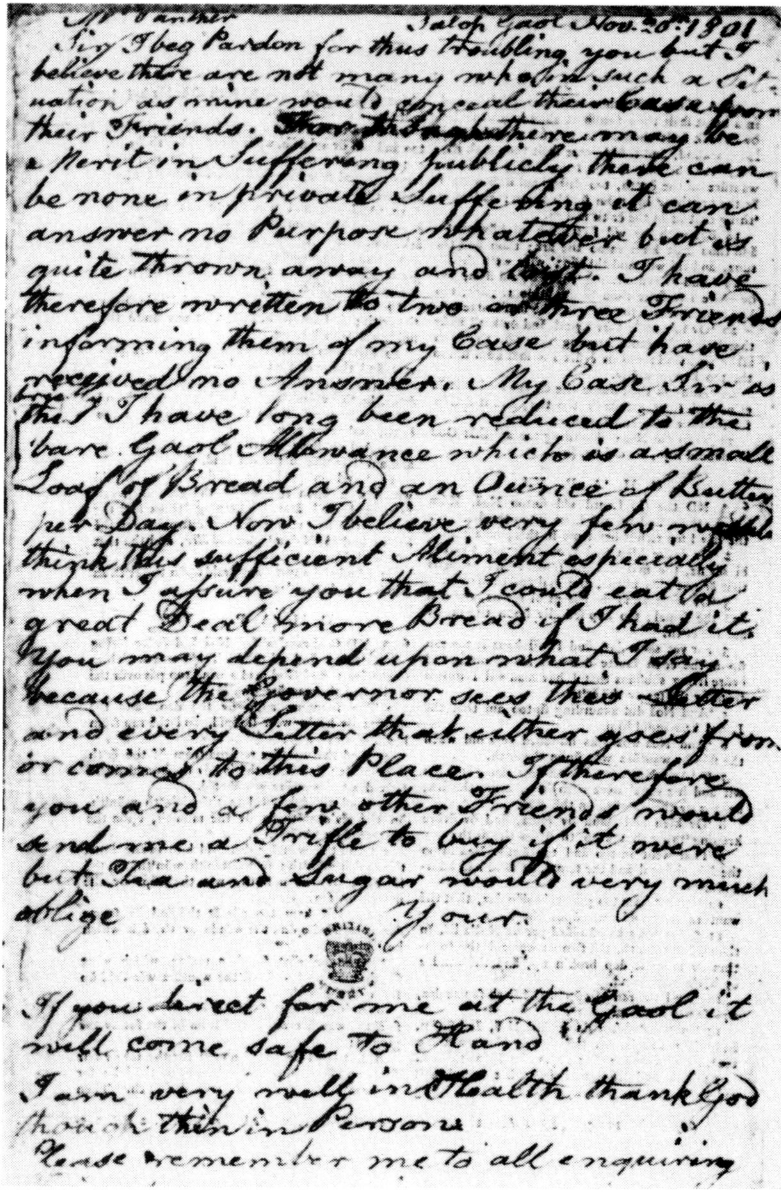
Mr Panther Salop Gaol Nov. 20th 1801

Sir I beg Pardon for thus troubling you but I believe there are not many who in such a Situation as mine would conceal their Case from their Friends. [illegible] there may be a Merit in Suffering publicly there can be none in private Suffering it can answer no Purpose whatever but is quite thrown away and lost. I have therefore written to two or three Friends informing them of my Case but have received no Answer. My Case Sir is that I have long been reduced to the bare Gaol Allowance which is a small Loaf of Bread and an Ounce of Butter per Day. Now I believe very few would think this sufficient Aliment especially when I assure you that I could eat a great Deal more Bread if I had it. You may depend upon what I say because the Governor sees this Letter and every Letter that either goes from or comes to this Place. If therefore you and a few other Friends would send me a Trifle to buy if it were but Tea and Sugar would very much oblige

Your.

If you direct for me at the Gaol it will come safe to Hand

I am very well in Health thank God though thin in Person

Please remember me to all enquiring

Letter from Spence to Mr. Panther written in Shrewsbury Gaol, 20 November, 1801. He asks his friends to send, "Atrifle to buy if it were but tea and sugar" and comments that he is "very well in health thank God though thin in person." Place MSS. B.M.

**The signature and last words have not come out.*

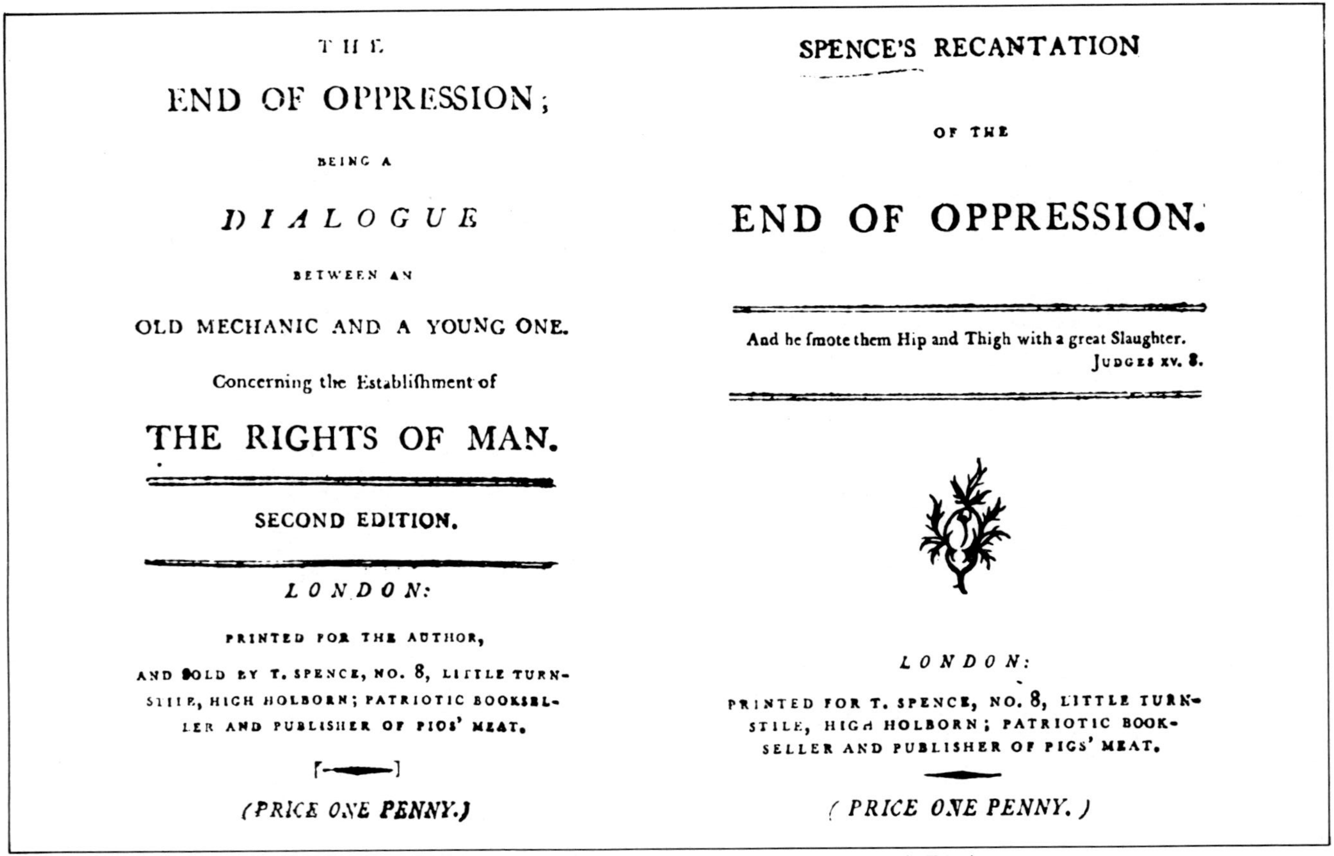

THE

END OF OPPRESSION;

BEING A

DIALOGUE

BETWEEN AN

OLD MECHANIC AND A YOUNG ONE.

Concerning the Establiſhment of

THE RIGHTS OF MAN.

SECOND EDITION.

LONDON:

PRINTED FOR THE AUTHOR,

AND SOLD BY T. SPENCE, NO. 8, LITTLE TURN-
STILE, HIGH HOLBORN; PATRIOTIC BOOKSEL-
LER AND PUBLISHER OF PIGS' MEAT.

(PRICE ONE PENNY.)

SPENCE'S RECANTATION

OF THE

END OF OPPRESSION.

And he ſmote them Hip and Thigh with a great Slaughter.
JUDGES XV. 8.

LONDON:

PRINTED FOR T. SPENCE, NO. 8, LITTLE TURN-
STILE, HIGH HOLBORN; PATRIOTIC BOOK-
SELLER AND PUBLISHER OF PIGS' MEAT.

(PRICE ONE PENNY.)

The End Of Oppression. Second Edition, ND (1795)
Spence's Recantation of The End Of Oppression. (1796).

THE

REIGN OF FELICITY,

BEING A PLAN

FOR

CIVILIZING THE INDIANS,

OF

NORTH AMERICA;

Without infringing on their national or individual Independence,

IN A COFFEE-HOUSE DIALOGUE,

BETWEEN

A COURTIER, AN ESQUIRE, A CLERGYMAN AND A FARMER.

PRICE ONE PENNY.

LONDON:

printed for T: SPENCE, No. 8, Little Turnstile, High Holborn; Patriotic Bookseller, and Publisher of PIGS' MEAT, and the END OF OPPRESSION.

1796.

THE

CONSTITUTION

OF A

PERFECT COMMONWEALTH:

BEING THE

FRENCH CONSTITUTION of 1793,

Amended, and rendered entirely conformable to the

WHOLE RIGHTS OF MAN.

Finis Coronat opus.

THE SECOND EDITION,

With a Preface,

SHEWING HOW TO STUDY POLITICS.

By T. SPENCE,

Author and Publisher of that best Repository of sound and standard Politics, entitled PIGS' MEAT, and of several Tracts on the imprescriptible Rights of Mankind.

LONDON:

Printed and sold by the Author,

AT No. 9, OXFORD-STREET,

Price Threepence.

1798.

XII XIII

Something to the Purpose.

A Receipt to make a

MILLENIUM OR HAPPY WORLD.

BEING EXTRACTS FROM THE

CONSTITUTION *of SPENSONIA.*

From the declaration of Rights.

ARTICLE.

3. All Human Beings are equal by nature, and before the law, and have a continual and *inalienable property in the earth*, and its natural productions.

4. The law is the free and solemn expression of the general will. It ought to be the same for all whether it protects or punishes. It cannot order but what is just and useful to society. It cannot forbid but what is hurtful

5. Social laws, therefore, can never proscribe natural rights. And every Man, Woman, and Child, *still* retain, from the day of their birth, to the day of their death, their primogenial right to the soil of their respective Parishes.

6. Thus, after a parish, out of its rents, has remitted to the state and county, its appointed Share or *Poundage* towards their expences, and provided for defraying its own proper contingencies, the remainder of the rents is the indisputable joint property of all the Men, Women, and Children having settlement in the parish, and ought to be *divided equally* among them.

From the Body of the Constitution.

4. Every man or woman born, or otherwise having acquired a settlement in a parish of Spensonia and of the age of twenty-one years complete, is admitted to the exercise of the rights of a Spensonian Citizen, as far as their sex will allow.

5. Female Citizens have the same right of suffrage in their respective parishes as the men: because they have equal property in the country, and are equally subject to the laws, and, indeed, they are in every respect, as well on their own account, as on account of their children, as deeply, and in fact more interested in every public transaction. But in consideration of the delicacy of their sex, they are exempted from, and are ineligible, to all public employments.

6 *Every man, woman, and child*, whether born in wedlock or not (for nature and Justice know nothing of illegitimacy) *is entitled quarterly to an equal share of the rents of the parish where they have settlement.* But before the division, the public aids to the state and the county must be deducted, and the expences of the parish provided for.

19. The right of property is that which belongs to every Citizen to enjoy and dispose of, according to his pleasure, his property, revenues, labour and industry.—Here his *property in land* is excepted, which being inseparably incorporated with that of his fellow parishioners *is inalienable.*

43 On quarter-day the rents shall be paid to the Parish Officers at their Counting-house.

44. During the ensuing days the parish accounts shall be made up, and after setting aside the poundages due to the state and the county, and settling all parochial pecuniary concerns and finding how much of the rent remains to be returned to the people, the accounts shall be minutely printed, including the names of all the men, women, and children, who are entitled to dividends as parishioners, distinguishing those of age to vote by an asterism.

45. When this business is all duly prepared the parishioners shall be summoned by *sound of trumpet* to come and receive their dividends, which, together with copies of the parish accounts is given to the heads of families, according to the number of their respective house-holds, and to single claimants.

124. The National Treasury is the central point of the receipts and expences of the common wealth.

125. It is supplied by a poundage raised quarterly, on the rents of the parishes by the Legislative Body.

126. This assessment being sufficient for all national purposes, and being sent up by the parishes every quarter without expence, renders *revenue laws and officers unnecessary.*

131. The National Accounts are printed yearly, sufficiently minute to give satisfaction, and sent to the parishes.

☞ *See the Rest of the Articles.*

Price One Penny.

Printed for T. SPENCE, Number Cutter and Bookbinder, No. 15, Princes Street, Soho, London.

THE

Important Trial

OF

THOMAS SPENCE,

For a Political Pamphlet, Intitled

"The Restorer of Society to its Natural State,"

On May 27th, 1801,

AT

WESTMINSTER HALL,

BEFORE

LORD KENYON and a Special Jury.

"A forbidden Writing is thought to be a certain Spark of Truth that flies up in the Face of them who seek to tread it out." *Milton.*

*** As nearly the whole of that offensive Book with suitable Remarks by way of Defence, was read by Mr Spence to the Jury, the whole of it therefore is reprinted herein, as a Warning to poor Old England. "And all the People shall hear, and fear, and do no more presumptuously."

And the Vision of all is become unto you as the Words of a Book that is sealed, which men deliver to one that is learned saying, Read this, I pray thee: and he saith, I cannot; for it is sealed; And the Book is delivered to him that is not learned, saying, Read this, I pray thee: and he saith, I am not learned.

(But) in that day, shall the Deaf hear the Words of the Book, and the Eyes of the Blind shall see out of Obscurity, and out of Darkness. **Isaiah 29.**

Second Edition.

XIV XV

DH'E

'Imp'ort'ant Tri'al

ŏV

T'OM'IS SP'ENS

F'or a P'ol'it'ik'al P'amfl·et 'entitld

"Dhĕ Rĕstorr ŏv Sosiĕte tw ĭts năteŭrăl Stat,"

'On Ma 27th, 1801,

'AT

W'ESTM'INSTR H'O'OL,

B'EFOR

L'ORD K'ENE'UN ănd a Spĕshăl Jwre.

"A fŏrbĭdn Ritĭng ĭz thŏŏt tw be a sĕrtn Spărk ŏv Trwth dhăt fliz ŭp ĭn dhĕ Fas ŏv dhĕm hw sek tw trĕd ĭt ŏwt." Mĭltŭn.

*** 'Az nerle dhĕ hol ŏv dhĭs ŏfĕnsĭv Bwk wĭdh sutăbl Rĕmărks wŏz rĕd tw dhĕ Jwre dhĕ hol ŏv ĭt dharfŏr ĭz reprĭntĕd herĭn, ăz a Wărnĭng tw pwr Old 'Inglănd. "'And ŏŏl dhĕ Pepl shal her ănd fer ănd dw no mor prĕzŭmptuŭsle."

And the Vision of all is become unto you as the Words of a Book that is sealed, which men deliver to one that is learned saying, Read this, I pray thee: and he saith, I cannot; for it is sealed: And the Book is delivered to him that is not learned, saying, Read this, I pray thee: and he saith, I am not learned.

(But) in that Day, shall the Deaf hear the Words of the Book, and the Eyes of the Blind shall see out of Obscurity, and out of Darkness. Isaiah 29.

LONDON:

Printed by A. Seale, Tottenham Court Road, for T. Spence.

1803.

DH'E

K'ONST'ITUSH'UN

'OV

SP'ENSONE'A;

A Küntre in Fare Länd,

Situatĕd bĕtwen

UTOPE'A 'AND OSHEAN'A

Bröŏt frŏm dhĕns Bi

K'APT. SW'ALO.

'And Printĕd in dhĕ Spĕnsoneăn Mänr.

Finis kŏrŏnăt opŭs.

Ee shăl la ŭp dhez mi wŭrdz ĭn ur härt ănd ĭn ur sol, ănd bind dhĕm fŏr a sin ŭpŏn ur hănd. ănd dha shăl be ăz Früntlĕts bĕtwen ur Iz. 'And ee shăl tetsh dhĕm ur Tshĭldrn, spekĭng ŏv dhĕm hwĕn dhŏw sĭtĕst ĭn dhin Hŏws, ănd hwĕn dhŏw wŏŏkĕst bi dhĕ wa; hwĕn dhŏw liĕst dŏwn, ănd hwĕn dhŏw rizĕst ŭp. 'And dhŏw shăll rit dhĕm ŭpŏn dhĕ Dor Posts ŏv dhin Hŏws, ănd ŭpŏn dhi Gats: dhăt ur Daz ma be mŭltĭplid ănd dhĕ daz ŏv ur Tshĭldrn. Dut. XI. (Fŏr) dhĕ wŭrk ŏv riteŭsnĭs [Jŭstĭs] shăl be pes; ănd dhĕ ĕfĕkt ŏv riteŭsnĭs (Jŭstĭs) kwiĕtnĭs ănd ăshwrăns fŏr ĕvr. 'And mi pepl shăl dwĕl ĭn ă pĕsăbl hăbĭtashŭn, ănd ĭn shwr dwĕlĭngz, ănd ĭn kwiĕt rĕstĭng plasĕz. 'Izaă, 32.

THE

Address

AND

REGULATIONS

OF THE

SOCIETY

OF

Spencean Philanthropists;

With an Abstract of

Spence's Plan.

London:

PUBLISHED BY ORDER OF THE SOCIETY.

1815.

Printed at Seale & Bates's Office, 160, Tottenham Court Ro[illegible]

XVII XVIII

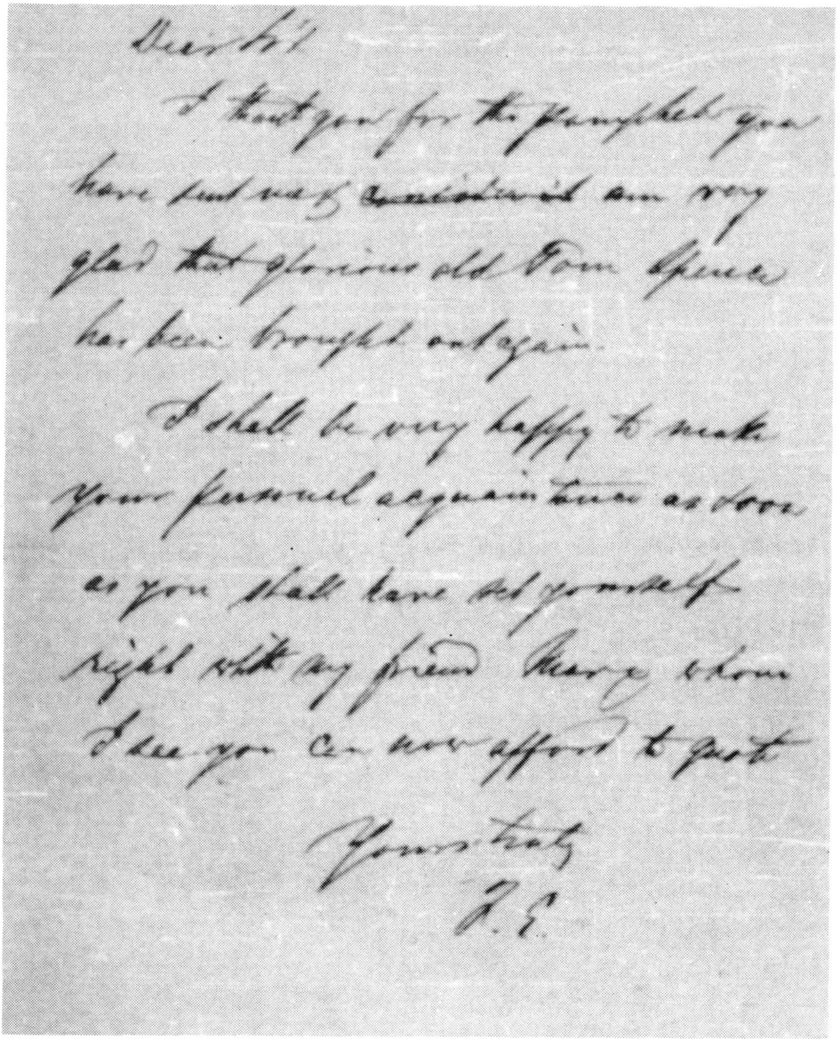

Dear Sir,

I thank you for the pamphlet you have sent me, am very glad that glorious old Tom Spence has been brought out again.

I shall be very happy to make your personal acquaintance as soon as you shall have set yourself right with my friend Marx whom I see you can now afford to quote.

Yours truly

F. E.

Letter from Frederick Engels to Henry Mayer Hyndman 13 March, 1882 calling him, "that glorious old Tom Spence".
Hyndman republished Spence's lecture in a pamphlet on land nationalisation, THE NATIONALISATION OF THE LAND IN 1775 AND 1882. He sent a copy to Engels in the hope that his properly annotated and acknowledged quotes from Marx would heal the rift between them.
Marx and Engels had objected strongly to Hyndman's free use of Marx's work without acknowledgement.
However, Marx died in 1883 and Engels continued to support the Socialist League that had broken away from Hyndman's Social Democratic Federation until he died in 1895.

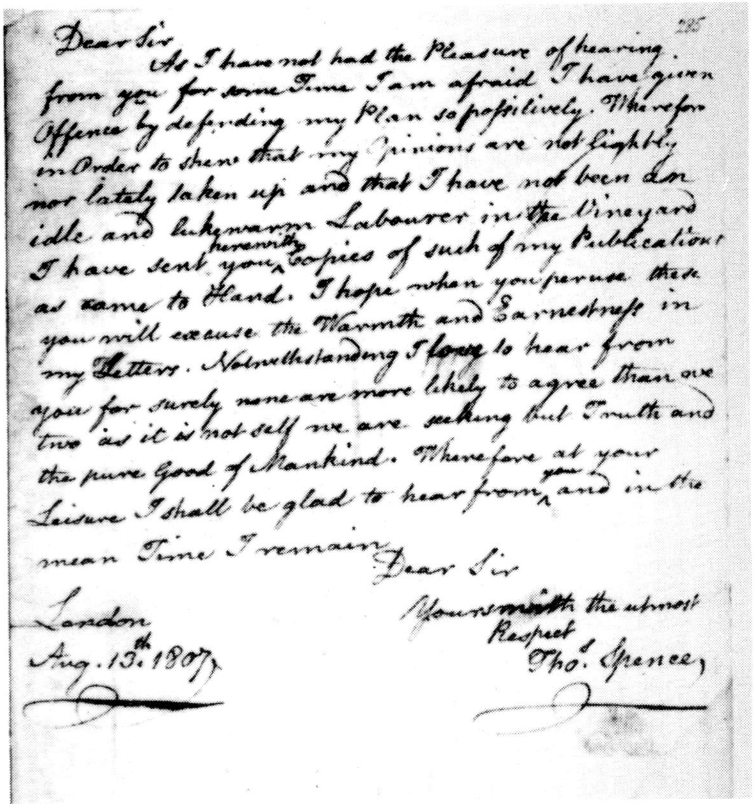

Dear Sir
As I have not had the Pleasure of hearing from you for some Time I am afraid I have given Offence by defending my Plan so possitively. Therefore in Order to shew that my Opinions are not lightly nor lately taken up and that I have not been an idle and lukewarm Labourer in the Vineyard I have sent you [illegible] copies of such of my Publications as came to Hand. I hope when you peruse these you will excuse the Warmth and Earnestness in my Letters. Notwithstanding I long to hear from you for surely none are more likely to agree than we two as it is not self we are seeking but Truth and the pure Good of Mankind. Wherefore at your Leisure I shall be glad to hear from you and in the mean Time I remain Dear Sir

Yours with the utmost Respect
Thos. Spence

London
Aug. 13th 1807

Letter from Thomas Spence to Charles Hall 13 August, 1807.

Thanks for permission to reproduce these illustrations:

Mr. Frank Graham (I)
Newcastle Public Library (II)
The British Museum (III, IV, V, VI, VII, VIII, IX, X, XI, XVI, XVII, XX)
Goldsmith's Library (XII, XIV, XV, XVIII)
Institute of Marxism-Leninism, Moscow (IXX)

impact of the French Revolution and experience of the London radical movement must have forced Spence to consider the real possibilities. "The whole nation" became "the working part" of it; the collective will became united action.

The three great revolutions had all begun in a political crisis within the ruling circles, in a deadlock between constitutional rights and prerogative. The Spencean revolution advanced no constitutional claims. The land was to be resumed without legal preliminaries. Up to this point the idea recalls the old peasant revolt, including the gesture of burning title deeds, except that urban and industrial property is included. With this echo of the past goes the imagery of the Jubilee and the Millennium, of the Trumpet and the Cedars' shout of joy when all men shall be kings. But Spence's disregard for constitutional means occurs when what had so long been the cornerstone of all Whig ideology was passing into the Rights of Man, on the one hand, and Burke's re-shaping, on the other. When the advanced working class entered politics through the London Corresponding Society, Spence was at pains to demonstrate how inconsistent their case was with accepted constitutional mythology *(Meridian Sun,* Preface). He must on this point have agreed rather with Burke than with Price, since the former, unwittingly Spencewise, held that the Glorious Revolution had re-enforced what he called "the entail" — the hereditary constitution of prerogative and property.

Spence's rejection of Parliamentary reform arose from his estimate of the growing economic stranglehold in the bid to monopolize world trade.[36] Before this hegemony was a reality, he declared that the promised prosperity was an illusion, for no matter how trade and agriculture might expand when it was freed of restrictions, all the real benefit would return to the landlord. "Thus all things work together for good to the landed interest, who are the visible elect". Hence his conception of the task:

> "In plain English nothing less that complete extermination of the private system of holding land . . . will ever bring the world into a state worth living in".

This he believes cannot be done "piecemeal". Unless the very roots of landlordism are destroyed royalty and aristocracy will grow again and prove ten times more savage than before. Writing to Charles Hall in 1807 he speaks of the hopes betrayed in the French Revolution and by the English reformers.[37] Names are changed but not the substance; new monopolies are established on the ruins of the old. Partial concessions only create delays.

> "For I labour all along to show that men cannot have their rights by piecemeal nor my system by any imperfect approaches and that the nearer they seem to come to partial improvements they are only more unlikely to adopt it and they must think of having it all at once or not at all".[38]

This complete "instantaneous" overthrow of "all establishments" is also necessary in order to have "clear ground to build on".

Spence's idea of revolution is based on the mass of people who must understand the aim in order to act together. The total overthrow of property is so violently opposed to existing interests that only this mass unity can succeed. It would be "foolhardy" for a few to take the initiative and begin to expropriate their landlords before the whole nation "were ripe and ready to join them". Conversely, he thought it unlikely that one section would reach that decision unless the understanding of the whole people had matured.

That day must come because the people "at this enlightened period" are in ever stronger conflict with "mixtures of right and wrong". "The nations will be in a continual State of Revolution"[39] until they are heartily "sick of the wars, the artificial famines" and all the rest, and seek the only real remedy — the destruction of all monopoly at its roots. The first concrete suggestion as to how this revolution could be organised is given in *The End of Oppression.* A volunteer revolutionary army is to be trained and a provisional government elected by it, but the main action is in the parishes, which immediately form their own committees of action and requisition the land and proceed to elect delegates to a central congress.

Even if popular representation were achieved by other means, the workers, who have to earn their bread, would not be able to "watch and resist" all the time to guard against the plots of the upper classes. Spence lived, be it remembered, before workers possessed organizations capable of holding out in a long strike. In those conditions he was not unrealistic in thinking that a popular revolution depended on the speed with which the rebels could get control of supplies and on the morale of united purpose and the solidarity possible in local actions. Instead of mobilizing large numbers away from their own districts, simultaneous action all over the country seemed the best way both to provision the people from local stocks and to paralyze or disperse the enemy.

This was the proposition in 1795. In 1800 it was further elaborated in *The Restorer of Society,* but without mention of the revolutionary army or the provisional government. Here neighbouring parishes form delegate conventions and discuss their plans. A few parishes combine, seize their lands and with them the "resources of war". The movement, already prepared by discussion, spreads immediately through the country.[40]

Great "Unions of the people" in recent times in France, America and England itself are evidence that the people can organize to achieve sweeping changes. In particular the recent naval mutinies had shown men so united and disciplined under their elected leaders that they were able to capture the fleet without bloodshed — a far more hazardous undertaking in view of their experienced officers than dealing with a parcel of landlords *(Restorer,* Letter V).

Most of the radical leaders believed that no initiative from below could ever produce anything beyond anarchic rioting. Spence on the contrary saw the necessary leadership coming from among the rank and file, like the obscure men who took command of the fleet and the unidentifiable but by no means unskilful captains who appeared in various mob actions.[41]

Spence formed no revolutionary organization. The small group around him in his latter years no doubt included his "field preachers" and there is some indication that a knowledge of his Plan had begun to penetrate more widely.

The war years seem to have deprived him of his earlier hope of a relatively peaceful and swift revolution. The power and ruthlessness of the existing regime and the support it could always have from interested careerists, showed that no government based on military power could be overthrown without an army. Spensonia, even more certainly than the French Republic, would be attacked by the foreign allies of reaction. A regular armed force had to be created and must incorporate troops deserting from the enemy on the promise of double pay for life. Clearly the same inducement to side with the people could be held out to English soldiers, although this could not be printed. The relevant passage shows that Spence took the matter very seriously. What else he may have talked about among his friends can only be conjectured. The role of the revolutionary army was his last important addition to his utopian romance in 1814, *The Marine Republic.*

From 1816 onwards the Spenceans paid special attention to the grievances of soldiers and sailors and recruited discharged men whose experience might furnish useful military leadership.[42]

The Mutiny on Land

Spence was speaking of the Mutiny of the Nore (1797) when he proposed a mutiny on land in *The Restorer.* But that was the word commonly used for the strikes of the miners and keelmen in the North and for other popular disturbances.[43] Spence had grown up near the lower streets and chares of Newcastle which Pennant described as "extremely narrow, dirty and ill-built . . . inhabited by keelmen and their families, a Mutinous Race, for which reason this town is always garrisoned". Memorable events in Newcastle history included the keelmen's great mutiny of 1710, and their armed rising in 1740, when they stormed the Guildhall, turning out the Mayor and the Council, sacked the Town Court and took £12,000 from the City treasury.[44]

The pitmen's riots in that terrible famine year and later made authority unwilling to meddle with them "as they all act in league and would stand by one another throughout the kingdom"; they attacked gaols to release imprisoned miners and took advantage of the fact that their labour was difficult to replace.[45]

Spence was a grown lad when the whole coal trade of the Tyne and Wear was brought to a standstill by a general strike through the coalfields in 1765 which frustrated the masters' plan to bind the men at will and won considerable wage rises.

Fifty years after the militia riots of 1761, the last words of the only man the authorities dared to hang as an example were remembered, giving bitter meaning to a well-known Border ballad — "Innocent blood is ill to shed". The centenary of the Hexham massacre was marked by a local history to honour the martyrs. Eyewitness accounts and oral tradition reveal not an undisciplined outburst but a well organized movement of miners, keelmen, workers and labourers, converging over a wide area to attack a formidable garrison. The listed dead alone represented no less than thirty-three parishes.[46]

The Tyne seamen provided the third important example of collective action. In 1794 when the miners came out in support of a keelmen's dispute and drew in iron workers as well, the situation resembled a general strike.

The major actions of these larger groups might not only combine but could involve other sections of the population and penetrate into surrounding areas. Food riots and industrial strikes often coalesced.[47] For most of the century food riots are recorded almost at regular five-year intervals, particularly serious in 1768 and again reaching threatening proportions in the eighties. Large donations by wealthy citizens to famine relief were less a charity than an insurance.

If we add the town demonstrations during the Wilkes campaign, the American war, the Town Moor anniversary, and the Catholic Bill, Spence's background offered rich experience of the power latent in the common people and the plebeian mob. The workers could be starved out, broken up, lacked major objectives and attacked property only by way of looting provisions or wrecking industrial equipment, but this was the prototype of the Mutiny on Land.[48]

Here in effect is the first hint of the political general strike and it is not surprising that Spenceanism was involved in the history of the industrial general union and general strike.

This connection in turn suggests that in the context of history Spence's ideas foreshadowed that fusion of political with social-economic aims which was the most striking feature of the working-class movement from the beginning of the eighteen-thirties.

From 1816 onwards the main body of the Spenceans particularly cultivated contacts with trade clubs and unions and encouraged the formation of new ones. From the spring of 1818 to the end of 1819 there are frequent references to John Gast, the shipwrights' leader, who spoke at public meetings called by the Committee of the Two Hundred[49] and attended inner meetings of Spencean leaders. It is not known when this connection began. Gast lived at Deptford and his visits to the centre of London would not have been frequent, but he might have known Spence himself. A passage in his pamphlet on the case of the shipwrights (1802) suggests that as a young man he held opinions about land and labour akin to those levelling tendencies which Spence represented.[50]

Masaniello, the Fisherman of Naples. Frontispiece to "Pigs' Meat", vol. III.

As is well known a movement for a general union, eventually called the General Philanthropic Society, was started at Manchester by the spinners, and at London under the name of the Philanthropic Hercules, led by John Gast. The Manchester delegates who came to London in this connection in the summer of 1818 met Gast, with Dr. Watson and other Spenceans at a meeting chaired by Edward Blandford, Secretary of the Committee of Two Hundred, at the White Lion in Wych Street — the usual meeting place of the Spencean committee at the time — when a report of the union of trades was discussed. Gast was seen at this period at inner meetings of Spencean leaders where matters of general policy and the progress of the journeymen's organization were discussed. The political commitment of the Manchester men may be gathered from the fact that Henry Swindells' colleague, Jones, on his return to Manchester in October took with him a quantity of a pamphlet by Dr. Watson.[51]

Before the end of August, at a public meeting sponsored by the Committee of the Two Hundred to put forward a Remonstrance to the Prince Regent, Gast appealed in a long speech to the mechanics who "had the club of Hercules in their hands" — that is to say, he proposed that the strength of the united trades should be used for political pressure.[52] Gast's article in the Spencean *Medusa* a little later reproaches the "tavern politics", mutual bickerings and trade jealousies which the workers allow to divide them, and again urges them to be "united in the bonds of a philanthropic Hercules" as the only way of defending their interest. If they use their real power they could cleanse the "Augean stables" of state corruption.[53]

There can hardly be any question that the name of Gast's society was only a variant of Spence's "philanthropic giant-killer" and implied some agreement with Spencean ideas.[54]

No doubt the immediate aim of the general union was a wider basis of industrial mutual aid, as set forth in the articles of the Philanthropic Hercules. This too was the aim of the London trades committee established by Gast and others in 1824 to campaign for the repeal of the Combination Acts. But that conflict between "middle-class Utilitarianism" and "emergent trade unionism" which Thompson has rightly seen as an important contribution of Gast's *Trades Newspaper,*[55] owed not a little to the legacy of Spence's class doctrine. The basis of Gast's criticism of Malthus and McCulloch is not an argument of economics but the belief that if a system or a theory cannot make the world "a place fit to live in" it cannot be said to work in any proper sense of the term.

Gast was a member of the founding committee of the Metropolitan Trade Union whose programme was 'trade and reform'.[56] From this body emerged the National Union of the Working Classes and Others, the nursery of Chartism.

William Benbow, once regarded as the first exponent of the theory of general strike, ever since 1816 had been one of the chief contacts between the London Spenceans and the Manchester Radicals. He also took part in the meetings which launched the general union of 1818, and on one occasion returned to Manchester with a large sum subscribed by the London trades on behalf of the spinners' strike. In 1831 he announced his National Holiday scheme in the National Union of the Working Classes,[57] and this was the basis of the Chartists' Sacred Month, the general strike policy adopted and then abandoned by the first Chartist convention.

The National Holiday was in fact a revival of Spence's Jubilee. The long passage on the Mosaic festivals in Benbow's pamphlet[58] recalls similar reference in the Preface to *The Restorer*; the Biblical allusions and figurative language echo Spence's millenarian tone, often in nearly identical terms. At the beginning of Benbow's Jubilee the people cease from work, operate through the vestry meeting, appropriate parish funds, send out deputations to requisition provisions and rents from the landlords, and eventually take over the land. Committees in each parish and district elect delegates to a National Congress which will "reform society", almost exactly according to Spence's recommendations. The moving reference to Thistlewood and other victims, betrayed by the workers' lack of unity, shows that the Spenceans must have been an acknowledged revolutionary tradition for a substantial number of Chartists, since the pamphlet had circulated for some time before Benbow's concrete proposal was made in the Convention.

The emphasis on land without developing the logic of Spence's Plan for the new situation, although the take-over in the towns was no doubt implied, seems to have proved misleading. The Convention sent out agents to discover what support would be forthcoming in rural districts, and as the reports were naturally discouraging, the general strike, which in this instance was contemplated as pressure tactics, was called off.

Spence himself is evidence that a consciously working-class point of view was taking shape and becoming articulate. Its actual demands naturally rejected the liberalism of the new democratic ideology of capitalism. But the conflict was often expressed as a condemnation of the old order which still prevailed, or in passionate denunciations that made no distinction between one method of accumulation and another.

> "But I contend that many Things are too sacred and of too great Importance to the Happiness and Dignity of the Human Race to be trafficked in, and in order to put a stop to all illicit Trade, I begin with prohibiting all Commerce in land, for that is the Root of all the other Branches of injurious Trade".[59]

The violence of the conflict during the last twenty years of Spence's lifetime was disclosed not in the Rights of Man literature but in the actual outbreaks of violence and in the character of the working-class associations which were becoming cohesive movements. This early distinction between a working-class interest and utilitarian radicalism is commonly recognized by English historians.[60] Spence's starting point was not the agitations of the political opposition, but the ethics of levelling, which were always repudiated by reform radicals.

Perhaps the reason why he has generally struck historians by his disconcerting mixture of insight and naivety as out of line with the main development of Utopianism, is because undercurrents among the lower classes in the early industrial revolution were understandably seldom put on record and even more rarely into any systematic form.

Place once called Spence "a typical specimen of those political poor preachers".[61] From time to time eighteenth-century documentation offers a passing glimpse of these humble non-conformists. But it is only by chance, because a great artist wrote an intimate memoir for his daughter, that we hear, for instance, of Gilbert Gray, in whose workshop Bewick met Spence among other lads who came to listen to unwordly wisdom and to read the books sent there for binding.[62] These old plebeian and working-class eccentrics preached reason, enlightenment and independence from the level of their own social status and seem to be the sign of changing values.

An inchoate tendency, not yet a movement, may be faintly perceived in the early formative period of the industrial proletariat. These tendencies were referred to by contemporaries in a general way as 'levelling'.[63] The condemnation of levelling is so frequent in the mid-eighteenth century that it may be supposed that people were aware of the existence of something of the kind. It is hoped that what has been said in these pages, however, will be found sufficient to discount as unhistorical any description of Spence as "the last of the orgiastic chiliasts",[64] and to connect his appearance with the problems of his age and sometimes with our own.
March, 1966

NOTES

1. This section on the Teachings of Thomas Spence is reprinted from Professor Ashraf's supplement: *Thomas Spence: The History of Crusonia and Other Writings* or *Essays in Honour of William Gallacher* Humboldt-Universitat zu Berlin 1966. For Professor Ashraf's modification of her views, see note 2. below.

2. The main changes I wish to make to the summary of Spence's teachings in the introduc - tion to reprints published by Humboldt University, 1966, are:

(1) I no longer accept the late Prof. Volgin's general assessment of Spence as an egalitarian rather than a forerunner of socialism. Volgin adopted a formal criterion: Socialist are those theories only which reject private property. He admits that Spence demanded the abolition of private property but this was merely formal and in reality cancelled by the terms of land tenancy. These are distorted by Volgin to mean long tenancies, even for life or heritable and that the land allotting authority then takes no further interest in how the land is utilized. This was not what Spence intended. The sole authority was the whole community of the parish as equal sharers in common property and continuously occupied with common economic and social improvement. This was essentially the way in which Spence related absolute democracy and equality to property relations. He also always emphasized that the welfare of the community had always been to take priority over all other sectional or individual interests.

(2) Marx and Engels in all references to Spence speak of him as one among many different utopian communists or early socialists and called Spence the arch enemy of private property. They welcomed into the First International the remaining members of O'Brien's organization who joined en bloc immediately after O'Brien's death. Marx regarded them as useful in strengthening the socialist element. It should be noted that Marx made extensive use of the "The History of Land Tenures" by Alfred Walton, their leading theoretician. (See "Capital", Vol. III).

The close similarity between O'Brien and Spence was first noted by Tillesley, particularly as regards the definition of land. O'Brien not only followed Spence's extended definition but the intention as to what must be included O'Brien emphasized by specifically mentioning railways and other new inventions which socialists treated as public utilities not to be owned by private persons.

The reflections of Spencean influence between the 1820's and the 1860's were many and modified the popular reception of Owenism. Only the name was often suppressed. Harney and his colleagues called themselves followers of Spence and the name came back with a fanfare in the 1880's.

(3) Spence's revolutionary theory, the concept of the Mutiny on Land and generally the social changes brought about by fundamental change in property relations contained undeniably socialist elements to be considered in deciding his historical place in the development of socialist ideas, always remembering that it was impossible for early thinkers to reflect anything but the fluctuating thought of those times. Spence belonged to the age of Adam Smith, the last days of manufacturing capitalism, so soon to be challenged by Ricardo and overtaken by the new problems and economics of Ricardo's critics. More than the few years in time divided Spence from Owen and the establishment of industrialism and the factory system.

(4) The concept of the callous elder brother depriving the younger served Winstanley, Sprigge, Trenchard, author of *Cato's Letters,* and other Commonwealth "republicans" to explain inequalities and justify a redistribution of property, or an agrarian law as sufficient. Spence declared that the landlord-oligarchy was an aggressive conqueror to be extirpated as a class in order to bring about equal partnership in the sources of wealth and thus made distribution depend on production. This was the decisive break from egalitarianism towards socialist ideas and demands.

The competition for land became more acute. Fears for property grew in the French Revolution. Patriarchal egalitarian theories had no place and the agrarian law debate soon disappeared.

(5) Spence was recognized in new movements. Fifty years after his trial, his *Restorer* was republished in *The Northern Star,* 1849, with portrait and other information.

3. *Pigs' Meat,* vol. II, p. 208.

4. E. Hughes, *North Country Life in the Eighteenth Century,* Oxford, 1952; p. XIX; C. H. Hunter Blair, *Members of Parliament for Northumberland and Newcastle-upon-Tyne 1559-1831, Archaeologia AEliana. 4th series, 1945; vol. XXII p. 132.*

5. *A Dream in Spence's Songs, Part Third.* London, n.d., p. 3 (not numbered).

6. The Spenceans in 1819 were reported to have made a list of urban properties as well as country estates. — H. O. 42.

7. Allen Davenport, *Life, Writings and Principles of Thomas Spence.* London, n.d. (c. 1835/6) p. 24.

8. For example:— "... The whole human family have the right to every advantage derived from the introduction of machinery ... which though of human invention may in a philosophical point of view, be ranked with the eternal elements of matter: it is the result of the advantages derived by the inventor from society ..." "... But where it is monopolized — as with the land — by an individual or by an oligarchy, whether it be by the originator or by the bloodfed capitalist ... machinery becomes a bane and a curse ... Until machinery of every description be approriated to the general welfare ... all the evils which we now complain of will progressively accumulate".— *The Man, 25 August,* 1833. "The possession of LAND is all that is necessary to transform the labouring classes from dependents into proprietors ... Having this land machinery would be employed for their own benefit ..." — *Republican,* 10 September, 1831, No. 25.

9. *English Chartist Circular,* 1841, No. 18, p. 75; No. 47, p. 185; *Bronterre's National Reformer,* 25 February, 1837, No. 8; Peter McDougall, *March of Serfdom* in *McDougall's Chartist and Republican Journal,* 1841, No. 1 seq.

10. A. R. Schoyen, *The Chartist Challenge,* London, 1958; p. 12.

11. *Democratic Review,* 1849; p. 141.

12. Place MSS. Add 27808, f. seq.

13. Rev. James Murray, *New Sermons to Asses,* London, 1819; pp. 19, 22.
The first statement as to a universal dividend is in the ballad *Rights of Man,* written at Newcastle in 1783. (Earliest copy known London, c. 1792). In *Meridian Sun* Spence only says he would prefer equal shares irrespective of age and sex. In *Rights of Infants* this is presented as an essential corollary from the natural right of all to the means of life.

14. *National Reformer and Manx Weekly Review,* 1847. No. 104, p. 3. See also O'Brien's arguments for parish ownership and seven-year leases in *Social Reformer,* 20 October, 1849; *Northern Star,* 23 June, 1838.

15. "His creed was — and Thomas Spence had taught it — that 'The Land is the People's Farm'. — *Northern Star,* 8 May, 1847. Quoted by Schoyen, op. cit., p. 148. Harney's

special interest in Spenceanism is shown by the tracts by and about Spenceans, as well as works by Murray, in his possession at the time of his death. See Catalogue of Harney Collection in Newcastle Central Library.

16. *Important Trial of Thomas Spence.* Second edition. 1807; p. 27, f.n.

17. *Medusa,* 24 April — 1 May, 1819; Nos. 10, 11.

18. The first and perhaps still the best scholarly treatment of Spence in England classified him with Ogilvie and Paine as an "agrarian reformer", v. M. Beer, *A History of British Socialism,* London, 1953; vol. 1, pp. 101, 105. Soviet scholars appear to associate him rather with Godwin as an exponent of egalitarianism. cf. V. P. Volgin, *History of Socialist Ideas* (Russian) Moscow, 1928, 1931; Part I, pp. 275 - 278. "Spence's Plan arose from the attitudes and beliefs of the masses rooted in an epoch when the land was the chief, and almost the sole condition of production". — Y. B. Chernyak, *The Mass Movement in England and Ireland in the late XVIIIth and early XIXth centuries* (Russian), Moscow, 1962; p. 318.

19. W. P. Hall, *British Radicalism 1791-1797. Studies in History, Economics and Public Law.* Columbia Univ., vol. 49, 1912; p. 152.

20. *A Dream* in *Spence's Songs.*

21. cf. *Register of Freemen chiefly of the Eighteenth Century,* ed. A. M. Oliver, *Pub. of the Newcastle-upon-Tyne Records Committee,* vol. VI, 1926; pp. 104, 121.

22. *Newcastle Courant,* 16 March, 1776, for Spence's appointment to Haydon Bridge School. His own school, advertised on the title page of *The Grand Repository of the English Language,* Newcastle, 1775, may not have been a full-time occupation. For his eight years service at St. Ann's School see *Common Council Books* in Newcastle City Records Office. Transcript. 1779, ff. 313, 314, 319; 1780, f. 342; 1787, ff. 54, 61.

23. *Marine Republic. Giant Killer,* 1814; p. 2.

24. *Restorer,* Preface.

25. *Meridian Sun,* Preface.

26. Thomas, Oliver, *A New Picture of Newcastle-upon-Tyne,* 1831; p. 42.

27. Thomas Houston, *A Congratulatory Ode to the members of the different Box Societies that lately entered into Resolutions to prevent Imposition and be their own Corn Dealers,* Newcastle, 1800; pp. 24-27.

28. J. Baillie, *An Impartial History of the town and county of Newcastle-upon-Tyne and its vicinity,* Newcastle-upon-Tyne, 1801; p. 131; W. Stanley Mitcalf, *"History of the Keelmen", Arch. AEliana,* 4th series, vol. XV, 1937; p. 2 passim.

29. *Marine Republic, Pigs' Meat,* vol. II.

30. *The Real Rights of Man. Pigs' Meat,* vol. II.

31. *Restorer,* Letter XII.

32. *Pigs' Meat,* vol. II, p. 206, p. 209.

33. *A Fable* in *A Suitable Companion to Spence's Songs,* n.d.

34. *Restorer,* Letter IV.

35. Loc. cit.

36. *Restorer,* Letter VII.

37. Place MSS. Add. 72808, f. 284.

38. *Important Trial.*

39. This was his prediction in *A Fragment of an Ancient Prophecy,* 1797, and is repeated in his *Important Trial* and *The Restorer.*

40. *Restorer,* Letter V. and f.n.

41. On the broad plebeian character of the mob see G. Rude, *Wilkes and Liberty,* Oxford, 1962; p. 13 passim. In J. Midon, *The History of the Rise and Fall of Masaniello the Fisherman of Naples,* London, 1729, which is reprinted almost entire in *Pigs' Meat* vol. III, the revolution begins in a food riot under an ideal popular leader, the humble fisherman. Spence does not give the name of the author but took his text from the above edition. The moral of the history was no doubt that the aristocracy can never be trusted.

42. P. M. Kemp-Ashraf, *Africans among Reformers,* (Russian) Moscow, 1960; pp. 318-319. On the role of the army see *Giant Killer,* p. 13.

43. "'Mutinies' of keelmen and pitmen were endemic in the eighteenth century". — Hughes, op.cit. vol. I, p. 249; p. 253.

44. H. Bourne, *The History of Newcastle-upon-Tyne,* Newcastle-upon-Tyne, 1736; p. 132.

45. Quoted in U. Neff, *British Coal Industry,* London, 1932, vol. II, p. 177. For disturbances in Newcastle see M. A. Richardson, *The local historian's Table Book,* Newcastle-upon-Tyne, 1842; vol. I, pp. 398-400.

46. J. Ridley, *The Hexham Chronicle,* Hexham, 1861; *A serious address to the Common People on account of the late insurrection at Hexham, 9 March, 1761,* Newcastle-upon-Tyne, 1761.

47. On the conscious intentions of early "negotiations by riot" see E. J. Hobsbawm, *Labouring Men,* London, 1964; pp. 5-8.

48. Spence uses the "official" term 'insurrection' of men leaving their work to attend to their political interests in *The End of Oppression.* The implication is the same.

49. The name of the radical reform body set up by the Spenceans, working in uneasy alliance with Henry Hunt, Cartwright and Cobbett.

50. John Gast, *Calumny Defeated or a Compleat Vindication of the Working Shipwrights during the late disputes with their Employers,* Deptford, 1802; p. 9. The tone as well as content should be noted.

51. The evidence of these meetings is found in H. O. 42, 179-182. The Hammonds, still the main secondary authority, used these documents and reports of the Select Committee on the Combination Laws (1824). — cf. *Town Labourer,* 1925; pp. 309-310; *Skilled*

Labourer, 1927; p. 358 passim. For another version see G. D. H. Cole, *Attempts at General Union (1818-1834),* London, 1953. None of these accounts refer to the Spencean connections and meetings.

52. *Globe,* London, September 7, 1818.

53. *"An Address to the Mechanics and Labourers of the United Kingdom", Medusa,* No. 20, 3 July, 1819.

54. "The extirpation of these (tyrannical giants, P. M. A.) should employ the philanthropic giant-killers, the deliverers of mankind". — *Marine Republic. Pigs' Meat,* vol. II, p. 209. "The Revolution it is true destroyed many evils of the Feudal System, but produced others. It destroyed the high-sounding titles of the old Giants; but left Giantism still in substance, and Giants though of other names arose". — *Giant Killer,* No. 1, 1814, p. 6 f.n. But the name puzzled later writers. "The curious name of the Philanthropic Hercules" — G. D. H. Cole, *A Short History of the British Working Class Movement.* Revised edition. London, 1960; p. 48. In eighteenth-century chap books Hercules' main labour is killing monsters.

55. E. P. Thompson, *The Making of the English Working Class,* London, 1963; p. 775.

56. *Penny Papers for the People,* 9 April 1830; p. 4 passim.

57. *Poor Man's Guardian,* 14 January, 1832.

58. William Benbow, *Grand National Holiday and Congress of the Productive Classes.* Printed and published for W. Benbow . . . London, n.d. The pastoral atmosphere in which Benbow's Jubilee begins might be associated with the Rechabites' return to the simple life in *The Restorer,* Letter X.

59. *Restorer,* Preface.

60. e.g. Erich Roll, *History of Economic Thought,* London, 1961; p. 234. cf. 1st edition for a more explicit statement.

61. Place MSS. Add 27789, f. 62.

62. Thomas Bewick, *Memoir of Thomas Bewick written by himself, 1822-1828.* Edited by Selwyn Image. London, 1924; pp. 54-55.

63. Spence defended levellers and considered himself to be one. See the last sentence in *Spence's Recantation of the End of Oppression; Giant Killer,* No. 2, p. 14, f.n. This did not imply for him any special association with or sympathy for Lilburne and the Leveller party of the seventeenth century. Like Godwin, Spence seems to have had more regard for the Republicans — Milton, Harrington, Sidney, Vane.

64. W. H. G. Armytage, *Heavens Below,* London, 1961; p. 70.

Works

All Spence's more important writings survived in one or more editions. The third issue of *The Giant-Killer* and *Eye-Salve* announced in *Pigs' Meat*, vol. II, may never have appeared. His tracts frequently mention or advertise previous ones, and these notices help to establish dates of publication. Not all editions of particular works have been traced and there is doubt as to what was meant by the third part of *The End of Oppression* or by *Spence's Plan* mentioned in *Spence's Songs*.

As regards slips and broadsides it is quite impossible to say how many of these were issued or what they all contained. These are now scattered in various private and public collections and many must have been entirely lost.

Some of the tracts do not have Spence's name as author on the title page. It is possible that he published others anonymously and that items hitherto not identified still exist. In the absence of other evidence nothing can be attributed to Spence which does not show his quite individual peculiarities of style. He seldom missed any opportunity of expounding his main teachings and writings which express decidedly different views. The only exceptions are topical ballads, e.g. on the British Convention, against the war with France, satires of Burke, Pitt or the Government. Some of these will be found signed 'T.S.' but are in one way or another characteristic of his approach.

Place left a description of Spence's works. Rudkin's monograph reprinted a bibliography originally published in the *Bulletin* of the London School of Economics, May 1926, with further details and descriptive comments. There are also bibliographical data in Waters' book, together with a catalogue of Spence's tokens, later amplified by Waters and other authorities.

1775

(1) Lecture to the Philosophical Society in Newcastle. The title quoted in the report of the Society was *Property in Land Every Man's Right.* All authorities agree that the Lecture was undoubtedly printed at Newcastle in that year shortly after Spence had delivered it. According to Mitchel, Mackenzie and Place the title was *The Real Rights of Man.* No copy of the first edition has survived. The two Newcastle writers may have taken the title from a later edition, and Place had his information presumably from Mitchel. Spence's ballad version of his Plan was called *The Rights of Man.* There was no need to stress "real rights" before Paine's *The Rights of Man.*

Thomas Evans says that the subject of the lecture was "on a plan, or mode of administering the landed estate of the nation as a joint-stock property", but in a short list of Spence's works he begins with *Rights of*

Man, evidently the Lecture. Davenport gives as the title of the Lecture: *On the Mode of Administering the Landed Estate of the Nation as a joint-stock Property in Parochial Partnerships, by dividing the Rent.* He might have substituted subject for title. The pretentious wording is unlike the brief colourful main titles so characteristic of Spence's publications. It is more reminiscent of Evans's phraseology and of the slant which he gave to the Plan. A similar formulation is found for example in the second *Address* of the Spencean Philanthropists composed by Evans.

The Northern Star (1849) says that Spence gave a lecture "taking for his subject: "The Mode of Administering the Landed Estate of the Nation as a joint-stock Property in Parochial partnerships by dividing the Rent", i.e. printing the words like a title with capital letters as in Davenport's *Life.* It is known that the writer in the *Northern Star* had at his disposal copies of *Pigs' Meat,* and *The Important Trial* with *The Restorer,* supplied by a reader, and no doubt Davenport's *Life,* and may therefore have had other pamphlets as well.

However a pamphlet with this title must have existed. It was not published at Newcastle and cannot therefore have been the original version of the Lecture. Morrison Davidson quotes a pamphlet with exactly the same title (with 'partnerships' in the plural as in all the other instances) published by Reeves of Fleet Street, but no date. If his quotations are all from the same pamphlet, it would appear to combine part of the Lecture (corresponding to the fourth edition) with part of the *Introduction* to *The Constitution of a Perfect Commonwealth,* including the additional passages given by Davenport in his *Life,* but not by Evans, and not found in the second edition of *The Constitution.*

As the edition of the Lecture, presumably the third, which led to Spence's arrest in 1792 was entitled *Rights of Man,* it seems unlikely that he would have used such a very different title for the London edition which could only recently have preceded it. Perhaps there was an entirely separate pamphlet, possibly not published in Spence's lifetime, since he himself made no reference to it in his advertisements nor does it occur in the advertisements of other booksellers who distributed his pamphlets(Lee, Eaton and Ballard), but compiled by one of his followers after his death.

The question of this title is more than a mere bibliographical detail. Although Rudkin did not mention this wording as a title of a pamphlet, she adopted the interpretation of the Plan which it implies. She maintains that what was meant by Parish property merely amounted to the Parish as an administrative unit for the management of national land. This might be a logical deduction, but it is clear from every first-hand description of his system that Spence always thought of it the other way round, namely that the state was a collection of federated small regions whose inhabitants enjoyed the absolute inalienable right to their land, and whose central government was composed of the representatives of these "landlords" (just as the existing government consisted of private property owners) who agreed on equitable contributions to the national rent and its expenditure. In *The Restorer* Spence made a point of rejecting the concept of nationalisation of the land, indicating that the question might have been raised at that time in connection with his Plan. It is not absolutely certain that Evans had already attached himself to Spence's circle.

The Land: and every Man's Right is the title of a much later anonymous pamphlet published at London perhaps in the late eighteen-forties. The title nearly coincides with that of the Lecture in the first notices. Although the arguments and proposals of a "partnership" and division of rents are very close to Spence it was obviously not written by him. It calls for the gradual nationalisation of land and could have been an attempt to adapt the Plan to changed circumstances and bring it up to date.

(2) The next edition of the Lecture of which there is any certain knowledge was in circulation in 1792 when a copy of Spence's *Rights of Man* was bought by the agent who visited his shop, in mistake for Paine's *Rights of Man.* (See: *The Case of Thomas Spence,* p. 3). It is not clear whether this was a second or third edition.

(3) The Rights of Man as exhibited in a Lecture read at the Philosophical Society in Newcastle. To which is now added an interesting conversation between a Gentleman and the Author, on the subject of the Scheme with the Queries sent by the Rev. Mr. J. Murray to the Society in Defence of the same. And a Song of Triumph for the People on the Recovery of their Long Lost Rights. The fourth edition. By T. Spence. Printed for the author and sold at the Corner of Chancery Lane, Holborn. 1793.

The Preface quotes Swift and disclaims that the Plan is intended for "a country so well-bred as this", but rather for American or African savages who have not yet learned to reverence "blood-sucking landlords and state leeches". It is signed 'London, November 19, 1792. The Author'. Either the volume which the police runner bought was printed between November 19th and December 6th, or it was an earlier edition without this Preface. The fourth edition might have been in preparation at the time and owing to Spence's arrest not published until the following year.

Eighteen of Murray's original twenty-two Queries are given. The *Hymn of Triumph* at the end of the pamphlet is a new version of the *Jubilee Hymn.* On the last page there is a quotation from Swift's *Letters* headed "Swift's Revolution Principle".

(4) The Real Rights of Man. Plainly shown in a Lecture, read at the Philosophical Society in Newcastle, on the 8th of November, 1775, for printing of which, the Society did the Author the honour to expel him.

This is printed in *Pigs' Meat,* vol. III, 1795; pp. 220-241. There is no Preface. The 'Conversation' and the 'Queries' follow the Lecture, which does not differ in any important respect from the edition of 1793.

(5) The Meridian Sun of Liberty on the whole Rights of Man displayed and most accurately defined in a LECTURE read at the PHILOSOPHICAL SOCIETY in Newcastle on the 8th of November, 1775, for printing of which the Society did the Author the honour to expel him. To which is now first prefixed by way of PREFACE, a most important DIALOGUE between the CITIZEN-READER, and the AUTHOR. By T. Spence. London, 1796.

The prefatory 'Dialogue' differs considerably from the 'Conversation' in the previous edition. In place of a "Gentleman" objecting from the point of view of landlords and ending with an appeal to religion, in the new dialogue the "Citizen-Reader" speaks for democratic reformers whose notion of the Rights of Man is limited to parliamentary representation and the enjoyment of their individual property. The Author points out that since they agree to a system based on property, which excludes them and treats them no better than strangers in a land entirely owned by others, they ought to acknowledge the perfect right of the landlords to manage their property in whatever way they please. But by demanding a share in government, control of taxation and financial reforms, they are in fact attacking property. One might well suspect that these democratic leaders only want to change one lot of masters for another and stir up unrest in order to fish in troubled waters. This is a very clear statement that Spence regarded the state as an instrument of the ruling class and not as an impartial regulator of different interests. Taken together with *The End of Oppression,* the 'Dialogue' marks the sharpening of his polemic against half-way reform. A verse on the title page brackets John Thelwall, who had now left the London Corresponding Society, with Burke.

Below the end of the Lecture on the last page is printed "An Important Query" advertising the three complete volumes of *Pigs' Meat,* forming a permanent "School of Man's Rights".

The most important change in the text of the Lecture itself is the addition of three final paragraphs establishing the public auction of leases limited to seven years and the distribution of a quarterly dividend.

In the original *Lecture* and *The History of Crusonia* the people of the parish form "a corporation" and use their revenue, after paying a portion to the central government, for any purpose they may agree upon. Spence's first audience did not need to be told that the Newcastle Burgesses had recently shared out their Town Moor rents or that many local Box Societies regularly shared out the whole or a surplus of their funds. The dividend was implied in the formulation. However only later it became a key point for the operation of the Plan. The dividend is expressly mentioned in *The Rights of Man* in verse in 1783, in the *Pigs' Meat* version of the Lecture and again in *The Marine Republic and A Further Account of Spensonia.* Here it is said that some dividend however small should always be distributed as a reminder of the people's partnership in the soil. In *The Meridian Sun* an equal dividend is tentatively extended to include all men, women and children since all have the same right to existence. It is put as a suggestion evidently anticipating possible objections to the inclusion of women and children. But as Murray used the expression "dividend" before Spence in the sense of the share of the earth's wealth to which all are entitled, it is probable that this was the source of Spence's idea and that he had always considered this right to be universal and inalienable.

1775. The Grand Repository of the English Language containing besides the excellencies of all other dictionaries and grammars of the English tongue, the peculiarity of having the most proper and agreeable pronunciation of the alphabetical words denoted in the most intelligible manner by a new alphabet, with a copperplate exhibiting the new alphabet both in writing and printing characters, intended for the use of everyone whether native or foreigner that would acquire a complete knowledge of the English language with the least waste of time and expense but especially for those who are but indifferent readers from not having been taught to pronounce properly.
By Thomas Spence, Teacher of English in Newcastle, Newcastle-upon-Tyne.
Printed by T. Saint for the Author and sold by him at his school on the Keyside, and by all the Booksellers in Town and Country. 1775.

There is a Preface, quoting Sheridan and Baron Biefield, on the need for a reformed spelling especially to aid "the labouring part of the people" to educate their children. A summary of grammar with rules of syntax and exercises is followed by the new alphabet and a dictionary giving new and old spelling. Immediately after the Preface there is an advertisement:—

> "Just published by the Author and sold by him at his school on the Keyside, and the Booksellers and Newscarriers. No. 1 (Price One Penny) of *The Repository of Commonsense and Innocent Amusement*".

This is described as a weekly miscellany of "extracts from the best authors". It is mentioned by Mackenzie and Thomas Bewick possessed a copy but none now survives in any of the main libraries.

1779. The Poor Man's Advocate.

An extract is printed in *Pigs' Meat,* vol. II, pp. 32-35, under the heading:

> "A Lesson for the Swinish Multitude. Being Queries of Importance. From a pamphlet entitled 'The Poor Man's Advocate', published at Newcastle by T. Spence, in the year 1779".

The contents of the pamphlet is nowhere indicated. Spence used the same pen name "The Poor Man's Advocate" as editor of *Pigs' Meat.* No copy of the original pamphlet is known. It is impossible to say whether this extract is an exact reprint of what was published in 1779. The phrase "the sheepish multitude" was of course newly inspired by Burke's famous "swinish multitude" in 1791. The questions introduce "gentle-horses" served by docile "landless horses", a parable of landlord and tenant relations suggestive of the Houyhnhnms in *Gulliver's Travels.*

These questions contain the first mention of Spensonia and it is evidently assumed that the reader knows what the word means. Place says that Spence published a Spensonia story at Newcastle after 1783, i.e. in addition to *The History of Crusonia.* All Place's information on Newcastle publications was at second-hand. Perhaps this reference was to *The Rights of Man in Verse* published in 1783 which also describes Spensonia, if there was not another prose narrative which has been lost. *The Poor Man's Advocate* may have been the first version of a story about a utopia called Spensonia and the name may have been changed in 1782 to fit the Robinson Crusoe context of the next story.

The extract is also of interest on account of a statement that those who acquire wealth by honest work or trade in Spensonia cannot force others to work for them. This would seem to indicate that Spence had had labour and production relations as well as property relations in mind from the outset.

1782. The Real Reading-Made-Easy: or, a Foreigner's and Grown Person's Pleasing Introduction To Reading English, Whereby all Persons, of whatever Age or Nation, may soon be taught, with Ease and Pleasure, to read the English Language.
Newcastle: Printed and sold by T. Saint. 1782.

This book contains "Eze Lesinz for Kruzoniin Skolirz" consisting of short Biblical sentences or sayings in Spence's "Crusonian" alphabet, arranged to familiarise key words by repitition. It could be counted on that grown persons and children from Bible-reading families would already have heard similar sentences. They are of the rhythmical and easily memorized kind. The selection is evidence that Spence must have worked out a real method of teaching based on practice.

This is the first time that Saint appears as Spence's publisher. Thomas Hastie's *The only method to make reading easy* was published with Bewick cuts by T. Angus in the 1770's. It had considerable circulation. The 73rd edition appeared in 1839. Angus and Saint were not only trade rivals but religious and political antagonists. The title, *Real Reading-Made-Easy,* suggests that Saint backed Spence's new method to compete with Angus's book.

The same year Spence invited subscriptions of a penny a week for a complete Bible in this phonetic or "Crusonian" script. The advertisement appears at the end of *A Supl'im'int too thi Histire ov Robinsin Kruzo.* Proof pages corrected by Spence giving title page, Preface, and an Alphabet, of *The Pronouncing and Foreigners' Bible. By T. Spence, Teacher of English, London,* printed by T. and J. Cook, Paternoster Row and J. Debrett, Piccadilly, are in the Place MSS (Add. 27808. f. 249). The proof is a single sheet of which seven pages are printed. Spence evidently attempted to launch his phonetic Bible in London. No Newcastle edition known. Nothing further is heard of it.

1782. A Supplement to the History of Robinson Crusoe being the History of Crusonia or Robinson Crusoe's Island down to the present time. Copied from a letter sent by Mr. Thomas Wishit, Captain of the Good Intent to an intelligent friend in England, after being in a storm in May 1781, driven out of his course to the said Island. Published by this said gentleman for the agreeable Perusal of Robinson Crusoe's Friends of all Sizes.
A New Edition. Newcastle.
Printed and Sold by T. Saint, in 1782.

The volume contains three additional stories, which are run on without separate title pages, viz:—

"An History of the Progress of Learning in Lilliput; and the changes it produced there in the manners and customs. Brought over in the Ship Swallow, by Master Ramble".

"The History of the Mercolians, communicated by Master Brolio of Lilliput".

"What Happened on a Journey with Old Zigzag. On Tenderness to Animals".

There is a full page woodcut frontispiece depicting Robinson Crusoe and three vignettes illustrating the Zigzag story. These are generally thought to be by Thomas Bewick. The Crusoe picture is crude and conventional and might have been one of the old blocks of which Saint had a large stock. He published various editions of Defoe's *Robinson Crusoe,* including one in 1784. The small pictures might well be by young Bewick trying to render lifelike movement and humour before he had overcome the difficulties of a crude medium and bad printing.

On page 3 (unnumbered) is a poem by Jeremiah Spence *On reading the History of Crusonia,* in this edition unsigned.

The *Jubilee Hymn* appears for the first time in *The History of the Progress of Learning in Lilliput* as the Prologue to a play performed in the Parish theatre every year to commemorate the establishment of the Jubilee. It is sung line by line in turn by four actors representing different trades "as if the words arose spontaneously from the Occasion".

A phonetic version with the same frontispiece was also published:

> A S'upl'im'int too thi Histire ov Robinsin Kruzo being TH'I H'IST'IRE 'ov KRUZONEA or R'O'INS'IN KRUZO'Z IL'IND down too thi prezint Tim . . .
>
> Nuk'as'il. T. SANT. 1782.

A Preface explains that the aim of spelling reform is "to free the poor and the stranger, the industrious and the innocent (i.e. workers and children, P.M.A.) from vecsatious, tedious and ridiculous absurdities: and also to make Charity schools and in a great measure, all schools for teaching English, unnecessary". The verses *On Reading the History of Crusonia* follow, signed "J. S. Newcastle, July 7, 1781", and some other verses, *The Universal Jubilee* (not the *Jubilee Hymn),* signed "S. T.", possibly in error for "T. S.". There is a "Postscript" at the end of the story with the Crusonian alphabet, and a passage from Priestley on progress through experience and observation as against the mental apathy induced by "rigid, unalterable establishments". *The History of the Progress of Learning in Lilliput* is included in this volume but not the other two stories.

It would seem from the date, May 1781, mentioned in the title and the date of Jeremiah Spence's verses, July 1781, that the book was written about six months before publication. Dates of publication of the two versions within three weeks of one another are established by two separate advertisements of them in the *Newcastle Courant* for 22 December 1781 and 12 January 1782. Place thought that the phonetic version appeared or was written first. That might account for calling the normal script version "a new edition". There is so far no trace of any earlier edition.

There was a further edition of *The Real Reading-Made Easy* followed by both versions of *A Supplement to the History of Robinson Crusoe,* in a single miniature 24-mo volume, "Printed and Sold by T. Saint. 1782. Price one shilling". This volume is described by Place and a copy was preserved in the Newcastle Public Library. These various editions might indicate that the book had a good sale.

Saint ran a line in toy books similar to Newbery's at London. The economy in paper perhaps enabled him to sell three books in one at two-thirds the price of the normal volumes. Probably the miniature edition was also sold in separate parts.

And it must therefore be recorded that the first and perhaps the most original contribution in England to utopian socialism in the period of the industrial revolution first circulated as a halfpenny pamphlet sold in public houses, then in the form of a children's story and finally in a toy book.

The History of Crusonia might be described as a utopian romance demonstrating the benefits of the system outlined in the Lecture. The descendants of the people left by Crusoe on the island intermarry with the Indians on the mainland. The young generation that results decides to abolish the inconveniences of the political system which the first settlers brought with them from Europe, and to combine the benefits of civilization with the free customs of their Indian ancestry. The results particularly brought out are:— Political democracy based on local autonomy of federated parishes, possible when private property in land is abolished; the functions of the Parish corporations and the use of revenue to provide public amenities and to encourage industry and enterprise; the reasons why the system once established will be permanent, and the means of defense by a people's militia. The really new aspect here is the insistence on human equality. Residence alone gives full citizen rights irrespective of origin. The parishes grow and strengthen through naturalizing foreigners attracted to settle among them. The system spreads by founding new free parishes in uninhabited lands, and by neighbouring people adopting a similar way of life. To prevent landlordism reappearing, colonisation by conquest is forbidden and no individual is allowed to settle on unoccupied land until it has been duly incorporated in the parish. All unsettled land is regarded as the common property of the state. The universal character of the original Plan is thus illustrated in an imaginery non-European setting. Hence the *The History of Crusonia* contains both the basic idea of the ideal democracy described in *The Marine Republic,* and part of the specific criticism of the whole domestic and foreign policy arising from the existing order of property and not from the 'mistakes' of foolish or of wicked men in power. It is not difficult to see that Spence's ideas were also influenced by the American war. *The History of Crusonia* shows how America could have been settled peacefully by Europeans without injustice to the native inhabitants and reflects an opinion then current in democratic circles that colonial conquest and plunder were one of the sources of the political corruption at home.

It has always been assumed that the whole book was written by Spence, in the first instance by Place.

> "The Supplement to Robinson Crusoe, the Learning of Lilliput and the History of the Mercolians are pictures of what he supposed would be the practice and condition of the people under his system, principally in answer to objections, to the account of Robinson Crusoe's Island. In these tracts he makes some good observations on voting by ballot, proving its necessity and utility".

John Bell only refers to *The History of Crusonia,* saying that after the failure of the Lecture, "to further his project he wrote the account of 'Crusonia' ".

Only *The History of Crusonia* is a full account of Spence's ideas. In *The History of Learning in Lilliput* there is the old facile convention that enlightenment precedes liberty (in flat contradiction to the alleged freedom of the primitive Golden Age), so that the "important revolution" which overthrows the Landlords, results spontaneously from "the introduction of learning". The Jubilee — "the former captives now were all set free, all Debts were abolished" — follows Moses not Spence. *The History of the Mercolians* presents constitutional reform as a possible half-way stage to full liberty. It may be that it was only after he came to London that Spence became completely convinced that neither the universal franchise, nor the ballot, nor any change in the form of government would suffice to bring about a change in the material basis of society. After 1794, while continuing to support the French Revolution and the principles of democratic rights proclaimed in England, he began to attack rather than lament the Reformers' aims even as a means to an end. The three stories however show something of the connection between Spence's political ideas and the Parliamentary Reform movement, particularly for example as regards the militia and the ballot, although at the time he published them the Reform movement was showing very little sign of activity.

Although *The History of Crusonia* is a political allegory its most interesting features are the practical uses to which the collective surplus of production, represented by the rents, can be put for public works and services. Idealistic as they sound, they were based on real contemporary needs and demands.

Crusoe himself stands for the enterprise of labour and in particular for his "Jack-of-all-Trades Disciples", "the Mechanics". The popular image in the eighteenth century was not always "the isolated economic man pitting his strength against nature", or the nascent capitalist, but very often "poor Crusoe". True, he set out to get rich by any means, including the slave trade, but through hardship and loneliness learned to respect labour and the social bond. There was an inn sign in Gateshead painted by John Collier in 1774 and the local poet's verses on it probably expressed what Spence also saw in the figure.

> "Stop my good friend, and cast your eyes around,
> Behold a *Figure!* rarely to be found —
> The figure of a *Man,* in veiled distress;
> Yet arm'd, as if he would defiance show.
> Is this the fancy of the sage Defoe?
> It is the same; — and now by memory led,
> *Robinson Crusoe* half the world have read.
> See him *thus* wreck'd upon his desert isle,
> Inur'd to patience, and inur'd to toil.
> His looks, though chang'd, betray no weak despair;
> Cheerfulness and gravity seem blended there.
> We'll not the painter's happy skill define
> But mark the moral meaning of his *Sign.*
> Old *Time* may have to Revelation brought
> Why *Selkirk* suffered and why *Daniel* wrote.
> And mark, my friend, if stray report say true,
> 'Twas in *this* place the bold design he drew;
> Gateshead, scarce known, the hardy *writer* chose,
> When sorely prest by persecuting foes;
> To teach frail mortals, as a friendly guide,
> In Providence to trust, whate'er betide.
> Reader, here's folly, come and laugh thy fill,
> He ne'er did good that never did ought ill".

There was something of this in Spence's own singlehanded struggle with poverty and persecution and his collectivism was very much the mutual aid of poor but self-reliant artisans. Crusonian happiness corrected the poverty of the isolated individual. Mutual dependence abolished Crusoe's landlord attitude to the island as his property and to other races as his natural slaves and inferiors. Crusoe is honoured as the founder in his character of husbandman, mechanic and worker, not as the adventurer after wealth. There are degrees of personal success in Crusonia but no one monopolizes the sources of wealth. One of the functions of the Parish is to provide good workshops for a population entirely of working people. From the common revenue they create a garden landscape, workers' homes "like the Habitations of Gentry", no more dirty patched windows, smoky houses, broken pavements, but all the refinements of living and learning that make every parish "a little polished Athens".

The History of Crusonia is an original continuation, a legitimate use of a popular classic. It borrows nothing but the symbolism of what was now a folk character. The other three stories in the book, however, are in a large measure word for word reproductions of earlier versions. It was not hitherto noticed that *An History of the rise and progress of learning in Lilliput* and *The History of the Mercolians* had appeared much earlier in Newbery's *Lilliputian Magazine,* a work which Francis Place had evidently not consulted on the theory of the ballot. The title page sets forth that ideal of simplicity and virtue which the working middle class liked to contrast with the corruption of idle wealth.

> "The Lilliputian Magazine or the Young Gentleman's and Lady's Golden Library. Being an Attempt to mend the World to render the Society of Man more Amiable and to establish the Plainness, Simplicity, Virtue and Wisdom of the Golden Age so much celebrated by the Poets and Historians.
>
> Men in that Age no Rule but Reason knew,
> And with a native bent did Good pursue:—
> Unforc'd by Punishment nor aw'd by Fear, —
> His words were simple and his Soul sincere.
>
> London.
>
> Printed for the Society and Published by T. Carnan at Mr. Newbery's Bible and Sun in St. Paul's Church Yard".

This was one of Newbery's toy books for children. What appears to be the oldest specimen is undated. It is not a magazine in the modern sense, but a collection of miscellaneous pieces. All the contributions are anonymous. They include *The Adventures of Little Tommy Trip,* sometimes ascribed to Goldsmith who has also been suggested as the editor. Accounts of the controversy over Goldsmith's connection and the date of publication did not offer any conclusive result. In the book itself the beginning of the children's society mentioned on the title page, is given as 1750 (pp. 8, 9), and a list of subscribers at the end is dated 1752 (which rules out Goldsmith). This date was taken as the probable date of publication for instance by *The Cambridge History of English Literature,* and is given with a query in the British Museum catalogue.

The book is illustrated and just as a famous writer was chosen as the hypothetical editor, so the pictures were ascribed to a well-known artist, Thomas Bewick, who was not yet born. The cuts have nothing characteristic even of Bewick's earliest efforts and the details of costume belong to an earlier period. They do not help to decide the date of publication as sometimes very old blocks were used for cheap books. The internal date also does not count for much as evidence. The *Magazine* was still being sold by John Newbery's grandson, Francis Power, in the 'seventies, when the society, if it had ever existed, could only have been a fiction. There was nothing unusual in reprinting such books after a considerable time without bringing them up to date.

At this time the Newcastle trade in children's books was nearly as extensive as that of London. Saint and White published a number of books similar in style to Newbery's, illustrated by the Bewick brothers. Saint had connections with Carnan and Newbery, printed or took over some of their books, and through this connection Bewick, while still unknown, was employed to make designs for the London printers whom he met on his visit to London in 1776. Hence it would not have been impossible for Spence to have been commissioned to write stories for them. If the date of publication of the *Magazine* could be pushed forward about twenty years or shown to be a new edition in the seventies of an earlier publication, he might have been the author of the original *Learning in Lilliput* and *The Mercolians.* However, it seems more probable that in order to make a more substantial volume Spence adapted these stories for Saint and that the plagiarism was not regarded as any infringement of the other publisher's interests. It might have been done by agreement while Newbery's book was out of print.

The Newbery's and Saint were businessmen, but that does not mean that their children's books were not genuinely inspired by certain benevolent and progressive ideals. Saint not only launched Spence's spelling reform with its much stronger emphasis on the needs of the working poor, as well as his utopian schemes which the Philosophical Society had outlawed, but at one time risked publishing handscript for another experimenter.

The editors or authors of *The Lilliputian Magazine* claimed that they were introducing "a new method of education" as well as 'Golden Age' precepts, "to remove that rusticity and awkwardness which appears in the common people when talking to their superiors". The price is so trifling that their book is within the reach of the poor also who are "in their station as much regarded as the rest". ('Common people' here evidently meant not the labouring poor but the lesser middle class in trade and employments where they had occasion to meet their 'superiors'). The aim is "to unloose the minds of children from the fetters of habit and custom". *The History of Learning in Lilliput* in this version is meant to make learning to read attractive by giving a rational explanation of the alphabet. Perhaps this attempt convinced Spence that the only way in which reading could be simplified was to adopt a system of regular phonetic spelling. His demand for universal education, as expressed in for example in *The History of Crusonia* and later extended to higher learning, is to be connected with this democratic movement in education, a necessity for the rising manufacturing and commercial middle class, and was only re-affirmed for Spence by the vague provisions in the French Constitution of 1793. He merely extends the demand to the lower classes, since the proletariat in its turn had similar reasons for making the same demand, and makes it a political matter, as the working class movement did later.

Spence's *Learning in Lilliput* up to p. 40, 1.2, coincides with the first instalment in *The Lilliputian Magazine.* The second part of the latter (pp. 105-108) only explains the normal alphabet, while Spence went on to the reform of the alphabet and the spread of learning. The now enlightened Lilliputians, driven by the oppression of the landlords, make "an important revolution", take over the land and cancel all debts. The annual commemoration of this Jubilee is described. Incidentally Spence satirizes certain local characters who had become notorious in recent dissenter battles over Free Grace, which could only have appealed to a more adult local audience.

Newbery's *The History of the Mercolians* exemplifies the evils of money, the dignity of labour — ploughman, artisan and tradesman — time-honoured themes for didactic literature for the young if not intended for adult practice. But here too the original writer went a little further than was usual. Money having corrupted morals, the King makes the people bring all their money every four years into the public treasury, when it is redistributed in equal shares to all alike. Those who have accumulated more "by honest means" earn "the thanks of the community" and marks of royal favour. This naive treatment of money and the clumsy device of periodic redistribution based on pure altruism, was cut out of Spence's version. *The History of Crusonia* had already given a better scheme. (It may be noticed in all his stories that the Crusonians or Spensonians were not of a saving disposition but spent most of their dividend as soon as it came to hand, enjoying the pleasure of the moment like sensible people, not to mention that saving in any form was considered sinful by his Glassite connections). On the other hand he retained the classical tale of corrupting the enemy's army with gold and perhaps this was the germ of the Spensonian strategy of offering double pay for life to deserters from an enemy (as in *An Infallible Way to make Peace at any Time)* in earnest of the benefits to expect from the establishment of Spensonianism. There is also a description of elections by open voting. The Mercolians are said to be far behind the Crusonians in political wisdom, "and carry on their improvements very slowly like the English . . . or the American Sluggard".

An Account of what passed on a journey with old Zigzag has never been discussed. On the surface it is simply a lesson about kindness to animals and has nothing to do with political theory. However, it is in fact a series of amusing fables with an application to human affairs — social inequality in the story of the bees and the ants, the ingratitude of cruel masters in the case of the cock or the plough horses. The comment on social ethics is not markedly more radical than other contemporary humane moralizing. The treatment of animal consciousness and natural rights extending throughout creation may be compared with William Godwin's more thoughtful and amusing fable-writing for children. It appeared as an ingredient of that broadly humane social harmony which was more important to these thinkers in the long run than any formal argument about political rights and essential for the enjoyment of life. Spence's story in *The Supplement to the History of Robinson Crusoe* is word for word a slightly abridged version of an older one in another Carnan and Newbery children's book, *The Valentine's Gift* (1777). This book was reissued unchanged by Francis Power, grandson of John Newbery and successor to Francis Newbery, in 1790. There may have been other editions. The last seems to be by J. Lumsden & Son, Glasgow, c. 1824, with new illustrations by Richard Austin. This is evidence of long-lasting popularity. The Zigzag story in these editions is entitled *A Lecture. To let down the Pride of Man or an account of what passed on a journey with Old Zigzag.* It is linked with the main Valentine story and there is a description of Zigzag. One of the passages omitted by Spence uses London associations for general illustration — "I never heard that the dogs of Islington went in a body to destroy the dogs at Newington" (p. 40). The style also shows that it was not by Spence.

These borrowings show that Spence in his youth was influenced by a progressive trend of humanitarian liberalism and non-denominational ethics which might be said to reflect criticism of the dominant norm from the point of view of the working lower-middle class and artisan sections.

1783. "The Rights of Man".

This ballad, often called "The Rights of Man in Verse", to the tune of *Chevy Chase,* summarized the Plan in 31 stanzas. (In some copies only 30 stanzas are given). No first print is known. It appeared in *Pigs' Meat* III, p. 250, in *Spence's Songs* and on numerous broadsides, usually with the heading *The Rights of Man. First published in the Year 1783.* The "dividend of rents", equal for all men, women and children, is mentioned. Generally there is a footnote briefly explaining Parish finance.

A new version in 20 verses, some entirely new and some slightly altered or rearranged, was published in 1819 with the title *The Wrongs of Man or Things as they Are by a Spencean Philanthropist,* and a companion piece, *The Rights of Man, or things as they were intended to be by Divine Providence.* These were by Thomas Evans.

Spence claimed that he was the first writer to use the phrase "the Rights of Man". When he visited the miner who had retired to live on Marsden Rock in 1780 to escape from a landlord, he chalked over the hearth

"Ye landlords vile, whose man's place mar
  Come levy rents here if you can,
Your steward and lawyers I defy
  And live with all the Rights of Man".

This anecdote is given in a note to another ballad, *The Rights of Man for me* composed during confinement in Newgate in 1794.

Sykes gave the year for the occupation of the cave as 1782.

> "In the summer of this year a man near 80 years of age and his wife made one of the caverns under Marsden rocks, near Shields, their place of residence. In the earlier part of his life, he had been a miner at Allenheads, but having removed to Shields, to avoid the charge of housekeeping, he and his wife formed the resolution to retire to one of these caves, which they furnished. The romantic situation and the singularity of the thing drew numbers of people to visit them, whom they accommodated with refreshments, even ladies and gentlemen in carriages drove to the place and partook of the old couple's cheer."

A more commercial-minded man took over the cave later and turned it into a refreshment room and tourist attraction. Local tradition knew the old miner as 'Jack the Blaster'. Mr. Alex Robson of North Shields, the veteran seamen's leader who figured in the S.S. Linaria case and was active in the Red International Seamen's Union of the nineteen-thirties, claims to be a descendant.

This completes Spence's known Newcastle publications. There are references and quotations in them which show that he already knew a number of important writers and that he had probably begun collecting the kind of extracts later published in *Pigs' Meat.* They show that the basic machinery of the Plan as a method of establishing and maintaining social equality had been worked out, but not the clearer conception of the class aspect or the revolutionary means which characterize his writings in the nineties.

1792. The Case of Thomas Spence, Bookseller, the Corner of Chancery Lane, London, who was committed to Clerkenwell Prison on Monday the 10th of December 1792 for selling the second part of Paine's "Rights of Man", and a bill of indictment found against him to which is added an extract from a letter from His Grace the Duke of Richmond to the Chairman of the Committee of the County of Sussex convened at Lewes, January 18th 1783 for the purpose of presenting a petition to the House of Commons to take into consideration the unequal State of representation in Parliament &c.
London, 1792.

The pamphlet contains precisely what is specified. It is a protest against unlawful detention, treatment under arrest and harassment of the victim and his family by the agents of Reeves's society. It was published while Spence was awaiting trial and announced that a fellow-bookseller, Mr. Hamilton, was collecting subscriptions to pay for his defence. An anecdote about the Duke of Argyle taken from the *Weekly Miscellany* for 8 February, 1779 is appended, apparently just to fill up an extra page. Some pages which appear to be wrongly numbered were put together in the wrong order and the culminating protest and appeal which should have come at the end is inserted in the middle of the narrative. There is nothing about Spence's theories, but the pamphlet is an energetic vindication of the right to freedom of speech and press.

1793. The Case of Thomas Spence . . . to which is added the affecting case of James Maccurdy a native of Ireland who was committed to Clerkenwell Bridewell for distributing certain seditious papers where he died in a few days.
London. 1793.

This is a second(?) edition of the preceding. The part relating to Spence's arrest is identical with the first. Both these pamphlets have usually been ascribed to Spence, although the style and the third person narrative certainly suggest other authorship, possibly Mr. Hamilton. The second edition makes this possibility almost certain.

The two paragraphs headed *Reflections* (pp. 10, 11) which interrupt the narrative in the first edition, are placed at the end of both narratives under the heading *Conclusions* and are followed by an appeal which no one can imagine Spence publishing anonymously, since in that limited circle of radical publishers everybody would have know who had written it.

The author of the pamphlet writes:

> "Britons! The two foregoing narratives will surely excite the indignation and compassion of every friend to society . . . One of the victims is gone . . . but one remains — he has braved the storm with more firmness than commonly falls to the share of a single individual. He has combated the enemies of the Law and of the Liberty of the Press at the repeated hazard of his life and liberty. His cause is yours — his punishment will be yours. It is earnestly hoped you will not desert him, and though you may be branded with infamy by those who wish to loosen the bonds of society, you will have the happy recompense of being satisfied that you have struggled to preserve the law of your devoted country uncontaminated.
>
> "Those therefore who feel an interest in the grand cause may have

an opportunity of contributing towards Mr. Spence's defense and support by applying to Mr. Hamilton, Bookseller, near Gray's Inn, Holborn, where a book for the purpose lays open".

There is no publisher's name or printer's imprint on either pamphlet. It will be noted that neither spelling nor language is typical of Spence's usage and that the ideas in the above quotation, for example, are not too clearly expressed. Had it been Spence writing, he would have found some equally telling argument without defending the sanctity of the existing laws. In what he himself said about the matter after his release, he merely shows the arbitrariness with which the law was applied or broken.

1793 — 1795 PIGS' MEAT

Vol. I

One Pennyworth of Pigs' Meat; or, Lessons for the Swinish Multitude. Published in weekly penny numbers Collected by the Poor Man's Advocate in the course of his reading for more than Twenty Years. Intended To promote among the Labouring Part of Mankind proper Ideas of their Situation, of their Importance and of their Rights, and to convince them That their forlorn Condition has not been entirely overlooked and forgotten nor their just Cause unpleaded, neither by their Maker nor by the best and most enlightened of Men in all Ages.
London:
Printed for T. Spence, at the Hive of Liberty, No. 8, Little Turnstile, High Holborn.

Vol. II

Pigs' Meat; or, Lessons for the People, alias (according to Burke) The Swinish Multitude. Published in penny numbers weekly Collected by the Poor Man's Advocate (an old persecuted Veteran in the Cause of Freedom) in the Course of his Reading for more than Twenty Years. Intended To . . . Ages. Volume II.
London:
Printed for T. Spence, No. 8, Little Turnstile, High Holborn.

Vol. III

Pigs' Meat; or, Lessons for the People . . . Volume III.
London:
Printed for T. Spence, No. 8, Little Turnstile, High Holborn.

Volume III began to appear after Spence's release from prison December 1794. The title page is similar to Volume II. The First and Second volumes have two different biblical quotations under the title. For Volume III these are replaced by the following verses:—

"The Pigs to starve, bad Men in pow'r.
Their Feeder sent to doleful Gaol,
And eager bent him to devour,
Long time the Pigs did for him wail.
But now the Storm is blown o'er,
That drove him from his blest Employ;
And to his Task return'd once more,
He feeds them with his wonted Joy".

Pigs' Meat is a collection of articles, extracts and verses from the works of a wide range of about seventy different writers ancient and modern, issued weekly in penny numbers. These were afterwards bound together to form three volumes of 284 pages each with a list of contents at the end of each volume. The three volumes were also bound together in one volume. The complete work went into second and third editions, also in one and three-volume sets, with and without minor additions, including illustrations, and odd sheets headed "Loose Meat for Pigs" which had probably been distributed separately at irregular intervals. Detailed description of sets in libraries and the evidence relating to dates of publication have been adequately dealt with by Rudkin. The complete volumes were sold over a considerable period and were advertised in Spence's other publications and by other booksellers. It is impossible to say how many copies were printed but it is the only work of his of which many copies survived, thanks no doubt to the greater durability of the bound copies. However, within a few years of his death *Pigs' Meat* was already a collector's piece. A catalogue of 1818 (when there was still a Spencean organisation in existence) for example, describes it as "very scarce" and prices a copy at 16/-. Extracts from various authors which appeared in *Pigs' Meat* are also found in Chartist newspapers in the 'forties. *The Chartist Circular* acknowledges that an extract from Sinclair has been taken from *Pigs' Meat,* Vol. I, second edition. It must long have retained its value as a source book for popular political information.

Among the more substantial pieces are long extracts from Sprigges's *A Modest Plea for an Equal Commonwealth* and nearly the whole of Midon's *History of the Rise and Fall of Masaniello.* Both of these are given without the author's names, but the reproduction is so meticulous that it is possible to identify the editions which were used, both of which would have been available at Newcastle. Certainly some of the extracts belonged to a common stock of quotations frequently used by democratic and Whig authors at that time or to be found in radical works of the seventeen-nineties, but many of Spence's selections were not the most frequently quoted, and it would be more difficult to locate secondary sources than to suppose that in most cases he used the books in which they originally appeared. Spence called *Pigs' Meat* "the Political Bible", not perhaps in the sense of infallibility, but as a collection of various writers who have sought for truth. "The Honey or Essence of Politics" was another epithet which showed his intentions.

A number of Spence's own political tracts and poems were printed in *Pigs' Meat,* including the above-mentioned edition of his Lecture.

1793. "The Rights of Man by Question and Answer".
Pigs' Meat, vol. I, pp. 261-267.

This satirical dialogue appeared before the reprint of the Lecture, but gives prominence to the dividend of rents. "The people in every parish or district should appoint collectors to receive the rents; and divide them equally among themselves, or apply them to what public uses they may think proper".

1794. "For the Swinish Multitude. The Rights of Swine. An Address to the Poor".
Pigs' Meat, vol. II, pp. 97-102.

Most of the items in *Pigs' Meat* show author or source. Pseudonyms or book titles without other identification are or were easily recognizable (with the exceptions above mentioned and some of Spence's own verses). This item is signed in *Pigs' Meat* and in other copies "A Friend of the Poor" at the end. It is found also bound up in the volume of Spence's pamphlets which belonged to his friend George Cullen. This copy is not a separate pamphlet but consists of pages from a copy of *Pigs' Meat.*

Spence said in his letter to *The Morning Post* (reprinted in *Pigs' Meat,* vol. III) that he had completed volume II when he was arrested on 17 May 1794. As there were 24 weekly parts of 12 pages each, pages 97 to 102 should have been the 9th issue, and allowing for discrepancies this should have appeared in the third or fourth week of January. Now at the trial of Thomas Hardy and others in 1794 the prosecution included in evidence among papers seized from members of the LCS, a copy of *The Rights of Swine* dated "January 5, Stockport". It appears to be identical with the *Pigs' Meat* version and with that printed by Lee except for the word "Stockport". Unfortunately we do not know whether "Stockport" appeared as part of the original printed text and no other Lancashire copy seems to have been noted so far to confirm the existence of a Stockport edition. The Lancashire origin is suggested by the description of the textile operatives' distress and the tyranny of the millowners. It might be supposed that a copy was sent to somebody in London after 5 January in time to appear in *Pigs' Meat* in the second half of January.

The opinions expressed in *The Rights of Swine* are undoubtedly akin to Spence's. The style could also be his. The oracular conclusion could be compared with *A Fragment of an Ancient Prophesy* or with *"A Dream"* in *Spence's Songs.*

1794. "The Marine Republic". *Pigs' Meat,* vol. II, pp. 68-72.
"A further account of Spensonia". *Pigs' Meat,* vol. II, pp. 205-218.

These two articles make up the second, or third, Utopian fantasy developing the story of Crusonia. There are two important additions: the example of co-operative enterprise and partnership based on the division of labour, and the international character of the system.

Several brothers receive a ship called The Spensonia from their father who instructs them to keep it as their common property and inheritance and to run it as a brotherly partnership. They are to elect officers and pay everyone according to their work, but share the net profits of every voyage equally among all. After shipwreck on a desert island they found a new country to which they give the name of the ship and the constitution of their Marine Republic. The second article begins from the Crusonian incident of intercourse with mainland Indians, which leads to the rapid progress of the country. This theme is expanded in a number of ways. (1) The speech of the first Indian visitor is an eloquent, ironical criticism of European society and condemnation of colonial expansion by conquest, fraud and missionary hypocrisy. (2) The rights of strangers in Spensonia. (3) The universal equality of all races of man insuring peace and fraternity. (4) The uniting of savage independence with civilized progress. The second article is in the form of a dialogue between a traveller from Europe and a Spensonian, in which various objections to the Plan are answered and the Field Day or Jubilee celebrations are described. The main topics discussed are:

1. The land system and its effects in encouraging industry.

2. The reasons why landlordism cannot revive in Spensonia; thanks to the ballot which prevents political corruption and the arming of the people.

3. A general indictment of the landowning class and the need to destroy it.

4. Practical functions of the Parish authority.

5. A long concluding passage justifying the Spensonian system as in accordance with God's intentions, and showing the material benefits of the progress of knowledge, invention and medicine which flow from it.

In touching on the two highly topical points, the ballot and the militia, as the guarantee of political liberty, Spence does not fail to point out that factionalism and a permanent "conflict of interest" are inherent in the system of private property. There must therefore be a radical change instead of futile "mending the constitution" and "the extirpation" of "your real monsters" who "toil (men) to death in their endless drudgery, harass and butcher them in villainous wars, and drag them from every social connection". Naturally it is landlordism not landlords that is to be exterminated but the whole tone of the writing shows that Spence had arrived at an uncompromisingly revolutionary position.

1795. *A Letter from Ralph Hodge to his Cousin Thomas Bull.*

This is a 12-page tract without title page or cover, the text beginning on page 1. At the bottom of page 12 is an advertisement of complete 3-volume sets of *Pigs' Meat* giving Spence's address, showing that the *Letter* could not have been published earlier than the spring of 1795 and that it could not have been an extra number of *Pigs' Meat,* as has been suggested.

Spence does not deal here with any part of his special doctrines but with topical grievances — enclosures, low wages, ministerial corruption and patronage, the national debt swindle, and so on, and above all the machinations of the Society for Preserving Liberty and Property against Republicans and Levellers. He appeals to those who earn "fourpence, sixpence or even a shilling a day" to understand their debased position in society and to be loyal to their own class. His appeal is more decidedly to urban journeymen and labourers. Taken together with *The End of Oppression* published in the same year, it might seem that Spence had gained more concrete understanding of the class struggle and that class interests not abstract principles determine the part that a man plays.

The *Letter* satirizes great placemen and their humble time-server, Thomas Bull, who are all alike worried about the safety of their jobs. Thomas Bull is very like the conservative working man of later Socialist satire and cartoon. After informing on fellow-villagers who tore down enclosure fences, he had been forced to leave home to escape their vengeance. His patrons found him menial employment in a public office of some kind, not at all the fine "situation" he had expected as a reward for his loyalty. But the story did not only satirize the system of patronage and its accompaniment of informers who repeatedly exposed themselves. The transformation from contented village blacksmith to down-trodden town worker without a proper trade was the typical case of many through no fault of their own. A contemporary writes:

> "It is no uncommon thing for four or five wealthy graziers to engross a large enclosed lordship, which was before in the hands of twenty or thirty farmers, and as many tenants or proprietors. All these are thereby thrown out of their livings, and many other families, who were chiefly employed and supported by them, such as blacksmiths, carpenters, wheelwrights and other artificers and tradesmen, besides their own labourers and servants".

The *Letter* is followed by Questions on the National Debt, showing how sinecures are financed and an extract from Volney's *Ruins* which reinforces the class character of government.

The *Letter* is a parody of *One Pennyworth of Truth from Thomas Bull to his Brother John.* This was the first tract for mass distribution published by the Society for Preserving Liberty and Property. A number of other Bull "letters" followed by various hands, attacking or defending the Associators. Spence was not only satirizing the original but some of the moderate Reformers' answers, like Ann Jebb's *Two Pennyworth of Truth for a Penny or a True Statement of Facts with an Apology for Tom Bull in a letter to Brother John* (1793), which asserts that the French would have been satisfied with Reform without overturning the Monarchy, and particularly insisting that Reform should not and could not entail equality of property.

A Few Words But no Lies from Roger Bull to his Brother Thomas (undated) is an answer to this line of reasoning and to *One Pennyworth of Truth* at the same time. The writer claims to speak "for the labouring interest", and remarks that "the rich" (i.e. Whig and middle class Parliamentary Reformers — PMA) invite the starving people to rejoice with them over the French Revolution and the Rights of Man but "snivel" if they think their own wealth is menaced. — "Poor creatures! They are much to be pitied. They cannot work and to beg they are ashamed". 'Roger Bull' condemns 'Tom' for the same reasons as 'Ralph Hodge'. "A poor man who is an enemy to the interests of the poor is an unnatural monster". The original 'Tom Bull' created by the Association's writer was precisely the dimwitted crawler whom Spence addresses.

One Pennyworth of Truth concluded with a warning. John Bull shouldn't think that he has nothing to lose. "If thy body goes to the Gallows and thy soul to the Devil, won't that be a *Loss* John?" — a pessimism neatly expressed in a similar effort in verse by a clergyman called *The Riot* intended to be bought in quantities by charitable or patriotic gentry for distribution to the poor.

> "And when of two evils I'm asked which is best,
> I'd rather be hungry than hang'd, I protest".

There were other angry replies to this cynicism besides Spence's. For example: Thomas Bently, *The Poor Man's Answer to the Rich Associates,* 1793, and James Parkinson's

> *Knaves' Acre Association. Resolutions adopted at a meeting of Placemen, Pensioners &c. held at the Sign of the Crown Knaves' Acre for the purpose of forwarding the Designs of the Place and Pensions Club lately instituted in London. Faithfully copied from the original minutes of the*

Society by Old Hubert. Dated 1793. (Copies of the last named exist with "Printed for T. Spence", and address on the title page, but Parkinson's authorship is confirmed by the advertisement of his pamphlets in *The Times* for 15 DECEMBER|, 1794).

1795/6

1. The End of Oppression; or, a Quartern Loaf for Two-Pence; being a Dialogue between an Old Mechanic and a Young One. Concerning the Establishment of the Rights of Man.

   Behold the grand, th' heav'n like simple plan,
   That soon will bring in use the Rights of Man.
   Then who'd be last such happiness to know?
   For hope of quick relief doth lessen half our woe.

   London:
   Printed for the Author, and sold by T. Spence, No. 8, Little Turnstile, High Holborn; Patriotic Bookseller and Publisher of Pigs' Meat.

2. The End of Oppression; being a Dialogue . . .
   Second Edition.
   London:
   Printed for the Author . . .

The title page of the second edition is the same as the first except for the omission of "a quartern loaf . . ." and the verses. There are a few minor changes in the text. *The Jubilee Hymn* is added under the heading: *"A Song, to be Sung at the End of Oppression, or the Commencement of the political Millennium, when there shall be neither Lords nor Landlords, but God and Man will be all in all. First printed in the Year 1782".* Neither edition specifies authorship or date of publication. A copy of the first edition has Ms. notes on the title page including "By T. Spence (Few issued)" beside the title. The title is given among other works by Spence on the title page of *The Meridian Sun* (1796) and in an advertisement in the second edition of *Pigs' Meat* vol. III. It is not certain when the latter appeared but probably in 1795 or 1796. A letter from a reader dated 17 May, 1796, printed in *A Fragment of an Ancient Prophesy* says that the writer bought a copy of *The End of Oppression* "a few days back". The probability is therefore that *The Meridian Sun* and the second edition of *The End of Oppression* both appeared in the spring of 1796.

1796? Spence's Recantation of the End of Oppression
And he smote them Hip and Thigh with a great Slaughter. Judges XV. 8.
London:
Printed for T. Spence, No. 8, Little Turnstile, High Holborn; Patriotic Bookseller and Publisher of Pigs' Meat.

There is no date, but must be taken to have appeared very shortly after *The End of Oppression.*

1796. A Fragment of an Ancient Prophecy. Relating, as some think, to the Present Revolutions.
(Being the Fourth Part of the END OF OPPRESSION).
London:
Printed for T. Spence, No. 8, Little Turnstile, High Holborn, Patriotic Bookseller; and Publisher of PIGS' MEAT &c.
1796.

In spite of its fanciful form and its brevity (three pages), *A Fragment* is a serious statement of Spence's reading of the most important events of his time. It was intended to be read as the final part of *The End of Oppression.* The complete series is not now known in a single volume edition as advertised. A footnote on page 1 of the *Fragment* states that all four parts were on sale. Inside the title page appears a letter signed 'A Democrat', dated 17 May, 1796 saying that the writer bought a copy of *The End of Oppression* "a few days back" and hoping that unless Spence stops selling it, the book will be publicly burnt and Spence hanged. After *The End of Oppression,* or perhaps simultaneously with it, Spence had re-issued his Lecture, with the new 'Conversation' addressed to the same class of plebeian democratic reformers as the two 'Mechanics' in *The End of Oppression* and the critics for whom the *Recantation* was written. I would suggest that *The Meridian Sun,* without which Spence's solution of the social problem would be incomplete, was to serve as the third part of the work, or perhaps the first part. However I have no other evidence to support this hypothesis.

When in real life there was speculation about a possible revolution among people like Spence's 'Mechanics', no doubt some reformer would ask "What about the French Revolution? Has it brought the people the Rights of Man as we conceive them?" To complete *The End of Oppression* it was therefore necessary to relate it to actual events, to define the revolution in France and examine the immediate prospects. He must also give a fuller answer to the question raised in *The End of Oppression* (page 5): "And what means the inveterate war commenced by the Aristocracy of the world against France?"

Spence's answer is that the French Revolution achieved "a mixed kind of Liberty", but the people having now aroused everywhere will continue to struggle for the full Rights of Man.

In contrast to the style of the *Fragment,* it is followed by two Odes. *Resignation; An Ode to the Journeymen Shoemakers, who refused to Work except their Wages were raised* by Peter Pindar (John Walcot), brings the reader back to the fundamental "quartern loaf for twopence". The other, *Ode to Burke,* is a reminder that the shortcomings of the French Revolution did not put the common enemy in any better light.

1796. The Reign of Felicity, being a plan for civilizing the Indians, of North America; without infringing on their national or individual Independence, in a coffee-house dialogue, between a Courtier, an Esquire and a Farmer.
London:
Printed for T. Spence, No. 8, Little Turnstile, High Holborn; Patriotic Bookseller, and Publisher of PIGS' MEAT, and the END OF OPPRESSION.
1796.

Inside the title page there is a short paragraph on the surplus revenue from the rents of the whole country that might be available as public property to "establish the Reign of Felicity". A note at the foot of the last page (p. 12) advises the reader to consult *The End of Oppression* in two parts, for further information about the Plan. This means that *Felicity* appeared before *A Fragment* and before part three of *The End of Oppression.*

There were two elaborate advertisements of *The Reign of Felicity.* A broadside headed *The Contrast* has a picture of an Ass laden with double panniers and two Indians, who say:

"Behold the civilized Ass.
Two pairs of panniers on his back.
The first with Rents a heavy mass,
With Taxes next his bones do crack".

The Ass says:

"I'm doomed to endless toil and care.
I was an ass to bear the first pair".

The design is signed 'W. Spence' (presumably Spence's son, William). *The Rights of Man* in Verse is given below in two columns, and finally

"Published 1 February 1796 by T. Spence, No. 8, Little Turnstile, Holborn. Publisher of a Plan to civilize the Indians".

A facsimile reproduction of the broadside is given by Waters.

A similar production, also signed "W. Spence" and dated 2 February, 1796, the *Disappointed Missionary,* is a more direct illustration of *The Reign of Felicity.* The Missionary exhorts the Indians as follows:

"God has enjoined on you to be Christians. Pay Rent and Tithes and become a Civilized people".

The Indians reply:

> "If Rents we once consent to pay
> Taxes on us you will lay
> And then our freedom's passed away".

Token dies of the Ass and of the Indians carry mottoes similar to these broadsides. The theme of missionaries as "dangerous civilizers" who introduce the buying and selling of land, reappears in *The Giant Killer* (No. 1, p. 7). The ass with double panniers will be found as a metaphor in *The End of Oppression* and in *The Rights of Infants.*

1797. The Rights of Infants; or, the Imprescriptable Right of MOTHERS to such a Share of the Elements as is sufficient to enable them to suckle and bring up their Young. In a Dialogue between the Aristocracy and a Mother of Children. To which are added, by way of *Preface* and *Appendix,* Strictures on Paine's Agrarian Justice.
By T. Spence,
Author of the *Real Rights of Man, End of Oppression, Reign of Felicity, Pigs' Meat, &c.*
London:
Printed for the Author, at No. 9, Oxford Street, lately removed from No. 8, Little Turnstile.
1797.

The title page has quotations from Peter Pindar's *Ode to the Shoemakers* and from *Paradise Lost.* The Preface is signed 'London, March 19, Tho. Spence'. The statement in a footnote to the Preface that *The Rights of Infants* had been written before the appearance of *Agrarian Justice* need not be doubted. Publication may have been delayed through Spence's bankruptcy(?) and removal from his shop in 1797 as seen from the title page.

The 'Preface' to *The Rights of Infants* ironically welcomes Paine's belated acknowledgement that the earth is common property. The 'Appendix' contrasts in parallel columns the different conclusions which the two authors draw from this common principle. A short 'Conclusion' elaborates Spence's theory of the claims of labour reinforcing the original right.

1798. The Constitution of a Perfect Commonwealth: Being the French Constitution of 1793, Amended and rendered entirely conformable to the WHOLE RIGHTS OF MAN.
Finis coronat opus.
The second edition. With a Preface, showing how to study politics.
By T. Spence, Author and Publisher of that best Repository of sound and standard Politics, entitled PIGS' MEAT, and of several Tracts on the imprescriptable Rights of Mankind.
London,
Printed and sold by the Author, At No. 9, Oxford Street. 1798.

The first edition does not seem to be traceable, unless this is to be regarded as the unrevised translation in *Pigs' Meat.* A third revised and corrected edition advertised as being reprinted at the end of the 1801 edition of *The Restorer* is also not known.

The French (Jacobin) Constitution of 1793 was published in three parts in *Pigs' Meat vol. I.* It is identical with the English translation published together with the French text by J. Debrett and by J. Ridgeway. It is presumed to be by Thomas Christie. Christie had published translations of the Declaration of the Rights of Man, the Draft and the final Constitution of 1791, together with his own narrative of the Revolution — a masterly account by an enlightened scholar and historian in answer to Burke's attacks. Christie, who was a friend of Horne Tooke, was appointed by the Convention to assist in producing the multilingual versions of the new Constitution, which it was the intention to circulate to all countries. The project was overtaken by the war and the Constitution itself was suspended. Only the English and Italian versions appeared in Paris and the English came out in two practically identical editions in London.

By his consistent support of the French Republic, Spence recognized the world significance of the Revolution, and this was still evident in *The Giant-Killer* in 1814. He did not fail to present the new Constitution to the readers of *Pigs' Meat* at the first opportunity as an advance towards popular liberty. It is true that the Jacobin leaders having come to power through wider plebeian support, gave with one hand what they took away with the other, and while granting a universal franchise even reversed their previous policy as to the mandatory character of the representation and reinforced the law against workers' combinations. But their still-born Constitution remained the primary charter of plebeian egality, providing the slogan of "bread and the Constitution of 1793" for the popular demonstrations and the rising of 1795. It was the demand around which the old militants too late attempted to form a unity of the left and the Act of Insurrection prepared by the Babeuvistes declared "The aim of the insurrection is the re-establishment of the Constitution of 1793, of liberty, equality and happiness of all". Possibly the inner circle of the Conspiracy did not intend to operate the Constitution, or not in its original form, but many must have regarded it as Spence did. It was the first state document that had in words recognised a primary right to existence and principles which could be logically extended to mean a great deal more.

The English translation was meticulously literal, and kept a number of French expressions. *The Constitution of a Perfect Commonwealth* added and adapted to bring it into line with Spence's Plan without altering a single word that could be retained. The Spencean Declaration has 38 articles only 5 of which are completely new; the French has 35. The rest of the document follows the same arrangement of subjects with 120 as against 124 articles. Nevertheless it must be read with an English not a French context in mind.

The resulting patchwork is evidence that Spence could still only systematize in the form of *a priori* generalities. It was always assumed that a constitution based on true first principles — "framed according to the exactness of Nature" *(Restorer* Letter XII) — must be universally applicable. Thus in taking over the prefatory Declaration, Spence appears to deduce economic rights from an abstract principle of liberty in spite of his repeated statement that liberty depends on or is equivalent to property relations. Similarly he accepts a large part of the original provisions regardless of their intention in the context and regardless of their local relevance, as though ready made for his purpose. He was not one to look an historic gift horse in the mouth. No doubt he wished to show that his sytem could be based on a coherent legal system which was not arbitrarily invented, but had a factual precedent in the decisions of a national legislature. In this adaptation he was no more naive than the revolutionary Secret Directory which discussed how the Constitution could be revised and supplemented in order to create the institutions of a true equality.

This apparently formalistic adaptation was at the same time a critique of the bourgeois essence of the Republic. Spence begins by adding five entirely new points in the Declaration, with the appropriate changes in the other articles. Thus while accepting bourgeois democratic or egalitarian principles at face value, these innovations destroy the illusion of class harmony which was the precarious basis of the French Constitution. The more radical leaders had foreseen that the Declaration of Rights was bound to inspire demands for greater economic equality in contradiction to the vaguely formulated freedom for capitalist accumulation and private enterprise. This was strikingly expressed in the struggle for a controlled economy in 1793 when in petitions from the Paris Sections demands for requisitioning and the restriction of prices and wages, even including a ceiling on private wealth, appealed to the Constitution where the Jacobin bourgeoisie only saw the need for practical measures in immediate economic difficulties.

Spence naturally did not understand the French Constitution as a reflection of contradictions within the Convention or as a compromise between the bourgeoisie and their all-important allies the sans-culottes. He saw factional struggles and imperfect conceptions of liberty. In *A Fragment* he regarded the revolutionary leaders as a "party" or a number of "parties", that is personal factions, not representative of the people or of a class, but clever politicians who had seized power by a compromise between popular rights and property interests. The Jacobin leaders and their successors were alike intent on securing the plunder of the aristocracy for themselves. Nevertheless he never doubted the historical significance of the Revolution which had awakened "the Multitude". In the Preface to his Constitution it was this that he had in mind when he said that the nations would now never rest until the true solution had been reached.

The Preface illustrates the working of the dividend, parish finances and public works as applied in the concrete example of the village of Little Dalby described in Nichols's *History of Leicestershire.* The dividend paid to each individual out of net profits from the rents is given special prominence along with more detail about the way in which such a parish could develop its resources. In order to show how the plan will benefit the people at large, Spence here gives a definition of social classes and how they will be affected by the change to the Spensonian system.

From the Little Dalby statistics Spence calculated a hypothetical yearly dividend of £10 per head. This was a little more that half the salary he had once enjoyed as a schoolmaster. It might not have sounded very tempting to a well-to-do landowner threatened with expropriation, but the total that would have come to a family with several children would have seemed luxury to those large numbers of the labouring poor who lived from hand to mouth, seldom had work all the year round and thought in terms of poor relief standards.

The Preface became the best known version of Spence's Plan. Most of it was reproduced in the Biographies of Spence by Evans and Davenport. It was probably known to Malthus.

The Preface ends with an appeal for the earnest study of "the chief of sciences, the science of the Rights of Man" to solve the problem of "abject servile poverty" in civilized society. "The dark ages will never more return; wherefore then should we prolong anarchy?" All nations have now a smattering of the Rights of Man and are tormented by uncertainty; "the rich know not what to fear, and the poor know not how far their rights extend". Those who can think must go deeper into the matter to discover a practical system of social truth and justice. The way to study politics is as in any other science, to put aside all other considerations and only concentrate on finding the right answer, as an upright judge hears a case or a boy sits down "to work a question in arithmetic".

> "This is undoubtedly the most likely way to arrive at the truth, and to make us adepts in the science we aim at. Surely you would not confine your pupil in arithmetic . . . to such and such a result of your problem, whether in truth it can be so according to rule or right reason? . . . If then we are not to sit down to politics in the same free state of mind as to our other studies, for God's sake, I say, speak out, and tell us to which side we are to incline at the expense of truth?
>
> I say, are we at the price of our sacred rights and interests to do violence to truth in favour of cannibals? Are we to determine right or wrong, that we and our children shall and ought to be less in the scale of animal beings, than worms and caterpillars? . . . Detested by the

mode of education that would confine us to believe so! Sophists come forward! Speak out, and tell us how we are to study the Chief of Sciences, the science of the Rights of Man! Tell us how to think, ay, and likewise how to feel! Tell us whether we shall study as with the unprejudiced minds of untainted youth, or with the determined, mercenary, warped sophistry of our critical literati?".

The Constitution therefore was presented as Spence's contribution to this search for a new system.

1807. The Constitution of Spensonia. A Country in Fairy-Land, Situated between Utopia and Oceana. Brought from thence by Captain Swallow.
The fourth Edition.
Finis coronat opus.

This edition was appended to *The Important Trial of Thomas Spence,* 1807, with which the pagination is continuous. It has a separate title page without place or date of publication. This is the same version which had appeared "printed in the Crusonian manner" in the phonetic edition of *The Important Trial* for private circulation in 1803, except for a different verse epilogue. There is a note inside the main title page in both these editions to the effect that *The Constitution* had been twice issued before the trial. As it was then out of print Spence could not produce a copy for which the Judge had asked and "it is therefore added to the Trial now". It must be concluded that the third revised edition advertised in *The Restorer* in 1801 had not yet appeared and its publication must have been postponed. As Spence says that this "fourth edition" was what he would have submitted in court had it been available, it may be understood that the third revised edition, while retaining the title *The Constitution of a Perfect Commonwealth,* did not differ from *The Constitution of Spensonia.* As in the case of *the Supplement to the History of Robinson Crusoe's Island,* the phonetic version of the *Constitution,* 1803, is to be regarded as the third and the 1807 edition as the fourth (normal spelling) edition.

The Constitution of Spensonia has no separate preface. *The Restorer of Society* serves as the enlargement or interpretation of the *Constitution,* or the *Constitution* can be seen as the codification of *The Restorer.*

This new version is considerably expanded and contains 155 articles. The parts taken from the French Constitution have been further adapted. 'Department' and 'District' taken over from the French in *The Constitution of a Perfect Commonwealth* are dropped and the only territorial — administrative divisions are the parish and the county. 'Republic' is everywhere replaced with 'Commonwealth'. Several additional articles clarify the concept of parish autonomy and its relation to county administration and to the national legislature and executive council. Minor changes in the wording adjust earlier inconsistencies and ambiguities. In the *Declaration,* Art. 7 of the old version is omitted and Art. 7 of the new edition (corresponding to the old Art. 8) is brought into line with Art. 5.

The most important changes and additions relate to:—

1. Powers and functions of the Parishes, including leases and tenancies, public works, provision of the means of livelihood (right to work) and settlement, public storehouses (to check speculation in provisions), Quarter-Day procedure and obligation to provide schools.

2. Status and rights of female citizens, children and foreigners. (Articles 5-10).

3. Citizenship. The triple citizenship (local, proprietory and general) in *The Constitution of a Perfect Commonwealth* is replaced by parish settlement (Articles 5-8).

4. Dividend rights (Articles 11, 12).

5. Holidays, five-day week, statutory past days. (Article 155, where for the first time animals are guaranteed the right to rest by a constitutional act).

6. Finance (Articles 107, 108, 131).

7. Size of the national parliament and of the equal electoral constituencies. (Articles 47-49).

8. Colonies. (Articles 152-154). These points are an extremely important addition although anticipated in previous writings. Better information as to French colonial policy during and after the Revolution and the course of the Anglo-French conflict in the East and West Indies must have brought the question of colonial possessions more sharply to Spence's attention (c.f. *Restorer,* Letter VII). The Draft Constitution of February 1793 (cap. XIII, arts. 2, 3) had renounced annexation by conquest (in Europe). Spence makes the necessary distinction between peaceful settler colonization in uninhabited territory and colonial conquest, peaceful or otherwise.

Spence had elsewhere attached great importance to the ballot to safeguard democracy. In the new version Articles 19 and 20 of *The Constitution of a Perfect Commonwealth* have been omitted. It is left to the primary assemblies, the parishes, to decide what method of voting they adopt. The ballot came to be regarded as a major demand of parliamentary reform in the nineteenth century or even as an essential principle of democratic government, instead of an expedient necessary to protect voters under certain conditions from improper influence. In Spence's time many democrats still objected to the ballot on the grounds that honest convictions should and could be openly declared.

Spence's Constitution took over the Executive Council indirectly elected and appointed and separated in function from the legislature, which had been created by the first revolutionary government and retained in the Constitutions of 1791 and 1793. The aim was to strengthen administrative uniformity and central authority. Spence may have regarded it simply as a means of abolishing sinecures and corruption in administration or as a substitute for a permanent bureaucracy. In neither of his Constitutions is there a full definition of his concept of the federation of parishes. In *The Restorer,* (Letter I) an important function of county and national executives seems to be to adjust inter-parochial interests.

The later Spenceans always stated that a new constitution would be drawn up by a national convention. The "provisional Government" (the self-appointed revolutionary committee in *The End of Oppression)* would proceed immediately to make arrangements for elections. Having taken over the land, the parishes would call meetings to elect representatives to the convention. They would present their proposals for the reform of society to the convention, expecting that truth and reason would prevail among disinterested delegates of the people. Exactly what plan would be adopted however was left to the delegates' deliberations.

Spence's *Constitution* broke new ground. It rejected the basis of a purified or 'corrected' or 'restored' English constitution identified by some with the Bill of Rights and by others with a Saxon original, together with the procedures and institutions elaborated by Harrington, or later by Cartwright whose "Saxon" organisation of the population was to serve as a model for a new electoral and parliamentary system and for a radical party at the same time. Spence swept aside all the arguments about the alleged perfection of the English system, and all the hallowed traditions of the True Whigs which had provided much of the ammunition for Parliamentary reform polemics. Such old shibboleths as 'no taxation without representation', the right of petition, the Habeas Corpus and so on became meaningless. Spence wanted to show that it was possible and indeed necessary to start as he said from "clear ground", and the French Constitution provided a concrete precedent arising out of the dissolution of the old order of aristocracy. The triple hierarchy — King, Lords and Commons — being abolished, new laws require the approval of nine-tenths of the parishes in more than half the counties. So little is left of the system which was supposed to enshrine 'English Liberty' that not even the word 'Parliament' is to be found in document. Most public offices are elective for short terms. Magistrates are annually elected, criminal judges are appointed for short terms by the national Executive and arbitrators in civil causes by the County Assemblies. This machinery is not without interest, for it foreshadowed some of the constitutions of later working class organisations.

Sharing some of the egalitarian ideal of the French *sans-culottes* and "attributing to the revolutionary demands of the bourgeoisie a meaning which they did not have",[50] Spence attempted to resolve the contradiction by basing equality on common property. At the same time he reversed the centralizing aim of the French Constitution by restoring a more Rousseau-like concept of universal democracy such as the Jacobins on coming to power has so decisively rejected. In taking over almost literally the French state machinery, Spence began by equating his parishes to the primary assemblies. There was of course an important difference which was further underlined by the wording in *The Constitution of Spensonia.* The parishes were not merely deliberative bodies or electoral constituencies through which in theory the popular will controlled the central government. Local autonomy and popular will were based on proprietorship. Hence the parishes were organs of economic power, representing citizens not only politically but as producers and as owners of property. Collectively as producers and as planners of local agriculture and industry, parishes appeared as independent economic units regulating mutual interests with other communities through county and national representation. The concept is perhaps understandable before the existence of great national industries or system of communications. Vague as it may be, there is no doubt that Spence had in mind the voluntary planning of resources related to consumption on a national scale.

Radicals generally in some degree shared a suspicion of all central or remote government. In *The End of Oppression* Spence asked ironically how working people were going to be able to watch what their representatives did in Parliament. This was in reply to various middle class Parliamentary reformers who argued that universal suffrage would be quite safe because the masses would naturally choose their representatives from among their superiors, who have time, money and education.

In Spensonia all proceedings and accounts of all public bodies were to be printed and circulated and all draft legislation distributed throughout the country. As in the French Constitution, national deputies were not mandatory or subject to recall (a matter hotly contested in the Convention in 1793). In England it was generally agreed that annual Parliaments would be sufficient guarantee, and make unnecessary the mandate which certain bodies of constituents had attempted to operate in the form of election pledges and Instructions to Members of Parliament. Spence thought that the popular will must be given power where people live and work. He repeatedly showed that parish autonomy was the way in which ordinary people and an increasing number of them could participate in public life, and laid it down that sovereignty should be not national but parochial *(Restorer,* Letter VII). Although it is not stated in his *Constitution* it is probable that Spence supposed that the parishioners would choose their representatives from among themselves. They would therefore know what was expected of them. In *The Restorer* the expression used was a "convention of parochial delegates".

The Constitution does not lay down how the parish runs its internal affairs. It is not said whether it should elect an executive committee or what officers should be appointed or whether they are to be paid. The functions of the parish are defined. It administers the common property, collects the rents, sends in the national poundage to the central government, divides the surplus on Quarter Day, provides its own police, annually elects Justices of the Peace, and is further obliged to provide a school, to provide work or the means to produce, and continually to extend its economic and social activities. Quarter Day proceedings and celebrations are prescribed in detail. Electoral Assemblies of parish delegates regulate inter-parochial matters, nominate to the National Executive Council, carry out various administrative functions, including county schools, hospitals and judiciary.

Taking the words of the Declaration of Rights at face value, Spence gave them positive force by defining property relations. The ambiguous property clause in the French Declaration could apply to any system. Spence first copies this clause exactly as it stands, since, as he put it, the aim was not to abolish property but to make all proprietors. He then added other articles which make the intention of the first precise. The citizen is guaranteed his right to two kinds of property — personal effects, earnings, movables honestly acquired which he can dispose of at will, and his parochial property which he cannot alienate "being eternally incorporated with that of his fellow citizens". This parochial property consists of land, its appurtenances and natural products including man-made "fixtures" (cf. *Rights of Infants).* It is clear from other parts of the *Constitution* that public property includes anything acquired in the name of the parish such as grain stores, tools and animals, materials for building, provisions and clothing supplied to parish deputies *(Restorer,* and so on).

As *The Constitution* only systematised and added more machinery to the basic plan, in 1793 Spence was further on the road to a socialist theory of property than any of his contemporaries. At that date Babeuf accepted Robespierre's rejected draft of Article 17 of the Declaration as his "manifesto". In this draft the absolute right to private property was only qualified but a vague statement indicated that it should not be to the damage of others and that society is obliged to provide work or the means of subsistence for the destitute. Full freedom to accumulate and employ capital is not in any way limited. The vague undertaking to assist the poor could have technically been satisfied by the English Poor Law as it then was or by the claims of liberal governments in the nineteenth century, although usually claiming poor relief to be humane charity rather than a right. The motive was stated almost cynically by Marat, who after the usual interpretation of natural right concludes that work or maintenance for the poor must be provided in order to secure respect for property and public order. In these debates it was not suggested that there should be any substantial change in the distribution of wealth.

It is true that a number of rank and file leaders in the revolutionary period began to move from an egalitarian to a more communistic position, the main left wing tendency in the plebian *sansculottes* did not go further than to demand some control of free enterprise and usury. A well known programme proposed a ceiling for almost everything including, prices, profits, wages, number of workshops and workers. This was an anti-capitalist demand in order to perpetuate small scale private production in which competition was to be regulated by government. Spence's constitution sets limits only to the amount of land and other means of production which individual may rent temporarily for his own use, in order to prevent the accumulation of large fortunes. Neither wages nor profit from individual labour are limited. These and wealth accrueing to the community will increase. Tenancies will continually change hands to allow as many people as possible to enjoy the best sites. How this scheme would work in the case of industrial sites and buildings is not shown. Possibly large workshops, factories and other enterprises in Spensonia would be run as co-operative partnerships or public works as suggested in *The Restorer.* Whether voluntary partnerships were to be treated like other tenants or as public works is not explained. Evidently a general levelling up process is envisaged. In *The Constitution of Spensonia* as the leases of large farms fall in after 21 years the land will be divided into smaller holdings, while public enterprise will continually extend to raise the standard of all and more townworkers will be settled on land.

The middle class defined in the *Preface* to *The Constitution of a Perfect Commonwealth* evidently included small manufacturers and those on their way to becoming capitalist entrepreneurs. Spence foresaw the danger of a new wealthy class arising from among small producers. The measures by which he hoped to prevent disproportionately large accumulations were strengthened in *The Constitution of Spensonia.* In addition to the above mentioned 21 years lease without renewal and the gradual division of large estates, large amounts of land are in the meanwhile only let to tenants who are prepared to build under parish supervision. Arrangements between parishes and local development boards *(Restorer)* were intended to counterbalance differences in natural resources. A separate clause enjoins on parishes the special responsibility for the efficient regulation of prices, by establishing public stores to counteract hoarding and speculation in provisions and fuel. Apparently Spence believed that control of essentials would automatically stabilize all commodity prices. In addition it is laid down that leases are only granted to those who do not harm public interest in any way, so that the highest bidder would not automatically be entitled to the tenancy without collective approval. In *The Rights of Infants* it was emphasized that the collective landlord, that is the majority of lesser husbandmen and wage workers, always control access to "every species of revenue from lands and fixtures".

The productive "middle class" would employ labour. But since none are compelled by poverty to work for a wage and there will be no more unemployed surplus labour wages will be high. The farmer or manufacturer depending on the goodwill of fellow parishioners for his use of the means of production, can only expect to employ a helper who shares in any increased profit which he helps to produce. The relationship which Spence evidently had in mind was in the nature of personal service in simple commodity production where the master himself works. The prototype would have been farmers and artisans who used the additional labour of their families, or independent millwrights, blacksmiths and masons who employed one or two journeymen and apprentices; or small farmers who supplemented farming with handicrafts and hired skilled seasonal workers and extra help at harvest time. Article 22 in *The Constitution of Spensonia* reproduced word for word a pious formulation in the French. "The law does not acknowledge servitude, there can only exist an engagement of care and gratitude between the man who labours and the man who employs him". This together with the other article taken from the French guaranteeing individual freedom of choice as to occupation and to engage in trade, established free contract. In the English context "servitude" could denote the legal apprenticeship, the yearly or indefinite binding of miners and farm servants, the whole Master and Servant Act and so on. That is no doubt why Spence included this clause.

On the other hand these provisions taken together with the right of choice and change of settlement, articles encouraging trade, including the prohibition of all local or national tolls, taxes and excise would seem to provide two important prerequisites for capitalist development — a free commodity market and free and mobile labour force.

In addition to the dividend the main rights which are given specific guarantees in *The Constitution of Spensonia* are:—

1. Right of settlement after a year's residence, backed by the Parish's obligation to assist newcomers and strangers.

2. The right to work secured by the parish obligation to find work or tenancies and strengthened by the right to education and by the duty of the Parish to build workshops for rent, extend agriculture, fishing, forestry, mining, public works and to assist artisans and farmers with equipment.

3. The right to leisure by instituting the five-day week, public festivals, weekly markets, cultural facilities.

4. The right to the weekly cash payment of wages on the fourth day of the week.

5. The right of each parish to select students for the university.

6. The right to aid in any kind of misfortune and to medical care in sickness, with the provision of hospitals. (Spence's ideas about the duties of hospital doctors and the notification of infectious diseases are found in *The Restorer).*

7. The right of voluntary association and meeting and the freedom of publication.

8. Universal male eligibility for all public office.

9. The obligation on the parish to build dwelling houses apart from farms, and single rooms for rent with the prohibition of sub-letting, taken together with other rights, implies the right to a dwelling at reasonable rent.

There is no positive right to work in the French Constitution, only a permissive clause which guarantees free enterprise and contract. The right to existence read into but not expressly defined in the Declaration was not supported by practical provisions. The right to work already concretised in *The Constitution of a Perfect Commonwealth* is reinforced by various other provisions in *The Constitution of Spensonia.* It is further backed up by channeling resources into public works and enterprises. The right to existence is distinguished from the right to work, since it applies to all ages and conditions in all circumstances. The Spensonian state "honours the unfortunate". The right to work is treated primarily as the right of access to common property in the means of production. This is further secured by the planning of local economy and the functions of the parishes (in *The Restorer)* as boards of agriculture, fisheries and coal. The right to work can obviously only really exist in a controlled economy. The regulation of common resources, planned development, and some supervision of how land is used by individuals which appear in *The Constitution* and in *The Restorer* provide this condition at least in an embryonic form. These proposals also show that Spence's ideas were based as much on actual material needs and demands of working people as on any abstract principles of justice and equality. In fact the practical needs are given priority over the theoretical right of the individual to free self-determination.

1801. The Restorer of Society to its Natural State, in a Series of Letters to a Fellow Citizen. With a Preface, countering the objections of a gentleman who perused the manuscript, and the answers by the author.
By Thomas Spence.
Printed for the author and sold by J. Smith, James Street, Covent Garden.
1801.
A. Seale, Printer, Fitzroy Place, New Road.

The Preface is dated "London, February 5th, 1801". In one copy it is signed in handwriting 'T. Spence'. Spence was prosecuted for this pamphlet and the date of publication given in the Indictment was April 10th.

1803. Dhe Restorr ov Sosiete tu its nateural Stat.

This appears without separate title page in the phonetic version of *Dh'e Imp'ort'ant Tri'al ov T'om'is Sp'ens,* 1803.

1807. The Restorer of Society to its Natural State;
In a Series of Letters . . .

This appears as part of *The Important Trial of Thomas Spence,* 1807. There is an inside title page similar to that of the first edition but without the author's name, date or printer. The text is identical with the first edition but with the addition of Spence's comments and explanations made in court which are given in footnotes.

The Restorer is Spence's longest and most complete work consisting of fourteen letters under dates between July and December 1800. It is essential for a full understanding of the implications which Spence drew from his Plan. It adds to the descriptive detail of the future society begun in the Preface to *The Constitution of a Perfect Commonwealth.* There are many suggestions as to the way in which the people might use their power to introduce practical reforms. These are generally given as optional, emphasizing freedom of choice in the spirit of Rousseau's absolute democracy, but certain changes are stated as inevitable and others as probable. Here is foreseen an increasing spirit of mutual aid or mutual dependancy which will result in higher moral standards and readiness to serve others.

The title of the book has sometimes been misunderstood to imply the aim of restoring a past golden age. On the contrary, it is markedly concerned with the idea of a material and intellectual progress which has never yet existed. The natural state did not mean some former time, but the condition of society which functions according to the laws of nature and not perverted by an unnatural inequality. 'Restore' is used here in the meaning of 'repair', 'restore to health'. Spence made it quite clear that in his opinion it was impossible to bring back the small proprietors who were then being pushed out, much less to reinstate the primitive hunting park. It is in *The Restorer* particularly that he speaks of the conflict between increasing wealth and increasing poverty which must ultimately force men to create a new order of society.

The Restorer does not contain fundamentals that have not already been put forward in other tracts. The rejection of illusory hopes of Parliamentary Reform is more incisive. Revolutionary direct action is proposed and the "Mutiny on Land" is put forward as the model.

1803. Dh'e Imp'ort'ant Tr'al ov T'om'is Sp'ens F'or a P'ol'it'ik'al P'amfl'et 'entitld "Dhe Restorr ov Sosiete tw its nateural Stat", 'On Ma 27th 1801, 'at W'estm'instr H'o'ol, b'efor L'ord K'ene'un and a Speshal Jwre.
London:
Printed by A. Seale, Tottenham Court Road, for T. Spence.
1803.

This report of the trial was produced after Spence's release from prison not for sale but to present to friends who had contributed to his defence or fine. The work contains a table of the Spencean alphabet with examples; the Defence; *The Restorer of Society* (as part of the Defence), *The Constitution of Spensonia,* and a verse *Epilogue.* The Indictment was not printed in the phonetic script but as a separate pamphlet in ordinary orthography, by A. Seale, Printer, 15 Terrace, Tottenham Court Road, without a date.

1807. The Important Trial of Thomas Spence for a Political Pamphlet entitled "The Restorer of Society to its Natural State", on May 27th, 1801, at Westminster Hall, before Lord Kenyon and a Special Jury.
Second edition.
Printed by A. Seale, Tottenham Court Road.
1807.

This includes the indictment, the Defence, including *The Restorer of Society* with its own title page, *The constitution of Spensonia,* and a new verse *Epilogue.* There are two copies in the British Museum, and one in the Goldsmiths Library. All have Seale's imprint inside the title page, but only the Goldsmith's copy in 8-vo gives the date. The type of all three copies is identical with the same minor irregularities and spacing. It is unlikely that the undated copies belonged to an earlier edition published in 1803 (as Rudkin suggests) since the type would hardly have been kept intact for four years. The Indictment in all three copies is identical but has been entirely reset since the first printing. No doubt the phonetic version is to be regarded as the first edition, as in the case of *The Supplement to the History of Robinson Crusoe's Island.* Spence sent Charles Hall a copy of the phonetic version in the summer of 1807. Hall complained that he found it difficult to decipher. Presumably the normal spelling version was not yet available or it may be that Hall's caustic remarks persuaded Spence that he should bring out a new edition. On the last page there is "A Serious Caution" to preserve the book in case it should be suppressed.

At the end of this note the author "Takes his leave". This sounds as though Spence now felt that he had completed his work of expounding his Plan, as is also shown by the *"Finis coronat opus"* on the title pages of both *Constitutions.* While by "former edition" he meant the phonetic one and no other first edition in normal spelling can have been issued, the note also hints that being familiar through his token trade with the ways of collectors, he may have had the first edition printed in phonetic script in order to give his friends something that might later have a scarcity value. Even during his lifetime, it is said, his publications were bought up by curiosity hunters.

On the title pages of both editions there is a quotation from Milton — "A forbidden Writing is thought to be a certain Spark of Truth that flies up in the Face of them who seek to tread it out", and one from Isaiah, 29. There is also the following note:

> "As nearly the whole of that offensive Book with suitable remarks by way of Defence, was read by Mr. Spence to the Jury, the whole of it therefore is reprinted herein, as a Warning to poor Old England. 'And all the People shall hear, and fear, and do no more presumptuously'."

Spence's address is not given anywhere in this book. In the first edition of *The Restorer* it is given with the advertisement of the third edition of *The Constitution of a Perfect Commonwealth* as "No. 3, Great Castle Street, Oxford Market, and keeps a Book-stall near the Pantheon, Oxford Street". A single sheet headed *Something to the Purpose* giving extracts from *The Constitution of Spensonia,* has "Printed for T. Spence, Number Carrier and Bookbinder, No. 15 Princes Street, Soho, London" (bottom right) and "Seale & Bates, Printers, Tottenham Court Road" (bottom left), and is evidently later than 1807.

1814. The Giant-Killer, or, Anti-Landlord
No. 1. August 6, 1814.
No. 2. August 13, 1814.

This is a small 8-page magazine described as a weekly miscellany. The two issues only survive in the Place MSS. The third, mentioned by Place, is not, known. The printers were A. Seale & Bates, 160, Tottenham Court Road. The first issue gives the address of "The Proprietor" at 71, Castle Street, Oxford Market. The second has "Proprietors" in the plural. This could be a misprint or it might indicate that several people were financing the paper. Spence's own name is not printed either as editor or proprietor, and actually is not mentioned anywhere in the two issues except for the single signature "T.S.". Correspondents address the editor as "Mr. Giant-Killer". A medal wrapped in a song is offered free to purchasers of the first number. The contents are various literary and general interest extracts, letters, verses, articles, several items on American and West Indian slavery. An unfinished article headed *"Of the Nobility"* is found in the Place MSS (Add. 27809 f. 332). It is in Spence's handwriting. Part of it is printed in *The Giant Killer,* No. 2. It traces the origin of the nobility to wars of conquest aided by the encouragement of the Church fathers, and shows conquest as the origin of private property and servitude. The matter owes much to James Murray's *Lectures on Genesis* and possibly to Sprigge.

1814. *The Marine Republic*
The Giant-Killer. or Anti-Landlord,
Nos. 1 and 2, August, 1814.

These two instalments in *The Giant-killer* form the last version of Spence's utopian romance. The second instalment is signed 'T.S.', but it breaks off abruptly with a relatively unimportant detail, unlike the way in which Spence usually rounded off a pamphlet or article with some eloquent peroration or striking sentence.

The first part repeats almost exactly *The Marine Republic* and part of *A Further Account of Spensonia* published in *Pigs' Meat,* vol. II, but condensing the passage relating to the Indians. The second instalment gives a completely new dialogue between a Spensonian and a visitor to the island. It illustrates a number of Spencean practices already touched on in *The Restorer* and *The Constitution,* and explains how poverty, unemployment, theft and envy have been abolished. The Parish provides newcomers or others in need, with employment on public works, or with land, tools and provisions in order to start as cultivators or tradesmen. Many visitors are attracted because the parishes hold their fairs on different days in order to encourage intercourse and increase festivity. The Quarterly Jubilee and Jubilee Fair stresses and describes the country's prosperity and inexhaustible resources.

Verse

1807? Spence's Songs.
Spence's Songs, Part Second.
Spence's Songs, Part Third.

All the above are printed by Seale, or Seale & Bates. The first part advertises *The Important Trial* and *The Constitution of Spensonia* in one volume. The date of publication of the *Songs* cannot be earlier than 1807. None of the books are dated. The price of the first is twopence; the other two are a penny each.

Evans in his *Life* mentions that Spence published some cheap song books after he came out of prison. Possibly there was an earlier edition. There are two complete sets in the British Museum and the Goldsmiths Library, and the latter also has an incomplete set. In one set on the first page of the first song book a few words have been changed and a biblical text added, probably as a correction for a re-issue without breaking up the rest of the type. Possibly the third part was published after Spence's death.

These Spencean songs are to be associated with the Free-and-Easy meetings advertised on the *'Humerous Catalogue of Spence's songs' by Mrs. Evans'* which is found together with *'A Suitable Companion to Spence's Songs'* and a few other songs and slips bound up with the three song books. A slip headed *Spence's Plan* announcing the regular meetings of three Spencean sections is also among them. One set from Truelove's library has a note dated 1900 to the effect that the volume was the property of William Herbert. Herbert's signature is found on *The Humorous Catalogue,* and in the footnote announcing the Free-and-Easy meetings 'Tuesday' has been corrected to 'Monday'. William Herbert was probably a contemporary of Spence.

There are songs by Thomas Evans in the first part, showing that it must have been published after Evans had joined Spence's circle. Evans was released from prison, after three years all but a month, without trial (during the Suspension of the Habeas Corpus), about March 1801, so he could not have met Spence again until the latter was freed in 1802. Evans's business had been ruined and it was not until about 1811 that he was again on his feet.

Whoever bound the song books together was evidently following the advice in a prefatory note to *Spence's songs.*

> "The Miscarriage of the Mighty Struggle made in our Day against Oppression, will astonish Posterity and stimulate them to discover the Cause. The History of our Times will be strictly scrutinized and our Opinions sought after with Avidity in order to weigh them in the Balance, and find wherein they are deficient. Let us then gather up the Fragments that nothing may be lost, and let the Wellwishers of the Human Race, bind up such valuable Tracts as fall in their way, thereby giving them a Chance of Preservation to future Generations, who will doubtless profit more by them than we have done, and avoid our Mistakes. The following Pieces containing Sentiments so singular, and what have never yet been acted upon, require no further Apology for collecting, and thus putting them in a way to be preserved".

In the first *Spence's Songs* there are 12 pages, containing 7 pieces by Spence which had already appeared in *Pigs' Meat* and/or separately, here unsigned; one by Thomas Evans, and *"The Spencean Jubilee"* by W. Tilley. *Part Second* (8 pp.) has 3 by Spence and 4 by Evans, and concludes with *An Address to All Mankind,* in prose which stresses the need for meetings as the primary means of spreading and discussing Spencean teachings and for mutual encouragement. *Part Third* (8 pp.) has no songs by Spence. There is one song by Evans; *The Dream* in prose; and *A Suitable Companion to Spence's Songs* containing *A Fable* (later used by Benbow in his *Grand National Holiday)* and *Most Important Queries for the Serious Consideration of all Mankind.* These questions are like radical debating club and lecture formulations of those days, that is to say, really statements of a foregone conclusion. They cover the main principles and arguments of Spence's Plan with some reference to the current problems of the working classes. The last question, No. 35, coincides with the last of Murray's 'Queries' to the Newcastle Philosophical Society.

Some of Spence's songs were also included in Evans's *Life* and odd verses are scattered in his pamphlets and title pages. Spence's broadsides included many of his own compositions and political verse or songs by others. The first English translation of the *Marseillaise,* generally attributed to Holcroft and performed at Sadler's Wells, appeared in *Pigs' Meat* and in a Spence broadside. It is impossible to estimate either how many broadsides were published or how many have survived. One sometimes comes across an odd Spence item by chance in miscellaneous collections and albums of broadsides and ephemera.

Spence's verse falls into three categories. (1) The topical political, generally satirical, ballad; (2) Serious lyric poetry like *"The Peasant's Lament"* published in *Pigs' Meat* or a pair of apocalyptic poems found on a broadsheet *"The Triumph of Tyranny"* and *"The Triumph of Freedom".* (3) Spencean Songs or Hymns like these in the Songbooks and later similar compositions by some of his followers. These are devoted to the themes of his principle theories, often echoeing images and ideas in his pamphlets and making use of biblical and traditional figures and symbols. They are markedly millenarian and have a style and tone of their own. They might be said to pioneer a special genre of popular verse, the political hymn. The distinctive character of the Spencean songs may be better appreciated when they are compared with the songs associated with the meetings and festivities of the Corresponding and other political societies of the late eighteenth century. The latter when not literary and in the manner of elevated sentiment, could be lively and colloquial, but seldom expressed their ideas through that particular poetic quality of the best traditional simple verse.

It is quite possible that Spence's own songs, which resemble both old popular ballad and sectarian hymn, were influenced by his Glassite connections. The Glassites were the pioneers of congregational hymn singing. Hitherto church singing by the congregation had been limited to the metrical psalms. The Glassites introduced a variety of popular verse forms and the more lively metres of secular songs and set them to traditional tunes rather than ecclesiastical music. The only collection of Glassite hymns known to me is in standard English, but decidedly in the ordinary language and vocabulary of the common people. There may have been others such as Scottish hymns. Although these hymns are naturally full of references to scripture, they are not in a special kind of language reserved for sacred subjects; the biblical expressions are those which were a normal part of the common language.

This peculiarity is very striking when these compositions are compared with, say, Watts, who aimed to write simple verse but produced something that sounds pious and not everyday in tone. Following the Glassites the singing of other poor sects like the Bereans introduced near-vernacular speech forms and traditional airs. The importance of the Glassite innovation for the history of Protestant hymnology is recognized, although church historians do not rate the quality of their contribution very highly.

Both John Glas and Robert Sandeman wrote longer songs expounding key doctrines in a very simple and direct style, as Spence did in his *Rights of Man.* The Glassites sang at their weekly meetings and at the Love Feast. Later accounts of the sect sound gloomy and their enemies called them "acrimonious", but the prevailing note of the hymns is warm and cheerful. They tell of the second coming when all men shall possess all things, and shall "reign on earth as kings", "Nations all shall broken be" and "Antichrist head o'er much land" shall be utterly destroyed. It is this social feeling of the poor and confidence in ultimate justice that is striking in the hymns, not the theology. Indeed the hymns rather ignore the doctrine of a narrow basis of divine election (perhaps because the hymn singers were presumed to be all elect). The positive assertion and the uncompromising destruction of tyranny in the shape of antichrist or landlord are common characteristics of both Glassite hymn and Spencean song. Taken at face value the Glassite hymn was an affirmation of equality, in as much as "the kingdom of this world" and its man-made hierarchies and pride had nothing in common with the true church. If poverty in itself was not a virtue it was certainly a necessary mark of a righteous man, since all hoarding for the morrow was positively sinful. These were the songs of poor men. When the "brother sinner" enters their humble meeting house he will see there "nothing finer . . . than the guilty clothed with grace" — the man himself.

Ultimately the Millenium was expected to take an entirely material form on the earth, when all the redeemed are naturally all equal, and there is no government because god and man are perfectly at one. The *'Epilogue'* to *The Constitution of Spensonia* may be compared with the picture of the future by William Leighton, a Newcastle elder:

"No hurtful beasts shall then annoy,
All jarring feuds shall melt away.
The child shall with the viper toy,
The lamb with lions frisk and play.
Then he shall set the poor on high,
And part the righteous from the vile . . ."

Meanwhile if the Glassite doctrines did not offer anything but hardship and contempt on earth until that general restoration took place, at least it did not justify the oppression and pride of the worldly rich, or teach that the poor should be resigned to a proper and unalterable inequality as did the other churches. The poor could not expect better under the rule of anti christ.

"When you see the world's disdaining
  Pouring forth the serpent's rage;
Then, companion, think of reigning
  When you leave this mortal stage.
'Twas in this world Christ was rejected
  He no place — no quarter had;
Say then, can it be expected,
  We should loll on downy bed?"

If 'the Jubilee Trumpet' were substituted for 'the Church of the First-born' and 'Tom Spence' for 'Jesus', the following lines by John Glas might easily be change into a Spencean Song like *"The Propagation of Spensonian-ism"* or Tilley's *"The Spencean Jubilee".*

  "And there 'tis declared, the help of distress'd,
The hope of the hopeless, the ease of oppress'd.
  The church of the first-born, with angels of light,
Shall sound forth its praises in endless delight.
  But fully unfolded it could be by none
  But Jesus among them, who knew it alone".

1795. The Coin Collector's Companion, being a descriptive list of the modern provincial political and other copper coins.
London.
1795.

Spence's token dies and his coins and blanks punched with his slogans are well known to collectors. Spence issued and dealt in tokens between 1794 and '96 as a sideline in connection with which he issued the above 'Companion', describing his own dies and explaining the meaning of the designs. He was reported in 1796 to have sold his stock and gone bankrupt. Mr. Thompson, of the Numismatic Society, remarks that Spence's finances were probably never sufficient to place him in bankruptcy.

Spence's token dies have been repeatedly studied and listed mainly by numismaticists not interested in his ideas or with any special knowledge of the history of early socialism. But thanks to Spence's singular ability and ingenuity in finding designs and wording which make their meaning unmistakably clear, what he intended to convey, if not its political significance or historical associations has always been well understood. This fact is in itself evidence that their message would have been even more obvious and more striking for his contemporaries.

Not that this always indicated approval. Thompson has given some amusing quotations from early writers who warned that Spence's tokens were unworthy of the collector's attention. More extraordinary is a modern numismatist who calls Spence "a minor — and crankier — Tom Paine" and takes all the trouble to defend XVIII century enclosures as allegedly good for employment. The reliability of this author as to Spence's biography is as dubious as his economic history. He says for instance that Spence "was never able to enjoy the publicity of a trial". He must have read Water's book with his eyes shut.

Spence developed a form of propaganda which was also used by the various corresponding societies. Several coins or medals were struck for the LCS, for example, to commemorate the acquittal of Thomas Hardy and others. Some, like the one commemorating Eaton's acquittal 14 March, 1794, showing a cock crowing with the names of the jurymen on the reverse, were stamped "struck by order of the London Corresponding Society". Others no doubt were contributions to the cause struck by individual supporters, among whom were many small manufacturers and tradesmen who handled tokens in the way of business. Mr. R. Thompson was, I think, the first to notice that Spence muled his dies in order to give different aspects or particular emphasis to his principles. Token specialists are seldom informed on the history of political thought and historians of socialism are not acquainted with the technical side and generally regard Spence's tokens as of minor importance and not as possible sources of ideas that supplement his writings.

Several designs advertised Spence's publications suchas *Pigs' Meat,* with and without a pig or a book, and with various mottoes. Waters describes a farthing die having a Cat on the obverse and a Book on the reverse, with the inscription "Hark how the trumpet sounds". The Book is described in the *Companion* as "the Political Bible" i.e. *Pigs' Meat. The Meridian Sun* is depicted as a disc with radiations. *The End of Oppression* is symbolized by men dancing around a bonfire of title deeds. An Indian, with the legend "If rents I once consent to pay, My liberty is past away", embodies the ideas on the broadside advertisement of *The Reign of Felicity*. The Ass with double panniers, inscribed "I was an Ass to bear the first pair"; Balaam's Ass, with "Am I not thy Ass?", and the Bull with Ass's head ridden by George III, are all variations on the theme of the taxed and exploited but passive people. The burdened Ass occurs as a metaphor or similie in many pamphlets, including the *Letter from Ralph Hodge* which ends with the announcement of Parson Bull's next Sunday sermon, the text of which was doubtless taken from Murray's first *"Lecture on Genesis"*. All editions of Murray's *Sermons to Asses* have a fine engraving of the indolent Ass resting with the panniers labelled 'Politics' and 'Religion' (i.e. Taxes and Tithes) on the title page. Spence put another pair of panniers on the beast to illustrate his contention that Taxes were an additional imposition resulting from the exaction of Rent by landlords. This Ass with double panniers is the subject of the illustrated broadside, *'The Contract'*, signed by W. Spence, 1 February, 1796. The Ass who is saying "I'm doomed to endless toil and care; I was an ass to bear the first pair", represents civilization contrasted with the figures of two Indians. A facsimile is given by Waters.

Another die showing a man on all fours with the words "If the law requires it we will walk thus" is also linked with an illustrated broadside by W. Spence found in one of the British Museum copies of *Pigs' Meat.* It was probably sarcastic reference to falling away of a number of leading reformers during 1795 and 1796, and the general return to the Sedition Act.

The subject of many of Spence's tokens was connected with the French Revolution. "Before the Revolution" depicts a man gnawing a bone chained to a block in a dungeon, presumably the Bastille. "After the Revolution" shows men feasting and dancing under a Tree. There are several variations of the Tree of Liberty, some of them satirical. A Lion with a Cock perched on its rump is inscribed "Let Tyrants tremble at the Crow of Liberty".

There are also Spence tokens in support of the LCS, in honour of Hardy, Thelwall and Horne Tooke. One in commemoration of Gordon is again an association with James Murray and a reminder that Spence must have known Gordonites among the members of the LCS.

A soldier and two citizens holding hands inscribed "We also are the people" illustrates the extract from Volney's *Ruins* printed at the end of the *Letter from Ralph Hodge. Three armed men with the legend "Who knows their rights and knowing dare maintain" connects with Sir William Jones's Ode in imitation of Alcaeus",* reprinted in *Pigs' Meat.*

The Plan itself is the subject of several different dies. One has 'Spence's Plan, November 8, 1775' with radiations, a design similar to the Meridian Sun, with an inscription running round the edge in two circles — "Spence's Glorious Plan is parochial Partnership in Land without private landlordism". On the reverse is a hand holding an olive branch, seals, and a cornucopia with "This just plan will produce everlasting peace and happiness or in fact the millenium". Waters noted a token celebrating the Glorious Plan struck at Newcastle, but was in error that it was struck in 1775, the date given as the origin of the Plan, i.e. the date of the Lecture. In fact it is not clear when Spence first used the phrase "Spence's Plan" or "Plan" in this way.

The token designs, then, are a visual record of many of Spence's favourite images, quotations, titles and ideas. Fortunate in the engraver, Charles James, who executed them, they are miniature political poems — lyrical, like the peace and happiness of Spensonia represented by a shepherd on a hill, or satirical, like Pandora's breeches or Pitt's head impaled on a tree of liberty. These designs contributed to a traditional symbolism of early socialist literature and art, and the figures would have conveyed similar associations thirty and forty years later. The themes and images were not all invented by Spence but were derived from many sources. He gave them a fresh meaning and often a humorous twist.

Typical of an old motif to which he gave a special meaning and which lasted long after him, was the murder of Abel, with the legend 'The Beginning of Oppression', i.e. the first crime of violence, the robbery of the land, which had divided society. It was a symbol of the unending war on the working people. "Abel seemed to resemble the Commonalty, Cain the Nobility, who being according to the Flesh, proud and cruel and a persecutor of him that was according to the spirit, meek and gentle, slew his brother". The Adam and Eve design was also given a complex significance. Standing for the innocence of the earthly paradise, the pair correspond to natural man or the condition of natural right, but they also by association recall the Fall of Man, and Milton's words, which are used for the legend, "Man over Man made he not Lord", affirm that the natural or desirable state is social equality.

Spence's head in profile appears on several tokens with different inscriptions, referring to his imprisonment for High Treason and signed 'James'. A number of copies of an engraved portrait survived in some copies of his works and separately. A specimen in Newcastle Public Library signed 'T. Spence, April 2, 1810' seems to be identical with the one owned and described by Waters. It is similar to the portrait on the tokens except that the head faces in the opposite direction. Hence it does not represent Spence as he appeared in 1810 at the age of sixty, but as he was 15 or 20 years earlier, round about 1795. Edwards, the government spy who brought Thistlewood and his companions to the gallows, sold plaster casts of Spence's bust. None of these are known to have survived.

Spence supplied his brother Jeremiah with tokens or with dies from which the latter had tokens made, e.g. a sailor with the legend 'J. Spence Slopseller Newcastle' signed 'James', with a man in a keel and 'Coaly Tyne' and the date 1795 on the reverse. Several halfpenny and farthing dies made for J. Spence have been described.

Spence also supplied himself with punches cut with short phrases which could be combined to form a variety of slogans. With these he countermarked current coin or stamped blanks specially supplied for that purpose, producing remarks like 'War is starvation', 'Read Spence's Plan. Small Farms', 'Landlords and starvation', 'Full bellies, fat bairns. No landlords and 'War or Spence's Plan'.

While *The Coin Collector's Companion* shows that Spence wished to sell to collectors, the dies themselves and the punched slogans show that the main purpose was political instruction. It is said that he produced large quantities of tokens and that he sometimes threw handfuls out of the window for passers-by to pick up. A medal was given free to purchasers of the first number of *The Giant-Killer* and tokens were distributed at his funeral, but whether these were old stock or newly cast is not clear. It does not necessarily mean that he had large stocks left over. The tokens then merely underline his persistent single-minded and single-handed endeavour to make known his discovery to the world by every means within his power.

BIBLIOGRAPHY

I. Miscellaneous Sources

The Act of Parliament obtained in the year 1774 for confirming the resident Freemen of Newcastle and their widows their full Right and Benefit to the Herbage of the Town Moor, Castle Leazes and Nuns' Moor. By a Burgess. Newcastle-upon-Tyne, 1811 (1810);

Anon.: *Opinions delivered at a numerous and respectable meeting in the country, lately held for the purpose of signing a declaration for the support of the Government in the present alarming crisis.* London, 1793.

Address and Regulations of the Society of Spencean Philanthropists. London (1815).

A serious address to the Common People on account of the late insurrection at Hexham, 9 March, 1761, Newcastle-upon-Tyne, 1761.

The Burgesses Poll at the late Elections of Members for Newcastle-on-Tyne. n.l. (1774) 1775.

Catalogue of a scarce and curious collection of books and engravings formerly belonging to Thomas Bewick ...To be sold at auction on Tuesday, Wednesday and Thursday, February 5th, 6th and 7th, 1884. Newcastle-on-Tyne (1884).

Common Council Books. Transcripts. Newcastle City Records Office.

Directory for the year 1801 of the Town and County of Newcastle-upon-Tyne, Gateshead and Places Adjacent. Newcastle-upon-Tyne, 1801.

Epitome of the Annals of Great Britain, or a succinct impartial History of England from the remotest period of Intelligence to the conclusion of the last war ...with an introduction on the Constitution of Great Britain. Useful for youth at school as well as all those who are desirous of relating what they read to the history of their country. Newcastle, 1773; *Epitome ...Second edition enlarged and corrected.* Newcastle, 1777.

Extracts from the records of the Company of Hostmen of Newcastle upon Tyne. Surtees Society, 1901.

Facts, Reflections and Queries submitted to the consideration of the Associated Friends of the People. Edinburgh, 1792.

A full Report of the Evidence and Discussion during the official investigations into the affairs of the Municipal Corporation of Newcastle-upon-Tyne before His Majesty's Commissioners &c. &c. Newcastle-upon-Tyne, 1939.

Hansard's *Parliamentary History.*

Harney Collection in Newcastle Central Library.

P. M. Horsley: *Some Frenchmen in Newcastle in the Eighteenth Century. Heaton Works Journal.* Summer 1957.

Howell, *State Trials.*

Hone, William. Letter to Place, 1830.

C. H. Hunter: *Members of Parliament for Northumberland and Newcastle-upon-Tyne, 1539-1831. Arch. Aeliana.*

Jacobin Grotesques: the deliberate Muling of Dies in late Eighteenth-century England. Actes du 8 eme Congres International de Numismatique. New York — Washington. Septembre 1973.

Law of the Literary and Philosophical Society of Newcastle-upon-Tyne with a list of members, 1794.

Letter of Administration granted to Sarah Murray 15 March, 1783. University of Durham, Department of Palaeography and Diplomatic Probate, 1783.

London Corresponding Society. *Address to the Friends of Peace and Parliamentary Reform.* London, 1794.

London Corresponding Society. *Address to the Nation from the London Corresponding Society on the subject of Parliamentary Reform. Together with resolutions which were passed at a General Meeting of the Society. Held on Monday the 8th July 1793 at the Crown and Anchor Tavern, Strand. Printed by Order of the Society and distributed (gratis);* London Corresponding Society. *Address to the Friends of Peace and Parliamentary Reform. November 15, 1793.*

The Report of the Committee of the Constitution of the London Corresponding Society. Printed for the use of the Members. Sold by Thomas Spence, No. 8 Little Turnstile, High Holborn;
Report of the Committee appointed to revise and abridge a former Report of the Constitution of the London Corresponding Society. Printed by order of the General Committee. nl.;nd.
An account of the Seizure of Citizen Thomas Hardy, Secretary to the London Corresponding Society; with some remarks on the Suspension of the Habeas Corpus Act. Printed by order of the London Corresponding Society (distributed gratis). (1794).
To the Parliament and People of Great Britain. An explicit declaration of the Principles and Views of the London Corresponding Society. Committee Room, Beaufort Buildings. November 23rd, 1795. (London, 1795).
The Origin and Plan of the General Association of Householders within the Kingdom of Great Britain united and uniting to procure A Reform in Parliament upon the Plan of their full and equal Representation in the House of Commons . . .digested by the Present Head Committee. London, Clerkenwell, 1796.
Place MSS. British Library.
Proceedings of the Stewards of the several companies of Newcastle respecting an Enquiry into the Rights by which any Roads over the Town Moor &c. are enjoyed with the Report of the Committee by them appointed for the Purpose. n.l., n.d. (Newcastle-on-Tyne, 1771).
Proceedings of the Friends of the Liberty of the Press on December the 22nd 1792; January 19th and March 9th 1793. Printed by Order of the Committee. London, 1793.
Register of the Ballast Hills Cemetery. Grave Books. Transcribed by C. E. Whitney, Newcastle-on-Tyne, 1930.
Register of Freemen chiefly of the Eighteenth Century. Ed. A. M. Oliver. *Publications of the Newcastle-upon-Tyne Records Committee.*
Report of the Committee of Secrecy to the House of Commons, 1794.
Second Report of the Committee of Secrecy of the House of Commons respecting seditious practices. 6 June, 1794.
Second Report of the Committee to the House of Commons . . .presented May 15th, 1801.
Report of the Committee to the London Reforming Society (June 18). London, 1795.
Report of the Investigation of the case of Messrs. Brunel, Walker and Angus before the Mayor, Aldermen and Common Council of Newcastle-upon-Tyne. Newcastle-upon-Tyne, 1835.
Report on the Proceedings of the Audit of the Accounts of the Corporation of Newcastle-upon-Tyne. Published agreeably to a resolution of the Court in Guildhall, on Michaelmas Monday in the year 1809. Gateshead, 1809.
Report of the Town Council of Newcastle-upon-Tyne on the Freeman's Quarry. October 10, 1842. Newcastle-upon-Tyne, 1842.
Reports, papers, catalogues etc., of the Literary and Philosophical Society of Newcastle collected by Anthony Hedley 1820-1821.
Sever, John: *Morrison of the 'Pioneer'. Notes on his life and background.* (Unpublished typescript). Oxford, 1963.
Thompson, R. H.: *The Dies of Thomas Spence (1750 — 1814). The British Numismatics Journal; — Additions and Corrections. The British Numismatic Journal.*
Town Moor Act 1774. Newcastle-upon-Tyne, 1811.
The Town Moor Case. (Newcastle-on-Tyne) 4 October, 1773.
The Town Moor Common of Newcastle-upon-Tyne. History and State in 1935. Issued by the Ratepayers' Union. Newcastle and Northumberland. January 1936.

Newspapers and Periodicals

Annual Register
Bronterre's National Reformer
Cobbett's Weekly Political Register
Democratic Review

English Chartist Circular
Globe
Freeman's Magazine or The Constitutional Repository
McDouall's Chartist and Republican Journal
Medusa
National Co-operative Leader
National Reformer and Manx Weekly Review
Newcastle Courant
Newcastle Journal
Newcastle Weekly Magazine
Northern John Bull
Northern Star
Penny Papers For The People
Poor Man's Guardian
Public Advertiser
Quarterly Review
The Tribune

III. Books and Pamphlets

Ahab Salem: *The new Maid of the Oaks. A tragedy.* London, 1778.
Manfred, Albert: *Essai d'Histoire de France du XVIIe au XXe siecle.* Moscow 1969.
An old fox tarr'd and feathered, occasioned by what is called Mr. John Wesley's Calm Address to our American colonies. 'In politics I dabbled too, Brave Jack of all trades!'. By an Hanoverian. Printed for the Author. n.l., 1775.
W. H. G. Armytage, *Heavens Below,* London, 1961.
Ashraf, P. M.: *Africans among Reformers.* (Russian translation). Moscow, 1960.
Ashraf P. M. and Mitchell J. (Editors). *Essays In Honour Of William Gallacher. Supplement: A Selection from the works of Thomas Spence 1750-1814.* Berlin, 1966.
J. Baillie, *An Impartial History of the town and county of Newcastle-upon-Tyne and its vicinity,* Newcastle-upon-Tyne, 1801.
Baker: *Biographia Dramatica.* London, 1812. vol. iii.
Bax, E. Belfort: *Jean-Paul Marat. The Friend of the People.* London, 1908.
Baxter, J.: *A new and impartial history of England.* London (1795).
Baxter, John: *Resistance to oppression; The constitutional Right of Britons* ..., London, 1795.
M. Beer, *A History of British Socialism,* London, 1953.
Bell, John: *Gatherings of scarce books locally printed in the counties of Northumberland and Durham or relative thereto* n.l.; n.d.
(J. G. Bell): *Historical memorials of Presbyterianism in Newcastle-upon-Tyne. By an Episcopalian.* 2nd edition. London, 1847.
William Benbow, *Grand National Holiday and Congress of the Productive Classes.* Printed and published for W. Benbow ...London, n.d.
Bently, Thomas: *The Poor Man's answer to the rich Associators.* London, 1793.
Bewick, Thomas: *Memoir of Thomas Bewick written by himself 1822-1828.* Ed. Selwyn Image, London, 1924.
Binns, J.: *Recollections of the Life of John Binns.* Philadelphia, 1854.
Black, Eugene Charlton, *The Association. British Extra-Parliamentary Political Organisation 1769-1793.* Harvard Univ. Press, 1963.
Boulanger, M. A.: *Christianity Unveiled.* (Translated by W. M. Johnson). New York, 1795
Bourne, Henry: *The History of Newcastle-upon-Tyne or the Ancient and Present State of that Town.* Newcastle-upon-Tyne, 1736.
Brown, John: *A short account of the customs and franchises of the Freemen of Newcastle.* Newcastle, 1823.
Brown, P. A.: *The French Revolution in English History.* London, 1918 (reprint 1923).
Buckle, H. T.: *History of Civilisation in England.* London, 1908.

Y. B. Chernak: *The Mass Movement in England and Ireland in the late XVIIIth and early XIXth centuries.* (Russian), Moscow, 1962.
Christie, Ian R.: *Myth and Reality in Eighteenth Century British politics.* London, 1976.
Christie, Ian R.: *Wilkes, Wyvill and Reform.* London, 1962.
Clarke, Joseph: *A friendly address to the Free Burgesses and other inhabitants of Newcastle-upon-Tyne.* Gateshead, 1809.
Clarke, Joseph: *Newcastle Freeman's Pocket Companion.* Gateshead, 1808.
Clarke, J.: *Newcastle Remembrancer and Freeman's Pocket Companion. A new edition.* Newcastle, 1817.
A. Burgess (i.e. Joseph Clarke): *The Town Moor Act 1774 ...with a full and interesting Detail of the public and private proceedings for obtaining a New Act &c. &c.* Newcastle-upon-Tyne, 1811.
A History of the Churches in England and Scotland. By a Clergyman. Newcastle-upon-Tyne, 1771/72.
'Clerus', *The lawfulness of self-defence explained and vindicated on Scripture principles. An evening lecture.* Glasgow, 1780.
G. D. H. Cole, *A Short History of the British Working Class Movement.* Revised edition. London, 1960.
G. D. H. Cole, *Attempts at General Union (1818-1834),* London, 1953.
Cragg, G. R.: *Puritanism in the period of the Great Persecution 1660-1688.* Cambridge, 1957.
Cushing, W.: *Initials and Pseudonyms.* London, 1886.
Dalton, R. and Hamer, S. H.: *The Provincial Token Coinage of the Eighteenth Century.* London, 1914.
Davenport, Allen: *Life, Writings and Principles of Thomas Spence, Author of the Spencean System, or Agrarian Equality.* London n.d. (c. 1836).
Davidson, John Morrison: *Concerning four precursors of Henry George and the Single Tax as also the Land Gospel according to Winstanley 'The Digger'.* London, 1899.
Dictionary of National Biography.
Evans, Thomas: *A Brief Sketch of the Life of Mr. Thomas Spence, Author of the Spencean System of Agrarian Fellowship or Partnership in Land &c.* Manchester. May 1st, 1821.
Evans, Thomas: *A Humorous Catalogue of Spence's Songs,* undated slip bound in with the collections of *Spence's Songs* in the Goldsmith Library, Univ. of London.
Thomas Evans: *Christian Policy in full Practice among the people of Harmony.* (London) November, 1818.
Evans, Thomas: *Christian Policy. The Salvation of the Empire.*
Ts. Fridljand: *Jean-Paul Marat i grazdanskaja Vojna.* Moscow, 1959.
Jones, John Gale: *A sketch of a speech delivered at the Westminster Tavern on the 9th, 10th, 23rd and 30th December, 1794 on the following question* ...London, 1795.
John Gast, *Calumny Defeated or a Compleat Vindication of the Working Shipwrights during the late disputes with their Employers,* Deptford, 1802.
Gerrald, Joseph: *A Convention the only means of saving us from ruin.* London, 1793.
Gibson, T. F.: *The Borough History of Newcastle-upon-Tyne.* Newcastle-upon-Tyne (1875?).
Gray, Gilbert: *The Complete Fabulist ...Designed for the instruction of both sexes as well as the use of English schools.* Newcastle-upon-Tyne, 1753.
Gray, Gilbert: *The Pleasing History or Impartial History of England* ...(1st edition), London, n.d.
Gurney, Joseph: *The Trial of Thomas Hardy for High Treason ...Transcribed in short hand by Joseph Gurney.* London, 1975.
The Hammonds, *Town Labourer, 1925. Skilled Labourer, 1927.*
W. P. Hall, *British Radicalism 1791-1797. Studies in History, Economics and Public Law.* Columbia Univ., vol. 49, 1912.
Handasyde, John: *A practical essay on the Lord's Prayer.* 2nd ed. Whitehaven, 1799.
Hill, Christopher: *Puritanism and Revolution.* London, 1962.
E. J. Hobsbawm, *Labouring Men,* London, 1964.

Hodgson, W.: *The Commonwealth of Reason.* London, 1795.
Hone, William: *Biographical sketch of the Rev. James Murray* in Murray, James: *Semons to Asses.* Ed. Hone. London, 1819.
Hone, W.: *(Memoir of Spence)* appended to *Riots in London.* Part 2. London (1816). Copy in Place Collection, vol. 39.
Thomas Houston, *A Congratulatory Ode to the members of the different Box Societies that lately entered into Resolutions to prevent Imposition and be their own Corn Dealers.* Newcastle, 1800.
E. Hughes, *North Country Life in the Eighteenth Century,* Oxford, 1952.
Hunt, H.: *Memoirs of Henry Hunt written by himself.* London, 1820-1822.
Inglis, Ralston: *The dramatic writers of Scotland.* Glasgow, 1868.
Johnson, Samuel: *Taxation no tyranny.*
Joyce, Jeremiah: *Sermon preached on Sunday February 23rd 1794 by Jeremiah Joyce. Twenty-three weeks a close Prisoner in the TOWER OF LONDON.* 2nd edition. London, 1795.
Law, A. R.: *Schola Novocastrensis.*
Lee, Richard: *The Happy Reign of George the Last.* London, 1794.
Lincoln, Anthony: *Some political and social ideas of English Dissent. 1763-1800.* Cambridge, 1938.
Mackenzie, Eneas: *A descriptive and historical account of the Town and County of Newcastle upon Tyne, including the Borough of Gateshead.* Newcastle-upon-Tyne, 1827.
Mackenzie, E.: *Memoir of Thomas Spence of Newcastle-upon-Tyne.* Newcastle-upon-Tyne, 1826.
Mackenzie: *History of Northumberland.*
Maccoby, S.: *English Radicalism 1762-1785.* London, 1955.
Marat, Jean-Paul: *Chains of Slavery.* London, 1774.
Marat, Jean-Paul: *Les Chaines de l'Esclavage.* Paris, 1793.
Marat, Jean-Paul: *Textes Choisis.* Editions Sociales. Paris, 1963.
Marx, Karl: *Capital.* Moscow, 1959.
Merivale, Herman: *Historical Studies,* 1865.
Middlebrook, S.: *Newcastle upon Tyne. Its growth and achievement.* Newcastle upon Tyne, 1950.
J. Midon, *The History of the Rise and Fall of Masaniello the Fisherman of Naples,* London, 1729.
Miller, F.: *St. Pancras Past and Present,* London, 1874.
Mortimer, Thomas: *The elements of commerce, politics and finance.* London, 1772.
Murray, James: *An alarm without cause; or the administration of peace supported by the sword of the spirit: An evening lecture delivered in the High Bridge Meeting, Newcastle. 'He that hath no sword let him sell his garment and buy one'. —Luke xxii. 36.* Published on behalf of the Protestant Association. Newcastle-upon-Tyne, n.d.
Murray, James: *The Contest. Being an account of the matters in dispute between the Magistrates and the Burgesses and an examination of the merits and conduct of the candidates in the present Election for Newcastle-upon-Tyne. 'Give the Devil his due'.* Newcastle-on-Tyne, 1774.
Murray, James: *An impartial history of the war in America.* 2 volumes. Newcastle-upon-Tyne, 1778-1781.
Murray, James: *Eikon Basilike. Or the character of Eglon, King of Moab and his ministry.* Newcastle-upon-Tyne, 1773 (Enlarged version of the earlier sermon in two lectures).
Murray, James: *The finishing stroke to Mr. Wesley's Calm Address to the people of England.* Newcastle-upon-Tyne, 1777.
Murray, James: *A grave answer to Mr. Wesley's Calm Address to our American colonies. By a Gentleman of Northumberland.* n.d., n.l.
Murray, James: *Lectures on the most remarkable characters and transactions recorded in the Book of Genesis.* Newcastle-upon-Tyne, 1771.
Murray, James: *The Magazine of the Ants. Or the Pismires' Journal.* Newcastle-upon-Tyne, 1777.

Murray, James: *Sermons to Asses* (v.supra); *New Sermons to Asses: Sermons to Doctors in Divinity*. London, 1771; *Lectures to Lords Spiritual. Or an Advice to the Bishops concerning religious articles, tithes, and Church power. With a discourse on ridicule*. London, 1774; *Sermons to Ministers of State*. Newcastle-upon-Tyne (1780).
Murray, James: *Sermons for the General Fast Day*. London, 1781.
Murray, James: *The travels of the imagination. A true journey from Newcastle to London*. (1773) Newcastle-upon-Tyne, 1828.
Namier, L. B.: *The Structure of Politics on the Accession of George III*. London, 1929.
Neff, J. U.: *The Rise of the British Coal Trade*. London, 1932.
Oldfield, T. H. B.: *The History of the original constitution of Parliaments*. London, 1797. *The representative history of Great Britain and Ireland*. London, 1816.
Oliver Thomas: *A new picture of Newcastle-upon-Tyne or an historical and descriptive view of the town and county of Newcastle-upon-Tyne, Gateshead and Environs*. Newcastle-upon-Tyne, 1831.
Parkinson, James: *An account of some perculiar manners and customs of the people of Bull-land or the Island of Contradictions: faithfully detailed by Old Hubert*. London, 1795.
Pigott's Political Dictionary. (Ed. R. Lee). London, n.d.
Preston Thomas: *The Life and Opinions of Thomas Preston, Patriot and Shoemaker*. London, 1817.
Reid, William Hamilton: *The Rise and Decline of Infidel Societies in this Metropolis*. London, 1800.
Richardson, *Local Historian's Tablebook*. Newcastle upon Tyne, 1842.
J. Ridley, *The Hexham Chronicle*, Hexham, 1861.
Erich Roll, *History of Economic Thought*, London, 1961.
Rude, George: *Wilkes and Liberty*. Oxford, 1962.
Rudkin, Olive: *Thomas Spence and his connections*. London, 1927. (Reprint. New York, 1966).
A. R. Schoyen, *The Chartist Challenge*, London, 1958.
Scott, Hew: *Fasti Ecclesiae Scoticanae*. Edinburgh, 1928.
Sinclair, A. G.: *The Critic Philosopher, or Truth Discovered*. 5th edition. London, 1791.
Skelly, George: *Alnwick in the past*. Alnwick, 1896.
Southey, R.: *Essays Moral and Political*, London, 1832.
Sykes, J.: *Local Records*. Newcastle, 1866.
J.S. (i.e. John Sykes): *Memoirs of the public life of Sir Walter Blackett*. Newcastle-upon-Tyne, 1819.
Tate, George: *A descriptive and historical view of Alnwick*, 2nd edition. *Alnwick*. 1822.
Tate, George: *The History of the Burgh, Castle and Barony of Alnwick*. London, 1866, 1869.
Thelwall, John: *Peaceful Discussion and not Tumultuary violence the means of Redressing National Grievance. The Speech of John Thelwall, at the General Meeting of the Friends of Parliamentary Reform, called by the London Corresponding Society and held in the Neighbourhood of Copenhagen House; on Monday October 26, 1795*. London, 1795.
Mrs. Thelwall: *Life of John Thelwall*, London, 1837.
Thomas Oliver, *A New Picture of Newcastle-upon-Tyne*, 1831.
E. P. Thompson, *The Making of the English Working Class*, London, 1963.
W. C. Townsend, *Life of Lord Kenyon*. 1846. Quoted in Fifoot, C. H. S.: *Lord Mansfield*, Oxford, 1936.
V. P. Volgin, *History of Socialist Ideas* (Russian) Moscow, 1928, 1931.
Wallas, Graham: *The Life of Francis Place*. London, 1898.
Waters, A. W.: *Notes of Eighteenth Century Tokens*. London, 1954.
Waters, A. W.: *The Trial of Thomas Spence in 1801*. Privately printed. Leamington Spa. 1917.
Watson, R. S.: *History of the Literary and Philosophical Society of Newcastle upon Tyne*. Newcastle upon Tyne, 1897.
Welford, Richard: *Men of Mark 'twixt Tyne and Tweed*. 3 vols. London, 1895.
Wilson, Jasper, *A Letter commercial and political addressed to The Right Hon. William Pitt* . . .London, 1793.

IV. Spence's Works

Short titles of editions quoted in notes.

The Rights of Man. London. 1793.
The Real Rights of Man. Pig's Meat. 1795. Vol. III, pp. 220-240.
The Meridian Sun of Liberty on the whole right of man. London. 1795.
A Supplement to the History of Robinson Crusoe. Being the History of Crusonia or Robinson Crusoe's Island. Second edition. London. 1782.
The Case of Thomas Spence, Bookseller. London. 1792.
One Pennyworth of Pigs' Meat or Lessons for the Swinish Multitude. Second edition. Vols. I, II, III. London. 1793-1795.
The Marine Republic. Pigs' Meat. 1794. Vol. II, pp. 68-72.
A Further Account of Spensonia. Pigs' Meat. 1794. Vol. II, pp. 205-218.
The Marine Republic. Giant Killer. London 1814. Nos. 1, 2.
The End of Oppression. Second edition. London. n.d. (1795).
Spence's Recantation of the End of Oppression. London. 1795.
A Letter from Ralph Hodge to his Cousin Thomas Bull. n.d. (London 1795).
A Fragment of an ancient philosophy. London. 1796.
The Reign of Felicity. London. 1796.
The Rights of Infants. London. 1797.
The Constitution of a Perfect Commonwealth. The second edition. London. 1798.
The Important Trial of Thomas Spence, for a political pamphlet entitled "The Restorer of Society to its Natural State". Second edition. London. 1807.
The Restorer of Society to its Natural State. Second edition. London. 1807. (Printed with comments from Spence's defence at his trial in *The Important Trial of Thomas Spence.* Second edition).
The Constitution of Spensonia. The Fourth Edition. London. 1807. (Printed at the end of *The Important Trial.* Second edition. 1807).
The Giant Killer or the Anti-Landlord. Nos. 1, 2. August 6th, 13th. London. 1814.
Spence's Songs, Spence's Songs, Part Second. Spence's Songs, Part Third. (London). n.d. (1803?-1807?).

INDEX